P9-DCV-108

THE
SEVENTH
SENSE

Also by Joshua Cooper Ramo

The Age of the Unthinkable
No Visible Horizon

THE
SEVENTH
SENSE

POWER, FORTUNE, AND SURVIVAL
IN THE AGE OF NETWORKS

JOSHUA COOPER RAMO

LITTLE, BROWN AND COMPANY
New York Boston London

Little, Brown and Company
Hachette Book Group
1290 Avenue of the Americas, New York, NY 10104
littlebrown.com

First Edition: May 2016

Little, Brown and Company is a division of Hachette Book Group, Inc. The
Little, Brown name and logo are trademarks of Hachette Book Group, Inc.

The publisher is not responsible for websites (or their content) that are not owned
by the publisher.

The Hachette Speakers Bureau provides a wide range of authors for
speaking events. To find out more, go to hachettespeakersbureau.com
or call (866) 376-6591.

ISBN 978-0-316-28506-3 (hc) / 978-0-316-39505-2 (int'l ed.)
LCCN 2015960065

10 9 8 7 6 5 4 3 2 1

RRD-C

Printed in the United States of America

For Nora

CONTENTS

CONTENTS

Part Three: Gateland

*A guide to power in the world that becomes
newly apparent with the Seventh Sense.*

THE
SEVENTH
SENSE

PREFACE

Three hundred years ago the Enlightenment and the Scientific Revolution began their pounding work on the foundations of an ancient order. Like twin hammers, these forces demolished most of what once seemed permanent: Kings, alchemists, popes, feudal lords — they were all undone.

Today, a fresh hammer is cracking our world. The demands of constant, instant connection are tearing at old power arrangements. The formation of networks of all kinds, for trade and biology and finance and warfare and any of a thousand varied needs, is producing new and still dimly understood sources of power. They are eroding the roots of an older order even as a new one is beginning to appear.

That last great shift of the Enlightenment was a violent and wonderful transformation. It produced winners and losers, triggered tragedy and lit fresh triumphs. What lies ahead of us is the same. A new landscape of power is emerging now. This book is its story, and the tale of the instinct that will divide those who master it from those who will be mastered by it.

PART ONE

The Nature of Our Age

CHAPTER ONE

The Masters

*In which the immortal problems of power are discussed
and the possibility of a new instinct is introduced.*

1.

One morning in the spring of 1942, a young Chinese scholar named Nan Huai-Chin packed his bags in Chengdu and began walking out of the city. He was headed south and traced a route along the Min River toward E'Mei Shan, several hundred miles away, deep into Sichuan province. E'Mei Shan — Eyebrow Mountain — was and is one of the holiest Buddhist sites in China.

Nan was an unusual young man. At eighteen, he had won a national sword-fighting competition against men twice his age. At twenty-one he had taught politics to China's top military officials. A year later he led a thirty-thousand-man army in the mountains of Sichuan. If you look at photos of Nan in those years, more or less at the moment he left Chengdu for the mountains, you see a clean-shaven and soft-skinned man. He is handsome, with electric eyes. You can see, if you know to look, the rough intensity of the man he'd become during the anti-Japanese war, a toughness in his stance; some hint too in his grimace of a sword fighter's mercilessness. This was long before Nan was regarded as one of the finest living exemplars of the Chinese Buddhist tradition, before he became known as *Master* Nan. This was before his flight from China with the Kuomintang in 1949, once the Communists came to power, before his decades of wandering and his eventual return to the mainland. All that lies ahead of the man you see in the photo. The man in the photo is young, energetic. He is certain.

In Nan's youth, in his early sword-fighting days, he had come to understand that mastering the blade of his sword meant first training his spirit to the highest possible level of sharpness. When attacked or when attacking, the spirit of a truly masterful fighter moves first, then—instants later—the sword. It was a desire to sharpen that inner blade that had led Nan to E'Mei Shan and to the study of Ch'an Buddhism. Ch'an—you may know it by its Japanese name, Zen—is the steeliest of the Buddhist traditions. Its adherents explain that enlightenment in Ch'an demands concentration intense enough to make and then smash diamonds. It promises, as a result, unmatchable insight into the nature of life.

So, with the anti-Japanese war still smoldering, Nan traveled through his convulsing country and up E'Mei Mountain, where he found a Ch'an lamasery near the peak. Once there, during three years of constant effort and meditation and deprivation, he achieved a breakthrough to *samadhi*, that state of spiritual alignment in which the world and your own soul become as transparent as water. Fear vanishes, as do lust and any real confusion about the deeper currents of life. You become, the priests like to say, as resilient as a mountain spring: No matter what mud is thrown in, it is simply and naturally bubbled away into clarity.

From the E'Mei temple, with this fresh, clear-running mind, Nan began a quest to sharpen his spirit even further. The journey took him, year after year, from master to master in China, from monastery to university to rural Tibetan huts. These were the places where the last bits of some of China's most ancient traditions had been carried, places where classical wisdom had survived a hundred years of national chaos. Nan's wandering education resembled the way in which, in millennia past, monks would make spiritual treks around China, seeking an ever-sharper edge to their insights by engaging in "Zen combat": arguments between sages to see who could feel the underlying nature of the world with greater fidelity. Solitary monks would stride into packed monasteries and engage the wisest abbots in winner-take-all tests of insight. The aim was to really know the secret sources of power that produced earthquakes, revolutions, and poetry. "Ten thousand kinds of clever talk—how can they be as good as reality?" the famous Ch'an master Yun Men once said in the midst of such a fight. True wisdom, it was believed, transcended mere talk.

Nan was trying to cultivate in himself deep ways of feeling and sensing the world. During his wandering study, he followed a path that would lead him to enlightenment in more than a dozen different schools of Buddhism. He mastered everything from medicine to calligraphy. His youthful success at sword fighting, it emerged, was a sign of a prodigal genius. He became, in the twentieth century, recognized as one of those crucial human vessels by which ancient tradition is preserved and carried forward for new generations.

After a few years of study, Nan left the mainland for Taiwan. He lived for decades between Taipei and Hong Kong and America. During this time his fame as a teacher grew. In the mid-1990s, as China opened itself to the world again, Nan returned. He had been invited by some of the country's most powerful families, the children of Communist revolutionaries who were groping for a sense of history and identity. They wanted to absorb the lessons of Chinese culture that Nan had internalized; they hoped to bend them into tools they could use to shape a Chinese future. Might the old habits of the country, with their ancient roots, have something to offer a nation nearly splitting with the energies of modernity? Master Nan agreed to set up a private school. He selected a site on the shores of Lake Tai, in Jiangsu province, not far from Shanghai. He chose the location carefully: The still lake water near his campus was like a giant bath of calming *yin* energy that balanced the urgent, aggressive *yang* energy of 1990s China into a kind of harmony. Ash trees shaded the study rooms in the summer. Wild peonies erupted in pink and white each spring.

It was here, when he was eighty-nine years old, that I first came to know him.

2.

What Master Nan was trying to teach at his Lake Tai campus was in the end not so different from what he had begun trying to cultivate on that long walk out of wartime Chengdu. How in the face of a burning, changing, and shifting world does one train an instinct for the essence of what is going on? At the turn of the last century, the German philosopher Friedrich Nietzsche suggested that humans needed a "Sixth Sense" to survive what then seemed like insane madness: the Industrial Revolution. He didn't mean by this that we should all go study history. At least that wasn't *all* he meant. He thought a Sixth Sense should be a feel for the rhythms of history. There was a certain pace and tone to human life, he said, sort of like a runner on a long race, and you or I would need a sense of the whole course in order to pace ourselves. Without it, we might end up slowing down at the wrong moments. Or—and this particularly worried him—we might run too fast and exhaust ourselves just as a big hill was coming up. Nietzsche thought the world was about to have to face a very steep, unforgiving incline on the way to a new kind of social order, and that most people in the 1890s were skipping along as if it was all downhill from there on out. A feeling for history, he hoped, might help. But he also felt pretty sure no one would develop this new sense. He expected tragedy. "The more abstract the truth you wish to teach," he said, "the more you must allure the senses to it." But no one was attracted to the idea of danger in those gilded days. Very few people tuned their instincts to the age. And, as two world wars later showed, Nietzsche had been sadly correct about the impending tragedy.

This book is the story of a new instinct, what I have called the Seventh Sense. If Nietzsche's Sixth Sense was tuned for a world of changing industrial power, the Seventh Sense is meant for our new age of constant connection. I don't just mean connection to the Internet, but to the whole world of networks that surrounds and defines us everywhere now. Financial webs. DNA databases. Artificial intelligence meshes. Terror or narcotic networks. Currency platforms. Connection—and ever faster, smarter connection—is transforming our lives just as trains and factories tore into Nietzsche's age. As a result, we live in a world that is both terribly exciting and awfully unsettling. A financial crisis that seems to drag on endlessly, despite the efforts of our best minds and most energetic central banks. A historically expensive decade of war against terrorists that produces more terrorists. A global ecosystem that seems beyond repair. New pandemic diseases arriving like clockwork every year. Endless refugee waves. Domestic politics that have been transformed into shouting extremism. The point of this book is that every one of these problems has exactly the same cause: networks. And by understanding how they work, we can begin to shape this age, instead of being used by it. "Man's habits change more rapidly than his instincts," the historian Charles Coulston Gillispie once wrote. That's us. We have all the habits of a new age. The phones. The emails. The ADD clicking of our keyboards. The hand sanitizers. Now we need to develop the instincts. Because anything not built for a network age—our politics, our economics, our national security, our education—is going to crack apart under its pressures.

In the first part of this book I want to tell the story of just how all our networks fit into that long marathon of human history that so concerned Nietzsche. How should we relate the way we think about the world now to, say, how we think of the Enlightenment, the Age of Reason, or the Dark Ages? This is important for all the same reasons a Sixth Sense once was: We need to understand that we're not living at a normal moment. The Enlightenment and the Age of Reason tore up almost every institution in Europe. The Industrial Revolution that followed produced our most violent wars. We'll come to understand how a world where we're all connected, all the time, represents every bit as profound a shift. Maybe more profound.

The second part of the book explains just how the networks operate. Here we'll travel in the company of hackers and activists and diplomats and terrorists who all have this new sensibility. They use the hidden lines of network power to build and destroy. Just as some people can look at a Picasso and unpack a whole story of meaning and passion, people who have the Seventh Sense can look at any object and see potential that is invisible to the rest of us. An entrepreneur with the Seventh Sense looks at a spare bedroom and sees the possibility of a network to unseat hotels. A financier looks at a currency and sees a way to make it algorithmically alive. A new and young discipline called "network science" will give us a framework for thinking about this because it shows how systems as different as the human brain and Facebook in fact follow similar patterns. We'll use these lessons. They will teach us where power really sits in the networks—and how it might be used.

Finally, in the third part of this book, we'll begin to feel out the future with our new sensibility. What can we actually do? This turns out to be an important question because if we don't act, if we just let the new age happen to us, it's likely to pretty quickly slip out of our control. Already many of the most important forces that affect our lives are hard for us to understand, obscured by technical expertise or by speed. Once we get to the root of the networks themselves, once we can see them with the same Seventh Sense that revolutionaries have, however, it will be obvious what we need to do. It's probably likely that we'll have to reinvent most of our politics and economics for the age ahead, for instance. And we'll talk some about that, but I'll linger particularly on the problems of war and peace. Just what might the future of world order be? Pretty much any expert you talk to describes a world heading into chaos, with an ever weaker America. In fact, once we look at the networks, they suggest a very different outcome. Yes, human history has been paced by wars and power struggles between nations. This is what Europe endured in the last five hundred years. But think about all of history. Some systems endure for centuries. The Roman Empire. Chinese dynasties. Assyrian or Mughal kingdoms. The decline of the United States is a popular subject now—in Washington and also in places that are less friendly to American interests. But the networks, when we understand them properly, suggest something very different is possible. In fact they tell us exactly how our most vexing problems—the very problems networks have created—might be solved.

Old-style ideas will, however, lead us down dangerous paths. Our leaders today are, as a result, often imperiling us in ways they can't understand. Honestly, these figures are not mentally prepared to fight any sort of battle on this landscape, whether it is against terrorists or income inequality or pandemic diseases.

They probably never will be. The language and habits of this new world are simply too obscure for them. This book is not, in any event, written for them. It is written for those coming to power and those already in power—even if they don't know it yet. It is written for those who are inheriting the possibility of that last generation's inventions and the price of their errors. By this I mean the cohort bred into the age of connected acceleration, the first generation of leaders and students and war fighters not to find the digital strange, but rather natural and curious and wonderful in its power. This book is for those who will have to build and manage machines that are smarter than humans, for those who will create a new network, and for all of us who want to turn the energies of a disruptive age to constructing an order that feels secure and just.

But before we can get to that point, before we can really begin building with the tools of this new age, we need to know how they work. And that demands an adventure of our own, one that leads us through our own burning world and toward a bit of enlightenment— not unlike Nan Huai-Chin's walk to E'Mei Mountain in 1942.

3.

Before I moved to Beijing in 2002, a friend took me aside and offered this thought: "Your life in China will change the way you see the world. But if you want to get the most out of it, you have to understand that, as important as being bilingual is, it is as important to be bicultural." I had not honestly thought of this as part of my plan, but it seemed like good advice. I have hewed to it as a personal law ever since. From my first days in China, I lived almost entirely among the Chinese. I can, for instance, nearly number on one hand the meals I shared with Westerners over my years there. This advice, to learn to be bicultural, really did change my experience of living in China. It changed how I saw the world. It presented moments of really honest and searching confusion. I had conversations in which I understood every word and yet had no idea what my interlocutor meant. But the decision produced, at least, a fortunate encounter that led me to Master Nan's school.

Several years after I arrived in Beijing, I was out for dinner one evening with a close Chinese friend. My friend is a remarkable woman. If you ask how China had progressed from poverty toward prosperity in record time, it is partly because of people like her. She had studied in China, had moved overseas and mastered the technical arts of economics and finance, and then returned eagerly to help in the construction of modern post-reform China. Nearly any time the government had some new and difficult financial problem to manage, she would be shuffled into the nervous hands of some baffled minister or vice premier. She had, in her various activities, helped put the Chinese stock exchange on its feet, rebuilt bankrupt banks, and overseen the construction of China's first sovereign wealth fund. Though only a few years older than I, her unique skills and absolute loyalty meant she had seen much of the development of China's speed-train economy — part miracle, part near accident — from zero-distance range.

As she and I were finishing dinner that evening, a door opened to a nearby private dining room. Chinese often eat out in private rooms, and the best restaurants are usually warrens of well-appointed secret spaces, a reminder that in China door after door after door leads to ever more secure sanctums — think of the nested power architecture of the Forbidden City. When the door near us opened, a stream of senior Chinese party figures paraded past, hovering around an intense, square-jawed, and smiling man who was soon to become one of the most powerful figures in China.

As this man walked past, he nodded hello to both of us. I asked my friend once he had left: "How do you know him?" I expected that her contact with senior leaders on financial matters would explain the connection. Her answer surprised me.

"We both have the same master."

I had been living in China then for only about four years, so I was still a bit surprised to learn in this unusual way about what I would later come to know—and see and even experience myself— as the spiritual life of China's Communist officials, particularly those at the absolute top. The master my friend was referring to was Master Nan. Though he was largely unknown outside China— I am sure you had not heard of him until a few pages ago—inside the country he was an icon. His books about Buddhism and philosophy sold millions of copies. His lectures are watched on DVDs and the Internet, and he owns a fond fame that reaches across generations and transcends politics and art and philosophy. You are as likely to find a copy of his book on the desk of a university president as stuffed into the back pocket of a tea server in Kunming.

As you can imagine, when my friend first introduced me to the idea of someone like Master Nan serving as a spiritual mentor to the figures leading this huge country, figures I had met and worked with in the brutally rational business of everyday life in a modernizing China, it raised all sorts of questions. *We both have the same master?* But in China, one thing you discover quickly is that honest understanding of anything isn't achieved by asking lots of questions, particularly not the direct sort. Yun Men, the old Buddhist sage, had it right when he said that ten thousand kinds of clever talk get you nowhere meaningful. But with my friend's one sentence, our dinner conversation, which had been moving pleasantly through the eddies of China's politics and economics, passed into deeper water, where it has stayed in the years since.

Master Nan's particular passion, I learned that night, was a branch of Chinese Ch'an Buddhism that had, about a thousand years ago, provided the seeds for the Japanese school of "instant illumination," known as Rinzai Zen. Rinzai is famed in the West for asking students to grapple with koans, the sorts of puzzles—*What was your face before you were born?* or *What is the sound of one hand clapping?*—that can never be approached or answered with reason alone. They require pure, trained instinct. Koans are not like math problems or word puzzles so much as questions that have to be answered with your whole soul. We don't really have an educational concept like this in the West, but the aim of Rinzai meditation and learning is to arrive at a sudden and complete understanding of the true nature of the world. Such "instant illumination" marks a very Eastern sensibility: Real truth resists the grasp of mere logic. It can't be simply explained, or taught with words alone. It calls on more immediate feelings, like a tumble into love or the pulled fuse of instant fury. In Rinzai study, the aim is to use meditation and focus and exercise—and the occasional slapping sharpness of a hardwood "enlightenment stick"—to tighten and compress your mind as a way to open it. A moment when all sorts of invisible relations become unforgettably obvious. The goal is instant, blazing enlightenment.

I had been a student of Rinzai since I was sixteen. So it was that, in the springtime of the year after that dinner in Beijing, I had the luck to be invited to Master Nan's campus.

4.

It is often said that during the days when Master Nan's Lake Tai campus is open for training, when hundreds of rich and well-connected elites from all over the Chinese-speaking world converge there, it is the best networking spot in the country. But on the weekend of my first visit, the Tai Hu Great Learning Center was closed to outsiders. Only about ten of us were present, my friend and I included. We were all, together, students. On our first morning we walked to a large hall overlooking the lake and sat down quietly on benches to meditate. And on our first evening, Master Nan sat with us during dinner, looking young and vital and twenty years short of his eighty-nine, barely eating. Above the bridge of his nose, I noticed, was a small bump. This is the mark that emerges, according to Buddhist tradition, when your self-cultivation and meditation have led you to deep breakthrough, when energy begins to slip out of your head at that "third eye" spot and into the world, leaving a little half marble of flesh as physical evidence.

As we finished dinner, Master Nan asked me what was on my mind. In later years I would learn that this was his habit, to hand the floor over to his guests for a bit—whether they were politicians or industrial titans or innocent visitors—before entering into his own reflections. He pursued me with careful questions, his voice purring with a thick coastal accent. At times, his questions seemed removed from my main points, but I quickly came to see them as needles. ("When he uttered a phrase," it was said of Yun Men, "it was like an iron spike.") Many of those present were jotting notes: Whatever Master Nan thought important, his students felt, must be worth putting down.

I knew that the records of Master Nan's lectures and discussions were often circulated by email. With subject lines such as "Understanding This Chinese Generation" or "Master Nan Answers Questions about Chinese and Western Knowledge," they were real-time maps of the usually invisible dance our daily lives do with history and philosophy. We live *now*, of course, but Nan was always aware that we live within a historical flow too, in a particular moment, amid constant change. Remember that the foundational text of Chinese civilization is the 3,500-year-old *Yi Jing*, the *Book of Changes*. Chinese begin consideration of any question with the idea that flux is the only constant. Problems rarely go away for good; they simply alter their shape. Victory never endures indefinitely. Anyhow, there is no "done." A world of ceaseless change means that a useful education involves not merely the mastery of facts, as it might at a Western university, but also the training of a vigilant instinct. A version of this same aim, to adjust and thrive amid change, was at the heart of Master Nan's teaching. It made his ideas, in a Chinese age of constant shifts, magnetically appealing.

The circulation lists on his lecture notes were the Chinese equivalent of a roster that included Alan Greenspan, Colin Powell, and Warren Buffett. "I just had a very senior leader here," Nan told me during a visit several years later. I had seen the high security at the compound and the military cars whipping in and out all day. "He asked me what books I could recommend to understand this period we are living in. I said, 'I could give you some books, but you wouldn't understand them.'" Master Nan laughed. The iron spike. "This can't be understood by reading!" Master Nan was trying to educate his students in the original principles of Ch'an: a set of psychological, philosophical, and physical tools to discover and then use the deeper patterns of our world.

5.

After wearing his guests down with relentless dinnertime questioning during my first night at the Lake Tai campus, Master Nan offered his own views of our age. What he saw, he explained, was a world pressing too hard on a fault line. We faced, he said, choosing his words carefully, an "epochal" quake. We were at a moment when the river of change he had spent a lifetime feeling out was about to shift its course over the landscape, drowning many of the reliable, old routes. The origins of this change were buried in the very things we hoped might, in fact, save us from shock: money, information, speed. "People are now constantly connected to computers and machines, and this is changing the way they think," he said. "People just cannot make sense of what is happening. There is no respite. The world is going to go faster and faster in this regard.

"In the nineteenth century the biggest threat to humanity was pneumonia," he continued. "In the twentieth century it was cancer. The illness that will mark our era, and particularly the start of the twenty-first century, is insanity. Or, we can say, *spiritual disease*." He paused. "This next century is going to be especially turbulent. It has already begun. And when I say 'insanity' and 'spiritual disease,' I don't only mean inside the minds of individuals. Politics, military, economics, education, culture, and medicine—all these will be affected."

I could sense the logic behind Master Nan's argument. The nineteenth century had packed much of the world into Dickensian urban pits. These became petri dishes for pneumonia. Too much industry and urbanization, too fast. The twentieth century of plastics and artificial, untested, unsafe materials had torn away at our genetic base and brought a plague of cancers. Too much science, too fast. In our age, in the twenty-first century, he felt that a wasting disease would be carried by information, by cell phones, by packets of data, by every bitstream we jacked into our lives—and it would go right for our brains. Our institutions and our ideas about power and stability would fall apart. A profound and destructive shift—what Nan called a *jieshu*, the Chinese word for a rupture in the fabric of human history—lay ahead. In such an era, once-reliable habits would become useless, even dangerous. All that would matter would be your instincts. Frankly, all you would have would be your instincts because no existing map could guide you through a completely new landscape. In fact, the existing maps, should you stubbornly continue to use them, would lead you along dangerous paths, toward catastrophes you could not even imagine.

6.

The dining hall around us was dark as Master Nan finished his discussion that night. At our table we sat in a pool of dim light and waited on the master as he considered his next thoughts. I knew that some of what drew China's great minds here to dinners with him was a sense that those old ideas of Chinese philosophy—born in an age of chaos and dating back to a time before rational calculation and scientific progress—offered hope. I asked Master Nan where he would begin on a quest to understand this age. How best to prepare?

"You know you can't just understand this easily," Master Nan said sharply. He was a little angry with me, I could see, for asking such a direct question—and he was also using the Chinese teaching technique of driving students through a range of emotions. Chinese philosophers believe we learn differently depending on how we feel. Terrifying, intimidating, or praising a student is often more effective than explaining an idea to them. Nan was working on my humiliation bone now: "This isn't like some idea I can *sell* you and then you can just go and use," he continued, his voice rising. I saw the focused intensity of the twenty-one-year-old who had recruited his own mountain army. "This is going to be hard."

Master Nan inhaled on his cigarette and waited a moment. "If you work, though," he said, "maybe you can be like Su Qin, the man who wrestled twenty years of peace out of three hundred years of war." Su Qin was a hero of the Warring States period two millennia ago. China had collapsed into total chaos. Su Qin penetrated the madness of that age and lashed together a stable peace.

"Su Qin started as an idealist, like you," Master Nan said. "He failed. Su Qin was humiliated in trying to advise kings. Even his kin were embarrassed. His sister and mother refused to let him return to the family home. He was in so much pain over this embarrassment that he sat in front of a desk and read every book of history he could find for seven years. He tied his long hair to a beam above his desk so that if he fell asleep it would hold his head up. Sometimes he would stab a knife into his thigh to keep awake." Master Nan's voice was rising, his speech picking up pace. "But in the end, he learned. Su Qin learned. You should study him. If you do this, if you are sincere, if you work hard, if you learn these ideas, you can understand. Can you be that disciplined?" The room was dead quiet now. No one looked at me. In the silence, one of the guests passed around a plate of cut fresh fruit and cherries and sweet dried dates.

Nan's relentless, intense Ch'an Buddhism sort of enlightenment, delivered only after painful years of study, expressed a clear ambition: to learn to feel through invisible relations and balances. Nan's long sessions of meditation and swordplay, his furious pursuit of philosophical dialogues that reduced students to an embarrassed, sweating state—these were all aimed at sharpening a blade so as to instantly carve at the energy flows of our age. Did madness really linger ahead of us as the twenty-first century advanced? What sort of tragedy did that suggest? What was it that, hair tied to the ceiling, penknife jabbed into his leg, Su Qin had learned in those long, effortful years of study? What secret had he penetrated? What sort of education had he finally received at the end of his humiliations and breakthroughs? He had mastered the energy of his age—and the exact right sensibility to use it. Nan seemed to be asking, might we do the same? What tragedy might occur if we did not?

This problem touches on one of the most elemental and interesting problems of philosophy. All of our ideas—from how we love to what we think of politics—are taken from our experiences. What we've seen and done and felt and learned is more than just "the past." We are, each of us, the sum total of our experiences. So what should we do when, as at this very moment, we are confronted with what we've never experienced? Never even dreamed of, perhaps? The answer is that we have to rely nearly entirely on instinct alone, not on "thinking." Every day becomes like one of those koan problems for which there is no rational answer, just an instinctive response. People continue to believe that our markets will work just fine without adjustment, that our politics will right itself eventually, that our world has transcended the experience of war because—for the most part—this has been the experience of their lives. Markets have adjusted. Politics never broke anything too badly. We have seen mostly peace. So you stand out immediately as different if you look at such a world, and feel an instinct that these ideas may be wrong. That something else is going on. And that it might not be a disaster, but hopeful.

Master Nan used to recall a famous story from the 2,500-year-old Daoist masterpiece *Zhuangzi* about the butcher who worked for a famous and powerful duke. One day the duke saw the butcher cutting meat, his blade singing and moving with almost no effort as it sliced apart a cow. "Ah, this is marvelous. Imagine such mastery!" the duke said. "How have you achieved this?" he asked. "What I follow is the Way," the butcher said, referring to the idea of a lively natural energy that Daoism tells us infuses everything, from ash trees to the human heart. "When I started butchering, all I could see was parts of the ox itself," the butcher explained. "Nowadays, I meet the ox with my mind and spirit rather than 'see' it." The butcher was not simply looking at his work; he was feeling the energy of the task. "A good butcher goes through a knife in a year, because he cuts," the butcher told the duke. "An average butcher goes through a knife in a month, because he hacks. I have used this knife for nineteen years. It has butchered thousands of oxen, but the blade is still like it's newly sharpened." He was cutting not with his knife but with an instinct—and the result was the highest form of mastery: accomplishment with nearly no effort. This is our aim: to see the expanding surface of connection around us not merely as a web of phones or data or refugees or markets, but to see its essence.

There will be moments ahead for all of us—the most terrifying or wonderful ones—in which things will happen that none of our old ideas or senses can help us understand. We've had previews of such shocks often enough in recent years. Surprising terror attacks. Economies slipped into sudden reverse. The demolishing of old governments and legendary companies. The Seventh Sense will explain why this is happening. Just as, hundreds of years ago, the demand for liberty or industry was a force that was only visible to a few revolutionaries, so we're likely still blind to what a network age demands.

The ability to hear these sorts of deeper chord changes in history has always been the decisive mark of leadership and success, particularly in revolutionary periods. Consider, for instance, Charles William Ferdinand, the duke of Brunswick-Wolfenbüttel, who faced down Napoleon on the fields of Jena in what is now central Germany in October 1806. Charles was then seventy-one years old. He was considered one of the most courageous soldiers of his age, possessing a record of astonishing victories. He looked over the sun-dappled fields along the Saale River on that fall day and foresaw nearly certain triumph. He had Napoleon outmatched two soldiers to one. His men were masters of the subtle techniques of Frederick the Great, tactics that had delivered victory in far more perilous moments. But Napoleon, just turned thirty-seven, stared across the same undulating land, studied the same poised armies, and saw in the landscape something completely different and lethally correct: an interlocking set of murderous gears that could be set loose by his artillery.

In the course of the French victory the next day, Brunswick-Wolfenbüttel was blinded by French musket shot and then bled to death. It was a poetic end. Like so many of the generals who would tumble before Napoleon in coming years, the duke had been absolutely blind to forces perfectly clear and visible and usable to the revolutionary upstart. Napoleon's European opponents would come to fear and admire nothing so much as the emperor's specific, almost mystical sort of battlefield vision. He could look at a battlefield and see possibilities—certainties, in fact—that eluded older, famous men. They named his masterful insight the "coup d'oeil": an instant, apprehending glimpse of power waves. He saw forces and facts in war that were obscured from his enemies by their own habits of mind and the limits of their creativity. The great Prussian military strategist Carl von Clausewitz, who was made prisoner by Napoleon during the massacre at Jena, used his time locked up to begin compiling notes for his classic work of Western strategy, *On War*. "Genius," he later wrote, "rises above the rules." Mastery of strategy, von Clausewitz explained, was not the result of steely courage, geometric calculation, or even luck, as earlier writers had figured it. Rather, it was derived from the ownership of a sensibility that could discern the secretly running lines of power that made the old ways instantly irrelevant and appallingly dangerous. The same is true today. The strategic genius of business or politics or war now has a similar apprehending glance: to look at the world and see, in an instant, the potential power of networks. And how to unlock it.

7.

Historians who study the long, century-by-century movement of humanity often divide time into "historic" eras, in which tsunami-like changes wipe clean old orders, and more sedate periods, in which time dawdles like a quiet lake. This is the difference between living in Warsaw in, say, 1339 and 1939. The first period was sober and silent; the second was awfully awake. Historic moments like 1939 are marked by the fact that change comes to find you. Your children are pulled into a world war. Your village is torn down. Your health is remade by science. The paleontologist Stephen Jay Gould called the march of these snapping changes "punctuated equilibrium"—when the world is jumped from one state to another and never turns back. He was largely considering the extinction of the dinosaurs, but we find the idea useful in considering history too—the Revolution of 1789 in France, for instance, which enabled the massive volunteer armies that Napoleon later brought to his wars, which were of unprecedented size. "Looking at the situation in this conventional manner, people at first expected to have to deal only with a seriously weakened French army," von Clausewitz explained later, recounting the comfortable, common view in most royal courts. Who would command in an age of *égalité?* France's enemies wondered. The country looked like a weak, easy target. But Europe's leaders had missed the essence of the revolution. It had accelerated France's development, inspired her citizens when called to arms. The age of industrial war had begun. "In 1793," von Clausewitz wrote, "a force appeared that beggared all imagination." The equilibrium of power had shifted.

There is a feeling of this sort of inevitable punctuation in what is under way around us now, the insertion of a single period at the end of one era and the first, italicized letters of a new one. Impulses and connections we don't fully understand and can't yet control are at play. Our imagination is beggared too now. Often. These forces are, we have to confess, wiping away one system. But they are also producing another.

Our problem is to learn to see both old and new, at once. The capacity to feel the real is as important as knowing the virtual forces at work. The capacity to feel the real world of cars, schools, and fighter planes and one of artificial intelligence, DNA data, and computer viruses—and to know that power flows through and between each. Flying-cars technological optimism is not the right mood for our age, but neither is resistant, grudging pessimism. We need an ability to contemplate the changing world ahead evenly, even coldly, and know what we want in politics, economics, warfare, innovation, genomics, and every other connected discipline. Unfortunately, there's not some switch we'll hit and move from today to the Jetsons. Our future will look less like an isolated technological paradise than an intermingling of real and virtual. It will not be an age in which we disappear into a blacked-out virtual reality—marked by a life lived on the digital side of an Oculus Rift, say, or inside the subversive and dystopian world of novels such as *Ready Player One*. Rather, real and virtual worlds will combine. We will be augmented by our connections, as reality is augmented by the HoloLens or Magic Leap goggles. Think of *Snow Crash*, Neal Stephenson's masterpiece novel, for instance, in which characters move effortlessly between net and city. Or of the elegant design of the video game *Ingress*, which drew hundreds of thousands of us to a game board that had been laid atop the world's cities in recent years.

These cultural landmarks matter. They are trail markers to a connected-age sensibility just as Nijinsky's twentieth-century dances and Goethe's nineteenth-century poetry once marked the path to modernism. The great art of a revolutionary era maps habits of mind; it expresses hopes and fears and innovation. To know Kokoschka and Klimt and Mahler and Musil is to hold the energy of Vienna in 1900. In our age, enduring art—work that shocks, upsets, moves us—will be made in virtual or fused reality. It will endure for hundreds of years, and the best of it will give future generations a sense of impossible tensions and profound joys. That advice from my friend about China—be bicultural *and* bilingual—fits the foreign country of our future. We'll have to be fluent both in the new language of networks and in their culture.

Most of us are starting to manage this. We flip back and forth between real and virtual in our everyday lives now, popping our head from screen to street, using our real-world fingers to manage virtual-world requests for sushi, movie tickets, and Yankees scores. Our health, our music, our finances—they are making the same passage. To see both real and virtual at once, to see the way they blend and pull at each other, does demand a new sensibility. And though, eventually, this new instinct will be commonplace, for now at least it must be defined, studied, and learned by each of us. (It also has to be taught to a new generation, in new schools with new techniques.) Such an instinct will make us like Napoleon looking at a battlefield and spotting the violent potential of industrial war. Or Einstein reaching the deeper, invisible truths of physics as he left Newton behind. "There is no logical path to these laws," he wrote later of the leaps that carried him to relativity, "only intuition." The rest of us followed these two men. We fought our wars on Napoleon's murderously industrial terms. We explored our universe with the tools of relativity. But others had to go first. They had to show us what we needed to be trained to see.

None of us yet knows whether the future that emerges from our confrontation with real and virtual phenomena, from a world where thick connection is normal, will produce an information paradise or a terrifying dystopia. That will be decided largely by choices made in the next couple of decades. It will be decided by people who do have the Seventh Sense. Even, I think, by people who are reading this book.

8.

Why start this journey into the churning, still-confusing, and affronting world around us now by the shores of Lake Tai? Why begin with the sentiments of the slower culture that Master Nan embodied, passed like delicate and still-warm tea, with so much calm in the face of all this urgency? It's not only because, as Master Nan said, the faster we move, the sicker we'll get. It's also something else: The training of an instinct, of a truly fresh way of looking at the world, demands a kind of calm. Understanding of anything, after all, is most durably assembled in slow conversations, in patient probing. It is developed as much from brushes with music and literature as it is from any direct confrontation with the truth. What Master Nan was trying to teach was the lesson of thousands of years of philosophy, Eastern and Western alike: The birth of a new instinct—for justice or truth or beauty— requires a rewiring of our minds, and this can be done only at the slow pace of contemplation. (It's the best way to keep the fear at bay.) In this early moment of a revolution, we should seek those stilled, freeze-framed moments when we can pause amid light-speed-fast networks to think about why they work and just what they are doing to us. Some version of Master Nan's own trek to a mountaintop is what we each have to make. We need the perspective of a new view. I guess we might say that Master Nan's model statesman Su Qin, knife stabbed into his own thigh and slouched with exhaustion, is a totem of sorts. *Knife in thigh.* Stop. Think. Even, hard as it may be, *wait.*

Let me tell you what is going to happen: In coming years there will be a struggle between those who have the Seventh Sense—who are born with it or trained to it—and those who don't. This is already under way. New, networked forces all around us are attacking old, established ones in business, politics, warfare, and science. Then—because those who don't have the Seventh Sense for network power will lose these contests, as anyone who tries to stop the future always loses—a new age will begin. This age will involve violent, historic wrestling among different groups with different versions of the Seventh Sense. Competing interests and ideals and aims will guide these contending forces. Networks will fight networks. Some of the plans of these connected-age groups will be good, others evil; and anyhow, the winners will be ruthless. Then—and this is where it will get particularly strange and incredible—there will be a battle between those with the Seventh Sense and the very systems of connection, machines, and intelligence they have built. Human instincts will compete against the machine instincts. That struggle? I'm not quite sure how it will turn out. But for now, at least, we can say this: The future sits almost like a cold-eyed dare in front of us. *Just try to avoid this!*

CHAPTER TWO

The Age of Network Power

In which the Seventh Sense reveals a fundamental insight:
Connection changes the nature of an object.

1.

Several hundred years ago the forces of the Enlightenment and the Scientific Revolution began working away at the roots of an ancient order. The powerful ideas of liberty, freedom of thought, science, democracy, and capitalism—these all layered one upon the other. They washed, like tides, across the institutions and kingdoms and beliefs of Europe, and in a process of revolution, of invention, of destruction and creation, they put a period at the end of one era and began the very first lines of a new human story. These forces produced what we know today as the modern world: Trains knit new markets, science tripled life spans, democracy liberated politics. Confronted with this really irresistible pressure, a gulf opened. The world started to cleave. On one side were the nations and peoples that our modern economists would come to know as and label a "convergence club." This group mastered and refined and then used the tools of their era to become industrial, democratic, scientific, and rich. They left the age of kings and feudal lords, of alchemists and all-knowing priests, behind.

At the same time, a "divergence club" appeared. These nations missed the essential turn. They were trapped. Old ideas, useless habits of power, inescapable history—varied shackles held them back from the punctuated shift to a new, more advanced equilibrium. China, much of Latin America, and Africa—for them, the leap to being honestly modern was fatally elusive. Even today, they struggle to catch up.

We are now in the earliest stages of a shift that promises to be still more consequential than the one that enlightened and industrialized our world over several centuries after the Dark Ages. What I want to do in this chapter is explain the nature of that shift. Fundamentally it involves a change in power. Those people and ideas that prospered in the past may not do so well in the future. And ideas that are coming out of nowhere, that look surprising and impossible and difficult to believe in, may fire up people whom we could never imagine to control our future.

The essence of the shift under way is best captured by the prodigious explosion of different types of connection emerging around us now—connections to finance, trade, information technology, transportation, biology—and the innovative combinations that follow these and other fast, fresh links. Modern, highly connected systems are different from those with less connection. And, as we'll come to see, they are particularly different from those with *slower* connection.

We experience power through networks now, as once we experienced it through brick-bound institutions such as universities or military headquarters or telephone companies. You can no more understand the operations of Hizb'allah or China's central bank or the most valuable Internet companies today without at least this frank admission: Their power operates as much through light pulses running inside fiber-optic webs as it does in any physical sense. Think of the most influential geopolitical forces. The most lethal militaries. The greatest new commercial or financial efforts. All now depend on and are nearly defined by their fluency with different sorts of connection.

Networks emerge when nodes—which can be composed of people, financial markets, computers, mobile devices, drones, or any lively and connectable object—link to other nodes. Networks can be defined by geography, or by language or currency or data protocols or any of a thousand particular features. *People who live in Bangalore* is a network. As is *switches on the Internet* or *businesses transacting in rupiah.* An engineer might say that network power is simply the ceaseless summing, at any instant, of all these bundles of connection. Real, physical networks hum in cities that now pulse and grow with accelerating, connected speed. New York City is a network, in this sense, as is Beijing or—in a less evolved way—the Alaskan steppe. So, while it's tempting to call the twenty-first century the Urban Century, in fact the billion-people-a-decade rush into cities is a symptom. A larger hunger for the constant knitting of lives together, for fresh and efficient connection, drives us. Of course completely, powerfully virtual instances of networks exist too: webs of computers teaching themselves how to read, or the fast, paranoid, and careful buzzing of cybersecurity firewalls. All these systems are defined by connection. Their power comes from the number, the type, and the speed of the relationships they establish and then use. Networks don't merely accelerate our markets, our news, and our innovation. They revolutionize the nature of their power. Broad-based interconnection can cause and even determine events.

These expanding, ever-thicker webs can be mapped, and, taken together, they reflect something we are coming to know as Network Power. By this phrase we mean not merely the Internet or Twitter or crypto currencies such as Bitcoin—though these are, of course, expressions of a kind of network power. Network

Power is something larger. It represents a potentially comprehensive grasp, new in human history and enmeshing billions of connected lives and tens of billions of linked sensors and machines. It is becoming, with every passing moment, more comprehensive: more sensors, more links, and more points. Cascades, epidemics, and interactions are ubiquitous on these networks, producing unexpected innovation in their collisions: the weaving of genetics and databases, for instance, or of terrorism and mobile messaging.

Scientists who study networks call this sort of change "explosive percolation," by which they mean an instant shift in the nature of a system as it passes a threshold level of connectivity. This melding of many nodes into a single fabric—think of the way phones tie together to make a telephone system—is not unlike the linking of water molecules, one to another, as the temperature drops. One moment you have something you can drink; the next you hold ice. So one day you have a few connected users; the next, a billion people are on Facebook or YouTube. A new entity has formed. Or: One instant you have angry fundamentalists; the next, a linked terror movement like ISIS or Al Qaeda. Terrorism—which is aimed at our psychology and sense of safety as much as at any physical structure—is an ancient problem, but it evolves and becomes still more effective when it occurs in a world of superfast networks of media and transportation. Network technologies do to terror attacks what gunpowder once did to projectiles. They make the impact larger. Which makes such acts more appealing to terrorists. Which, in turn, brings still more of these strikes.

Such elemental phase transitions, in which "more" means "different," appear everywhere in nature—the formation of crystals, for example, or the collapse of an ecosystem when the last of a keystone species is hunted down. They appear on networks too. Take out a map of the United States and start randomly drawing lines between cities. At first you'll have a few isolated pairs. Then, as you keep drawing, these pairs clump into groups. Finally, after a few dozen more roads, everything connects to everything. *Just this sort of phase transition lingers ahead of us in our security, our finances, our politics.* It's why the age we're entering now will be as different from the age we're leaving behind as the Enlightenment was from the Dark Ages.

The Enlightenment's seventeenth- and eighteenth-century revolution of free ideas and citizens and trade and capital demanded a new sensibility. So does our age. Already it insists on a feeling for the power that emerges from connection. There's an irony here. At the very moment we might expect to be most free—liberated by mobile phones, easy jet travel, and never-off communications—we find ourselves, inescapably, enmeshed. What is true for the machines all around us now is true for us too: We are what we are connected to. And mastery of that connection turns out to be the modern version of Napoleon's *coup d'oeil*, the essential skill of the age.

Centuries from now, our great-great-grandchildren will look back at our age and name it, as we have named the Enlightenment. Perhaps they will call this era the "Great Connection" or the "Great Enmeshment" or some such. They will spot the winners and losers of our time, as we do when we tell the story of the Age of Reason or the Renaissance. That distant generation will surely identify a new "convergence club" emerging among us now, even if we can't quite name its members yet. Already we can see lavish rewards accumulating to nations, companies, and people who have established a grip on the new sensibility. They understand connective power. They know how to manipulate it and profit from it. What they all share is a feeling for what it means to be enclosed, constantly, by an ever-growing thicket of connection.

This new set of forces, invisible to many, is now applying a merciless and grinding pressure to the familiar structures of an older age. The struggles of our cherished institutions—the U.S. Congress, the military, the news media, our universities, our once-inclusive capitalism—to achieve the very aims that they once elegantly and efficiently met is visible evidence of this shift. Repeated government shutdowns. Years of unwinnable war. No news source we feel we can rely upon. Expensive, debt-funded degrees that don't fit our modern economy. An ever-more-skewed distribution of profits. Pull your focus wider to encompass Europe, the Middle East, and Asia, and you find similarly vexing struggles as nations try to dig their economies out from financial landslides or resist nationalism and unrest. Power is now passing with a rip-pling, ripping energy from old, once-useful people and institu-tions. If this passage has so far wiped out only encyclopedias, telephone companies, and taxi medallions, it is merely because it is just beginning. Buried underneath these failures and the impend-ing collapse of many institutions is a common force.

2.

The Seventh Sense, in short, is the ability to look at any object and see the way in which it is changed by connection. Whether you are commanding an army, running a Fortune 500 company, planning a great work of art, or thinking about your children's education, this skill marks an understanding of power now. It means the ability to contemplate not just the extraordinary fea-tures of modern life but also the quotidian—a soldier, a share of stock, a language—and immediately know that connection changes the nature of an object. A medical diagnostic machine is impres-sive; one that is connected to a database of information that can accelerate and improve or perfect a diagnosis is revolutionary.

The act of linking our bodies, our cities, our ideas—everything, really—together introduces a genuinely new dynamic to our world. It creates hyperdense concentrations of power. It breeds fresh chances for complex and instant chaos. To follow the logic of the French philosopher Paul Virilio for a moment, "When you invent the ship, you also invent the shipwreck. When you invent the plane, you also invent the plane crash." Surely we can count on the network to invent the network accident—and many of them. The emergence of surprise, of tragedy, of wealth and hope will be more common now than in less revolutionary times. We all face possibilities and vulnerabilities we only dimly understand.

The great insight of the Enlightenment was that the nature of an object—a person, a piece of land, a vote, a share—changed when it was liberated from fetters of tradition, ignorance, habit, or fear. A peasant pulled from serfdom became a citizen, which changed his politics, his economic hopes, his ability to learn and teach. That shift triggered centuries of disruption. The world realigned itself. Our Seventh Sense era will be no different. When we are connected, power shifts. It changes who we are, what we might expect, how we might be manipulated, attacked, or enriched. We are relatively early in our age of connection. It's not just that so much of the world remains to be linked; it's also that the nature of connection itself is changing. It is becoming instant. It is increasingly sharpened and enhanced by the use of artificial intelligence. Basic connection has already become a powerful force. You can imagine what instant, AI-enabled networks might be capable of.

Let's take as an example a tool you and I are both using right now, the English language. Any language is a tool of sorts, the power of which depends on who uses it and why. Just as widespread use of the dollar or the British pound or gold—to buy cotton, invest, or stash under a mattress—reveals a network of exchange, so English is a mesh for information sharing. When Spanish and Lebanese and Russian researchers gather to design a drug molecule, when astronauts talk in the International Space Station, when bankers settle finance policy in the midst of yet another unexpected crisis, they are using a powerful, standardized, shared tool that makes their work possible and efficient. English in this role, like French before it, has an appealing leverage: The more people who use it, the greater the incentive to learn it. But when we think of English in a network sense, in an age of connection, this calculus shifts.

English is a means of connection, as important to linking two people in some settings as a cable is to linking two computers. Information scientists call English a "protocol." You may know the word from the realm of diplomacy, in which protocols decide everything from where a president sits at a dinner to how a letter to an envoy must be addressed. Protocols are what keep any possibly confused situation—a treaty negotiation, a banking seminar, a wedding—from becoming a mess of shouting chaos. English prevents the International Space Station from turning into a floating tower of Babel. HTTP, a protocol that translates digital bits into organized Web pages, makes the Internet function. SWIFT, a protocol for banks and consumers, is the reason we can easily shop in Paris with our American credit cards. Protocols are rule books. On the Internet, for example, protocol rules place each bit of data in a reliable, predictable order, just as diplomatic protocol might seat ambassadors at a negotiation. This is why computers can speak to each other. But protocols are about more than bits. They can be used to organize trade networks or stock markets too. Designing and controlling a protocol, then, means that you can control almost everything important about a system. "Protocol," the technology theorists Alexander Galloway and Eugene Thacker have written, "is a system for maintaining organization and control in networks."

In a world of older, more traditional power distributions, Americans might have worried about a day when another language, another protocol for communication—Chinese or Spanish, say—would overtake English. But this would be difficult. Protocols are hard to change. So many people have learned English. So many essential activities depend on its use. To suddenly switch the world's airline pilots, bond traders, and computer programmers to Chinese or Spanish would hardly be worth the immense cost. But it's here where that Seventh Sense axiom, that connection changes the nature of an object, comes into play. For the first time, as a result of constant connectivity, a once-unimagined possibility exists: real-time machine translation. Fast, ubiquitous networks mean that the central role of English will be boiled away someday not by another language but by an intelligent translation computer, available anytime, anywhere. You'll say, "Good morning," as you climb into a taxi in Barcelona and your taxi driver will hear *Buenos días*. As a result, "Good morning" is less likely to be replaced by a greeting in some other language than it is to be effortlessly, invisibly transmuted into 早上好 or *Bonjour*. Reliable access to a great translation algorithm will one day be more important than the ability to speak English (or Spanish or Chinese). Those American parents now nervously plowing their children into Chinese classes are missing the point. Fluency in any second language in the future will be an arcane specialty. Better to teach the kids how to build an artificial intelligence program, or to debate the moral reasoning of Confucius and Socrates, than how to order dinner in another language. The machines will take care of that. Power in a connected age will pool not in the mouths and minds of English speakers but rather in the hands of anyone who controls the best translation server. That's what the kids will need to understand.

Connection has changed the nature of several objects here: the language itself, the people who use it—pilots, commodity traders, machines, you and I. You can see how the ability to design, build, and turn on (or off) the fastest, smartest, most connected language machines becomes a nexus of power. What will replace English isn't Spanish or Chinese but a protocol. This sort of specialized data pipe will permit instant, always-improving translation. It will become as crucial to the operation of the global economy or research laboratories or entertainment companies as English now is. *More* crucial, in fact, because machines will enable us to really talk to each other. These systems will consider not only what we say but also what they suspect we *mean*.

The pre-network instinct to *fear Chinese!* or *fear Spanish!* is the wrong one. As is the idea to teach the world Chinese or Spanish as a source of power. Or, eventually, to demand that everyone in the United States speak English. Rather, *Can we control this turbo-smart connected language protocol?* is the right question. Many of the threats we worry about today have been similarly simplified and misunderstood. *Fear deflation? Fear ISIS? Fear the RMB?* Such fear reflects a blindness. Finance, terrorism, and currency change when they are connected. It's the network we should be nervous about.

We will see, over and over again, networks shifting and even destroying the nature of even the most solid-looking objects. New links, exploding into operation around us everywhere now, alter everything from how doctors operate to how investments perform. The failure to spot, understand, and use this connected power will be a source of our biggest future tragedies. Actually, it is already causing some of our most vexing present dangers.

3.

On paper, Ben Bernanke must have looked like the ideal figure to head the Federal Reserve in 2008. The world was tumbling into a financial crisis whose speed, depth, and dimension rivaled nothing since the Great Depression of 1929–1939. And Bernanke, a Princeton economist before his appointment to the Federal Reserve in 2006, was *the* expert on the Great Depression. His papers in the 1990s had helped redefine the way central bankers around the world thought about that tragedy, one that had demolished a generation of human hopes and helped spark the Second World War. Bernanke's essential insight about the 1930s was that the global depression was worsened fatally by a melting of faith in financial institutions. When no one could trust their banks, no one wanted to save or spend or invest. It was like stopping the very heart of the markets.

Bernanke thought that this sort of financial cancer had accelerated what economists know as a "deflationary cycle," a period when prices collapse to impossible levels. No one wants to buy, no matter the price. Economists and citizens alike worry about inflation too, of course, because that cycle drives prices constantly up: "I should buy this today, because it will be more expensive tomorrow!" consumers think as they rush to the store. But there are good policies to handle this problem: Interest rates can be used to encourage people to delay spending, for instance. Deflation is a different and more terrifying monster. In a deflationary environment people stop spending entirely. They think prices are going to be cheaper tomorrow, so they wait to spend. And wait. "Deflation," Bernanke concluded in one seminal analysis of the Great Depression, "creates an environment of financial distress in which the incentives of borrowers are distorted and in which it is difficult to extend new credit."

Bernanke's reaction to the 2008 financial crisis—and the path of most of his fellow central bankers around the world—was what you would have expected, then: to avoid that fatal financial distress by flooding the system with money. "I was not going to be the

Federal Reserve chairman who presided over the second Great Depression," he reflected in 2009. The U.S. monetary base grew fivefold, from $800 billion to $4 trillion, as a program known as "quantitative easing" pressed money into circulation. But something unusual and unnerving became apparent after a few years. Despite massively increasing money supply, prices remained largely the same. Consumption remained stagnant. Usually the injection of tremendous amounts of money into the system creates demand, it builds pressure for inflation: Suddenly everyone has money and wants to spend it. "Inflation is always and everywhere a monetary phenomenon," the Nobel Prize–winning economist Milton Friedman famously said. But if all that money was being pumped into the system, why weren't prices rising?

The answer, it emerged, was something largely invisible to Bernanke and many economists: networks. An age of connected markets was different from one with less connection. Global networks of trade and data and finance were doing two things at once, both of which were producing exactly the sort of pressure on prices that Bernanke was hoping to avoid: They were reducing demand for purchases by concentrating wealth and increasing supply of many important goods. On the demand side, the problem was simple enough to see. The rich were getting richer. And any member of the world's 1 percent has a lower "marginal propensity to consume"—less chance they will spend any additional dollar you give them—than someone in the middle class. Give a billionaire a dollar, he'll save it. Give it to a teacher and he'll spend it. But the design of capital markets at the time of the 2008 crisis ensured that most of the benefits of a loose monetary policy accumulated to those who already had money. (Among other reasons, because they were connected to networks of credit, investment, and information that elude most citizens.) At the same time, new technology and networks of trade, finance, and information meant that middle-class jobs were being exported or automated. So the once prosperous middle class, an essential element of any stable capitalist system, was being pulled apart. The rich were getting richer; the poor in other countries (or the machines) were taking the jobs. Though financial and monetary stimulus were pouring into the system, there was no trickle down. "The extent and continuing increase in income inequality in the United States greatly concern me," Bernanke's successor Janet Yellen remarked in 2015, after seven years of quantitative easing policy. "The past several decades have seen the most sustained rise in income inequality since the nineteenth century." Even with more money floating around, there was, paradoxically (at least using traditional thinking), less demand.

But that wasn't the whole story. Networks were also working insidiously on the supply side of the equation. Remember that markets always set prices by balancing supply and demand. On a hot day when more people want lemonade, the kids on the beach selling it can charge more than on a rainy day. In the years after 2008, much of the cheap credit of "quantitative easing" was used to fund projects that massively increased supply. More oil rigs were built. A whole fracking industry was financed on cheap credit. More ship keels were laid down. Mines were excavated in Australia and Brazil. Factories were built in China and Vietnam and Malaysia. This created a historic excess of supply of everything from jet planes to iron ore to shoes. Cheap money made usually unprofitable investments possible; technology accelerated their impact everywhere. Think of how businesses like Airbnb or Uber have liberated once unused assets—spare bedrooms and empty car seats—and brought them to market. This is a historic, rapid increase in supply. Similar technologies are at work in manufacturing, logistics, and information technology. It was as if hundreds of gallons of lemonade were suddenly available on that beach. Prices collapsed. And because demand had also collapsed in the face of that inequality that so worried Janet Yellen, there was no one to buy up all the new supply. Traditional economic policy tools would not be able to rescue the world, not merely because they had run out of ammunition, but because the problem was in the networks. The old ideas, if anything, were making the crisis worse.

In trying to stop deflation, Bernanke's policies had in fact made it inevitable. They had not helped the middle class as much as needed, and they had flooded the market with supply and then finally distorted prices to an unrecognizable level. In a speech in 2014, Larry Summers, the former Treasury secretary and perhaps America's most pedigreed economist, summed up the problem this way: "I think it is fair to say that six years ago, macroeconomics was primarily about the use of monetary policy to reduce the already small amplitude of fluctuations about a given trend, while maintaining price stability." In other words, the main preoccupation of figures like Bernanke and Summers and Yellen was trying to keep lemonade prices within a manageable bound. But by 2014, that had changed. "Today, we wish for the problem of minimizing fluctuations around a satisfactory trend," Summers said. His real concern, he vouchsafed in that speech, was that the system had undergone what is known as *hysteresis:* a term for a moment when something breaks and can never be put back together again. The markets, he worried, were like a shattered and irreparable crystal glass.

The source of that cracking pressure was networks, which had both boosted supply and destroyed demand. A perfect deflationary storm. Bernanke's initial moves were important and essential, but the wiring of even the world's most sophisticated capital markets to networks has made them dangerous. It was like putting a Ferrari engine in an old Beetle. Networks had accelerated the machine of global markets to a point where breakdown was inevitable, a crisis of the sort that the usual tools could not fix. Capitalism worked well enough in an age of puritanical values, where people saved, where markets moved slowly, where finance was an isolated part of the economy and the middle class received the bulk of the benefits of progress. But just as networks change the nature of something like the English language, so, too, they change the nature of a dollar of your savings. They really change the nature of anything to which they are connected. Our puzzle as citizens now is to understand why this happens. And to do so before the superfast networks crack much more of our world apart. Then, like it or not, we will have to throw ourselves into the business of combating the dangers of networks by using the possibility they contain. Most of us don't know how to do this today, which is the purpose of this book. But at least we're game to try. We're not nearly as dangerous in a sense as another group: our current leaders.

4.

At this early moment in a new revolution, most of our leaders are blind. It's not simple technical fluency that eludes them—though this is among the most embarrassing of their deficits, marked by their leaked emails and overheard voice mails. It's certainly true that listening to some of our leaders talk about technology resembles nothing so much as trying to explain Snapchat to your grandparents. But the problem is more profound. Avoiding cyberaccidents, controlling the spread of nuclear weapons, handling global warming, stemming financial crises, restoring equitable growth—all these puzzles yearn to be tackled with a new sensibility. They are *produced* by new forces, after all. These problems linger not as independent fractures on some solid base that can be easily patched, but rather as markers of connected cracks that are growing over time.

Even as this new age advances, most of our leaders still think in terms of disconnected dangers. They are like cosmologists before the discoveries of Copernicus and Galileo. These men (and, yes, they are mostly men) see a world of risks that can be reduced to nouns: atomic bombs, fundamentalists, derivatives. To be sure, plenty of these sorts of dangerous nouns confront us. But the sharpest edges of our problems come from the fact that these nouns are part of networks, which spring them into surprising action. Our era is one of connected crises. Relationships now matter as much as any single object.

"A commander-in-chief," von Clausewitz wrote of an older age of land warfare, "must aim at acquiring an overall knowledge of the configuration of a province, of an entire country. His mind must hold a vivid picture of the road-network, the river-lines and the mountain ranges, without ever losing a sense of his immediate surroundings." This sort of command mastery is what we should all seek in the age of networks, even if the terms are different or if the rivers are fiber-optic. But which of our current leaders holds in his or her mind such a vivid map? Who owns that subtle overall knowledge and then acts with the confident sensibility such wisdom would produce?

Our leaders don't yet see or feel the essential links of power that join these and other disruptions. They fight them in industrial terms, with predictable results. Networks are, even now, making the familiar dangerous and the dangerous familiar. Capitalism on networks is different. Politics as well. And military action. "We got to know the *nature* of calculating by learning to calculate," the Austrian philosopher Ludwig Wittgenstein once observed. So it is with networks. We must get to know them by operating them. But our leaders have never had such a chance. Partly this is age, I think. But honestly it is also temperament. Networks are packed with tremendous potential. Many of our current leaders like things as they are. The words "potential" and "threat" rhyme in their consideration. They don't appreciate that puzzles such as the future of United States–China relations or income inequality or artificial intelligence or terrorism are all network problems, unsolvable with traditional thinking.

At the same moment in time that so many of us are alive with the joy of being around something that is beginning, most of our leaders are locked, sadly or with terror, into the ending of something else. Same exact moment. Different instincts. It reminds me of Virginia Woolf's novel *The Years*, in which the once-commanding Colonel Pargiter finally passes away, liberating his daughter Eleanor into a world of adventure even as the change dooms Crosby, the family's long-serving maid. "For Crosby it was the end of everything," Woolf writes. "She had known every cupboard, flagstone, chair and table in that large rambling house, not from five or six feet of distance as they had known it; but from her knees, as she scrubbed and polished; she had known every groove, stain, fork, knife, napkin and cupboard. They and their doings had made her entire world. And now she was going off, alone, to a single room at Richmond." The people now lamenting the decline of television, of newspapers, of a disconnected age, who are baffled by constant connection or apps of the moment or machines that learn, should be given their quiet moments with the old structures. They knew that world from their knees and built and maintained it as much for us as for themselves. Elements of that slower, unconnected era must be preserved. But we must move on. These people will never grasp the opportunity in front of us now.

But a full-throated endorsement of our technological elite is not quite right either. Yes, it's wonderful that we are at the beginning of a new period. But it's not quite right to say that where the network age begins, the old one ends. In fact, that's a dangerous conclusion. We're at an extremely primitive point in our understanding of networks, comparable to where economics was in the 1800s or medicine was in the 1700s. We have a modest collection of tools we can use to analyze and think about and consider the complex physics of a network world. We barely understand the operation and evolution of many networks today. And networks of networks? Instant networks? Artificially intelligent ones? We have almost zero experience with these.

The headlong rush into a world of constant connection will, of course, be balanced, resisted, braced against, undermined, fought, and manipulated. Networks touch everything, remember? The idea that such elemental control—of you, of me, of our finances or our nations—would move with anything less than a few explosions is naive. Revolutions don't occur quietly. Consequently, the very qualities that make many of the greatest tech minds of our age so magnificent—a sense of unstoppable determinism, a disregard for history, a slavish and instinctive urge to connect everything—can be disadvantageous to us at times. I know many of these men and women; their iron certainty is only slightly more dazzling than their success in building something from nothing in a human instant. But that confidence in all things new is already leading to crushing collisions with older notions— privacy, localism, slowness—that have endured for so long precisely because they touch in subtle ways on the human heart, on what it means really to live.

A friend of mine who runs a leading technology company told me of the unnerving realization that some of the most important figures at the firm were twenty-something programmers, embarked in most cases on activities barely comprehensible to managers at the highest levels of the company. They fingered algorithms that determine some of the most essential functions of our modern world. And though it was impossible to argue with their technical virtuosity, for the most part it was also frankly tough to figure out just what sorts of people they really were. What did they think about liberty and fairness? Did they understand those ideas? Of course the biggest tech firms still rely on a few old figures, expert graybeards who know where the old, essential switches are. But they are in a fight to shape the values of the system ahead. The inevitable youth bulge of new tools and ideas is the type of power inversion that marks a moment of potential fracture: The greatest power in a stable world accrues to those with the most experience and judgment and perspective. The past is usually not a bad predictor of the future; maturity and its habits of conservatism have a certain wisdom. To place a gray-haired fighter pilot–turned-general in charge of a nation's nuclear weapons made sense. He could understand both the technology and its dangerous potential. Today, tremendous, even decisive, influence in our markets or our biology or our war fighting clusters in the hands of a young caste. Their very fluency with the norms of a network age is not yet matched with comprehension of the language of philosophy, history, and even tragedy.

"It happens that programming is a relatively easy craft to learn," the MIT computer scientist Joseph Weizenbaum observed in the 1970s, as calculating machines began to penetrate academic life. "Almost anyone with a reasonably ordered mind can become a fairly good programmer." The mistake, he warned, is to think that easy programming of a machine is really a predictor of anything other than getting a machine to follow commands. Mastery of programming doesn't mean mastery of the systems a machine might influence. It doesn't express a command of science, say. And it doesn't mean that anyone in front of a keyboard should believe, God forbid, that the world might be so easily programmed. Programming, he warned, "appeals most to precisely those who do not yet have sufficient maturity to tolerate long delays between an effort to achieve something and the appearance of concrete evidence of success."

Tempting as it may be to call for our world to be turned over to entrepreneurs or technocrats, to let their tools of wired efficiency tear into our politics and economics, the reality is that the world (thankfully) does not respond like a cold machine. The delay that Weizenbaum named, between an effort to achieve something and its realization, is the essence of being human. That delay is filled with worry, hope, debate, exploration, error, success. In short, it's a hitch that should never be polished out of our system, no more by technology than by authoritarian or totalitarian or fundamentalist doctrines. *Just let the entrepreneurs do it* or *Just let the machines do it* is no more a solution than *Just let the central planners handle this* could have been.

If these two groups of elites, old power and new, are united, at least, in their power over forces that shape our world, they share as well an unnerving feature: a near total lack of diversity. Women and minorities remain a rarity in these worlds; they handle real power only from a distance in most networks. Though they fill many of these networks as customers or investors or voters, to spend time amid the power centers of the network age is a jarring time trip. Elements of the future look disappointingly like the past. A strange, white male feudalism reigns: Millions of women, for instance, permit the very existence of online social and shopping services, which are commanded largely by men. But other kinds of diversity are absent too. Few of the figures in either world—the old power centers or the new—have lived overseas for any length of time. They don't speak a foreign language. Their close friends mirror themselves. Such an arrangement, which was merely immoral or ahistorical in the past, has now become dangerous. In fact, the very best tech firms have begun to redress this—they understand the irreparable disadvantage of a monoculture.

An instantly linked world means that the rapid apprehension of the real nature of any danger is essential. Time is the one thing we have ever less of in our crisis-filled world. And, honestly, the chances of a team of white American men making much sense of the totally foreign puzzles cascading back at us now are too slim to be a sensible risk. The chances that the macho culture that still influences Silicon Valley or Wall Street or Washington can really adjust to a new era are low. The failure of our old institutions means they'll have to be rebuilt. And, one way or another, they will be rebuilt and designed by people who are themselves diverse in experience, temperament, and background. Otherwise, they will fail. The only durable institutions in our future will be those that evenhandedly regard ideas and skills, no matter where they come from.

This is our dilemma: Old, network-blinded leaders (and the young people who think like them) pull us from Washington and other capitals and traditional power centers into a world in which their ideas and policies constantly fail. We trust them less and less as a result. At the same time, a rising generation lashes us into amazing meshes. We welcome this connection. Centered in places such as Menlo Park or Seattle or Zhongguancun or Tel Aviv, these figures understand networks perfectly, but—so far—not yet much else. Old and new, each group works anyhow on our freedom. We are pulled dangerously between these forces. Problems seem to get worse. What we need to find is a way out of this trap. A fusion. A blended sensibility of both the edgiest ideas of connection and the most unshakable requirements of power.

5.

Many of the technical choices we're about to make will be strikingly political. Who has access to what data? Where is the line between human choice and machine intelligence? Why is one

computer architecture better than another? These decisions—
and the people who make them—will determine power's new
aspects. Banal technical choices will reverberate through our
future with the same influence that the Bill of Rights, the Magna
Carta, the Analects of Confucius, and the Koran retain long after
they were first written down. The real contests ahead will concern networks—but this means, in fact, a deeper conflict over
values. Networks are like churches or schools or congresses; they
reflect the aims and ethics of the people who build them. The
price of meshing so many passionately held aims and sensibilities,
hopes and hatreds, will be high. We can already see how wrong
the idea of easy globalization, once promised to us, has become.
National identities, religions, biases—these aren't erased by connection. They are merely (and dangerously) linked.

"Modern societies," the French philosopher Bruno Latour has
written, "cannot be described without recognizing them as having a fibrous, thread-like, wiry, stringy, ropy, capillary character
that is never captured by the notions of levels, layers, territories,
spheres, categories, structure, systems." Familiar borders, like the
ones dividing science and politics or military power and civilian
safety, begin to erode when everything is linked. Computing
machines and networks were once locked into usefully narrow
silos, unconnected: An ATM. A heart monitor. A power grid. But
now they overlap and inform one another.

Engineers know the idea that network design shapes the real
world as Conway's Law. Melvin Conway was a scientist in the
1960s who noticed that the design of a telephone network had an
impact on the businesses, communities, and research labs it
touched. Who could call whom was a kind of power map, just as
who can share photos or who can trade with each other is now.
The physical world, Conway realized, could be shaped and influenced by something other than a physical force; it could be

reshaped by connection. The expansion of airline routes to Indonesia in the 1980s, for instance, was a network-design change that tilted real-life economic patterns. Hong Kong–to-Bali flights brought manufacturing, investment, tipsy expatriates, and then surfers. In our connected age, the design of research studies, voter databases, genetic-information sharing networks, financial webs — all of these — will change many usual patterns even as they establish some completely new ones. The networks will be used in ways their designers never imagined — Twitter turned to terror recruitment, Bitcoin as an alternative to central banks. But Conway's insight retains all its original power: The physical world can be reshaped by the virtual. Networks will create bumps in the surface of our everyday lives. "When you decide what infrastructure to use for a project, you're not just making a technical decision," the programmer and investor Paul Graham has written. "You're also making a social decision, and this may be the more important of the two."

You might ask: What drew tens of millions of people to watch as Steve Jobs, live, unveiled some new Apple device? Of course, partly it was the cool technology, the warm charisma of the man. But something else was at work, I think. What Jobs was unveiling atop those black stages over the years as we waited for him was nothing less than whole new worlds, connected landscapes that emerged entirely from ideas Apple was secretly developing. He wasn't merely introducing a phone; he was changing how we were going to experience life. "Every once in a while, a revolutionary product comes along that changes everything," Jobs began in his famous speech introducing the first iPhone, in 2007. "In 1984 we introduced the Macintosh. It didn't just change Apple. It changed the whole computer industry. In 2001 we introduced the first iPod. It didn't just change the way we all listen to music. It changed the entire music industry."

Apple devices were cracking open paths to whole new worlds in this sense. The company develops an app for podcasts; a new media form is born. It builds an architecture for video calling; our relations to each other deepen a bit. What Jobs was presenting were new and—until that very instant—unimagined universes of possibility that we would all explore. No wonder the world tuned in.

Power pulses through structure as molten metal might pass hot into a mold, leaving behind something solid and hard to snap—forms for politics, wealth, and influence. The Orientalist scholar Karl Wittfogel followed this link between form and power as he developed his famous "hydraulic hypothesis" in the 1930s. Ancient agrarian societies such as Egypt and China were formed not least by the need for large-scale irrigation. Chinese dynasties tumbled and Egyptian prosperity collapsed as unpredicted droughts and flooding tore them apart. Without water, these societies were dead. Without control of that water? Exposed to constant chaos. Taming rivers and canals and reservoirs became the aim of all politics. An unusual, centralized effort emerged as the most efficient approach. It screwed these scattered, nomadic societies into a tight authoritarianism. Wittfogel argued that the irrigation societies of Egypt, China, Mesopotamia, and South America all shared this link between water control and survival. Power pooled in the hands of a liquid elite, a "hydraulic bureaucracy." China's Yu the Great, for instance, rose to power around 2800 BCE because of his skills in throttling the unpredictable and deadly Yangtze. "Contrary to the popular belief that nature always remains the same," Wittfogel wrote, "nature changes profoundly whenever man, in response to simple or complex historical causes, profoundly changes his technical equipment."

Control of water in those ancient ages and control of information in our own are not so different. We are in the midst of a change in our own "technical equipment." A new elite is emerging. We should read Wittfogel with one eye on our own age, particularly his warnings: "Like the tiger, the engineer of power must have the physical means with which to crush his victims," he wrote of those older orders. "The agromanagerial despot does indeed possess such means." As networks come alive around us now, as they move power from languages to servers or as they rewrite the rules of economics, we should ask: Are we watching the emergence of a network despotism?

6.

In the 1930s, as the Austrian economist Friedrich Hayek watched Europe both struggle against and flirt with the ideas of Nazism and Soviet socialism, he spotted what he felt would be the fundamental conflict of his age: individual liberty versus central planning. Recall that at that moment America and much of Europe were in a deep depression, their political systems struggling. The rapidly growing economies in the Soviet Union and Germany — racing ahead some years at triple the U.S. rate — looked appealing to many. As Spain and Italy and Japan followed authoritarian, nationalist paths as well, it became popular to wonder if these nations had found a system better suited to an industrial age. Hayek found such a conclusion frankly terrifying. Europe, as the title of his bestselling book suggested, was walking nothing less than a road back to serfdom. Was man happier, better off, more justly fulfilled by the chaos of a market and democracy or by the orderly machine of authority, of clicking heels? Hayek voted with his feet. He fled the Nazis in 1938, but he worried for the rest of his life that in the attempt to manage the risks of free markets and minds, the Europe he loved was running into socialism. There was *nothing* appealing about socialism or fascism to him, and he made it his life's work to prove this urgent truth. "Is there a greater tragedy imaginable," he wrote, "than that, in our endeavour consciously to shape our future in accordance with high ideals, we should in fact unwittingly produce the very opposite of what we have been striving for?"

Hayek thought two safety catches might protect mankind: The first was an unkillable human instinct for individual freedom. The second was the inefficiency of centrally planned systems. No bureaucrat sitting at his desk, no economist with a slide rule, could possibly outperform the self-ordering chaos of a market or an election in the long run. Finding the right price, balancing political interests—it was impossible to think this could be done by some technocrat. Churchill's famous line "Democracy is the worst form of government except all those other forms that have been tried from time to time" contains a certain truth. The clicking heels sounded efficient, but they were anything but. History proved Hayek right. People wanted to be free; markets knew more than planners. The dream of central economic control collapsed with the fall of the Soviet Union in 1989.

In our own age, a fundamental conflict lingers as well. This is the struggle, just begun, between individual liberty and connection. We have to ask a version of Hayek's question: Are we happier, better off, more justly fulfilled through ceaseless linkage to the fast systems all around us? The appeal of constant connection is not a mere economic fact. It's become a feature of our personalities and psychologies and even the biochemistry of our brains. To be disconnected, in so many senses, *hurts*. And, while the human twitch for freedom remains alive as a protection for us all, Hayek's second safety catch is eroding, I think. Networks of deep connection, speed, and machine intelligence may appear powerfully more efficient than central planning; they will know more than any central bureaucrat might. They may yet be even more productive at times in their connection and intelligence than our existing structures or markets or electoral systems.

Fortunately, a new sensibility is emerging. This isn't a normal moment. And so we each should develop our understanding of the networks—to know network power by knowing networks, as Wittgenstein might have said. It turns out this is not very difficult. Because the networks are already all around us. And to study the mismatch between the old instincts and the new networks, there's no better place to start than the baffling global headlines of our day. Two hundred years from now, when the great companies and billionaires and revolutionaries of our age are crushed down below the horizon of history, it is the movements of states and populations, the alternations of war and peace, that will remain in the collective human memory. Just as some of the clearest signs of a feudal order breaking down came on the battlefields of Europe, so the collapse of our industrial-power habits now is marked out by the way we fight wars or try to secure peace or tackle problems that really do affect the future of humanity as a whole. And our leading politicians and intellectuals? As you can probably guess, most of what they have in mind is more or less the opposite of what the Seventh Sense suggests.

CHAPTER THREE

War, Peace, Networks

In which the Seventh Sense reaches toward the questions of war
and peace and power that will flavor our lives, like it or not.

1.

One afternoon in the fall of 2009, I received an unexpected call
from the Pentagon. The United States was then nearly a decade
into the wars of Afghanistan and Iraq. Each in its own way possessed a strange and shifting character, the sort of dim premoni-
tion of a greater violence that has always most unnerved warriors
and politicians. The old soldier's saying—*Fear chaos as much as the
enemy*—seemed to animate, constantly, the progress of these two
fights. Once, before I gave a speech to an audience of newly promoted one-star generals, a four-star general pulled me aside for a
moment. He explained that I'd be speaking to a crowd of officers
who had come of age pacing the murderous streets of these wars,
watching soldiers under their command killed by an often invisible enemy. "You have to remember that these men have been
seared, *seared*, by a decade of combat," he said. The best American
military minds had tried, with characteristically direct and relentless energy, to box in the wildness of these wars. In books and
papers and thousands of patrols, through millions of hours of lan-

guage training and endless risky nights, they had tried. It never quite seemed to work. There would never be a durable sense of mastery. The wars, which had at first appeared so winnable, had run longer than any in the nation's history. They were engines of chaos and fear.

Victor Krulak, an American counterinsurgency expert and a lieutenant general in the U.S. Marine Corps, once observed, "The war you prepare for is rarely the war you get." You could find this phrase whistling through the years of American combat after 9/11. One of the lessons of both Afghanistan and Iraq was that the Pentagon and the fighting services had been unready for what they would face. Soldiers had arrived in Baghdad with forest-colored uniforms, thin-skinned Humvees, and tank-led battle plans—all wrong and mostly dangerous. The deadliest weapons of these wars were the improvised explosive devices, or IEDs—hidden amalgamations of dynamite, duct tape, cell-phone detonators, and as much stubbly, impaling iron as could be found. They were impossible to deter. The IED threat, one officer later reflected, "is a contemporary example of conventional militaries being confronted with a tactical surprise with operational—if not strategic—implications." Like so much in our age, small problems were spiraling rapidly into crises of strategy. One hot battlefield instant—say, an explosion under an armorless truck— could freeze the operations of a billion-dollar division. Nearly everyone began to ask, sometimes out loud: *"Why did that happen?"* That question was followed pretty quickly by: *"What the hell are we doing here?"* The little bombs were shaking more than the Humvees; they were rocking America's entire conception about how to go to war.

Walking into the Pentagon, one is struck by its immensity and volume and, frankly, gravity. Surely, you reflect, there must be someone here with a plan for everything. But there was not;

there is not now. Yet the massiveness, the ineffable historical density and weight of American power, is so breathtaking that its frequent impotence in the face of a changing world represents a particularly unforgettable shock. The soldiers who had experienced those cold, failing nights at the edge of a superpower's reach rippled with unease. This was the slim comfort of life inside big, old structures confronting the fast and unstoppable future.

By 2009, with the wars in Afghanistan and Iraq settling into a low boil, America's generals again began wondering what other cracks were spreading around the world. The diplomats worried about this too, of course, but with soldiers dying every day, the question had a particular urgency for the military. The top brass asked incessantly about what they might be missing. What fissures were running through even their own building, masked by its scale but waiting quietly to make their best plans look foolish and dangerous? And how could they possibly confront this world with 30 percent less than what they had a decade ago? So they made a few phone calls.

2.

If you picked up one of those incoming queries from Washington and were asked to draft your views on how to approach this uncertain world, it was hard not to notice that one of the U.S. military's main aims in recent years—reducing the number of terrorists—appeared to be backfiring. This dynamic was an irritating feature of many global problems. In spreading market capitalism ever wider, for instance, the world was also digging an ever-deeper moat between rich and poor. In trying to make the world modern with more connection, we were lashing ourselves to some very unmodern risks. And in waging the most expensive war on terrorism in human history, the United States was uneasily discovering that it was creating more terrorists. Secretary of Defense Donald Rumsfeld had sketched the nature of this puzzle in an October 2003 memo. He asked: "Are we capturing, killing or deterring and dissuading more terrorists every day than the madrassas and the radical clerics are recruiting, training and deploying against us?" Though this was a simple question, six years later it was still hard to answer. There were a lot of dead terrorists. There were also a lot of new ones.

This puzzle, it turned out, marked a surprising and important feature of our age, one that resonates far beyond the war on terror. Big, expensive, and well-designed systems that thrived and dominated for decades now increasingly find themselves demolished by new, fast-moving forces that live on networks. It's not just militaries. Think of giant global media companies or manufacturing plants. Partly this pressure comes from what is known as the "innovator's dilemma"—the way in which companies that are world class at the old thing miss the new. The best companies making magazines, for instance, struggled with a leap to the digital world. Everyone working in those famous firms had been hired, rewarded, and promoted after all because they were great at making print magazines. The Web? It was a puzzle.

But the real reason the new baffles the old is deeper. And it's what I want to explore in this chapter. Our usual language, we'll see, fails to convey the power of networks. It's hard to let go of old notions, not just because we're attached to them, but because in many cases what we're being asked to hold on to next makes no sense to us. We honestly don't understand what network connections can do to a market or a military enemy any more than figures hundreds of years ago knew what steam engines might do to sailing. History remembers the steamship builders, of course, but there were decades of perplexity and resistance to new ideas until fresh language and science could justify the switch. We're in this same sort of early moment with networks.

It's only human to say that the more confused we are, the more hopefully we cling to the old ideas. Maybe they will work out, we think. They always have. In fact, the higher the stakes and the more powerful the figure, the harder it seems to be to dislodge the old ideas. In the world of international affairs now, at the level where the hugely important and possibly devastating questions of war and peace are discussed, there is almost no detailed discussion of how networks work or what they are doing to our safety. Well, that's not quite right. There is a lot of discussion about it—it's just taking place among those who would attack and erode the existing order. Those forces watch the impotence of old-power assaults on markets or territory or economics and they see an opportunity to try something new staring right back at them. That head-scratching worry of Rumsfeld's—How could the greatest power in human history be *behinder?*—skated right over a much more interesting question: Could that new source of power ever make the country *aheader* again? The group that worried most about this was, naturally, the military. They are, after all, where the shock of the new lands first.

As the war against terrorism had progressed in the years since 2001, it produced at least this: a huge amount of data. Inside the Pentagon, analysis teams pored over records of phone calls and text messages. They examined maps of personal relations and studied granular statistics about who had been killed and why and when. All this was fed into targeting computers and databases, and it became apparent with each passing year that the spread of terrorism after 9/11 looked like nothing so much as the spread of a disease. This was, at first, no great insight. After all, revolutionary ideas, dangerous ideologies, and just plain panic often look like epidemics. But what was shocking as you studied the Pentagon numbers was the speed of this virus. Disease epidemics, even the most virulently aggressive ones, such as Ebola and drug-resistant tuberculosis, move at the pace of human contact; they can be watched and blocked and even quarantined. But the contagions associated with terrorism were spreading at a pace well beyond what the soldiers and analysts could match or even fully monitor. "Is our current situation such that 'the harder we work, the behinder we get'?" Rumsfeld asked in 2003.

To be constantly behind. This was a commander's nightmare. Among other things, it was that sense of never quite catching up that had so seared the new generals in the audience of my speeches. But it seemed like an inescapable reality. One day a guy in Baghdad would figure out how to make an explosively formed penetrator—a sort of pipe bomb that becomes a flying chunk of red-hot steel and can smash through a tank from a hundred yards away—and ten days later the same style of projectile would take out an official thousands of miles away in rural Afghanistan, before U.S. troops had had a chance to update their defenses. *Behinder.* An American commander would arrive in a new town in Iraq, receive a list of people he could really trust, and discover a week later that half of them were showing up on terrorist call logs. *Behinder.*

The Americans knew why this was happening. The data made that clear enough. The proliferation of roadside IEDs, for instance, provided an example: Obviously there was no Al Qaeda Institute of Technology where bomb makers could gather to safely study trigger design or leisurely swap placement ideas. Such a place would have been flattened by a Tomahawk or a Hellfire within hours of its discovery. And though tomes such as Tariq Mahmoud el-Sawah's famous four-hundred-page guide to bomb making were often picked up on raids, they were out of date. (El-Sawah recommended using Casio watches as timers.) No, the force at work was buried inside a network of personal and technological ties, sometimes explicit, other times almost ethereal, until it was made real in a blast. By 2011, you could peel back some corner of the Web and find sites like "Al-Shumukh's Special Explosives Course for Beginners," where dark diagrams were uploaded and debated — a sort of hobbyist site for car-bomb geeks. Deeper still, encrypted chat rooms and messaging services pulsed invisibly, firing off real-time tips (*Use aluminum, not copper, for detonation packs*) and suggestions (*Marines are easier to target in the morning*). When soldiers said they were fighting a "terrorist network," they really meant it: The force arrayed against them was a self-repairing, growing, constantly learning web.

After a few years of facing IED attacks, the Pentagon organized a task force called the Joint Improvised Explosive Device Defeat Organization (JIEDDO). The group specialized in miraculous engineering, and it absolutely lived up to the can-do, American spirit captured in the sound of its name: *"Gee! Do!"* Scientists and war fighters in JIEDDO devised ways to secretly surveil streets so that they could fire on bomb-planting terrorists. They developed slick designs for cars that deflected explosions, and they pioneered armor that could absorb the hit of repeated surprise blasts. JIEDDO was, as its motto went, trying to "defeat the IED as a weapon of strategic influence."

That made good sense, of course. It was a bit weird that $100 pipe bombs were disrupting America's $15 trillion national interest. But you could sense a limit in the way JIEDDO's mission statement was written. Defeating *the device?* It wasn't enough. Beating the devices wasn't the same as chewing apart the network that produced them. That was the real target. JIEDDO developed one clever patch after another, but the devices kept coming, in their own innovative, murderous rush, with the gotta-have-it new pressure we know as the desire for the latest phone or video game or flat-screen TV. This raised an important question: Just what did it mean, really, to beat a network? Could you win? Could you ever get *aheader?* The struggle of JIEDDO is, in a sense, similar to something all of us face now: the old versus the new. Here was the most powerful nation in human history, backed by hypersonic missiles, the world's best radars, and endless jet fuel, unable to stop a group of half-educated and promiscuously backward terrorists. What had gone wrong? And did the failure suggest something even deeper about the position of the dominant international power of the era? About the nature of our age? It did. But making sense of it requires that we step back for a moment and review a bit of history.

3.

A few days before Christmas in December of 1787, Thomas Jefferson sat down in Paris to write a letter to James Madison. Madison was on the other side of the Atlantic, in Philadelphia, and struggling with refinements to the new American constitution, which had been drafted in the spring and summer just passed. The two men were frequent correspondents and wrote to each other with the easy familiarity of fellow revolutionaries. Jefferson was then forty-four and had settled hungrily into his role as the American minister in France, "violently smitten," as he wrote, by the charms of the Continent. Madison was thirty-six, twenty years removed from the election of 1808, which would elevate him to the presidency as Jefferson's successor. Madison would become, in a sense, America's first real foreign policy president, prosecuting the War of 1812 and implementing the Louisiana Purchase agreement with France. He was known already in 1787 as "the Father of the Constitution."

Jefferson begins his letter with a few of the charming literary asides we expect from him: He asks Madison about some nuns he wants to help teach his children and about a packet of carefully chosen South Carolina rice that has gone missing in transit, delaying his plans to impress French palates with an American crop. But then Jefferson turns to what he knows must be on Madison's mind, the new constitution. "I like much the general idea of framing a government which should go on of itself peaceably," he says, admiring the elegant balance envisioned in the document. The American constitution, Jefferson felt, reflected political arrangements new in the history of human governance, between people and power, between states and the center, between agriculture and commerce. He is, he says, "captivated" by the details of what he has seen.

Such a system, Jefferson wrote, was particularly appealing to him because it contrasted so sharply with the violent shearing of daily life then under way all around him in Europe. "France, with all its despotism, and two or three hundred thousand men always in arms, has had three insurrections in the three years I have been here," he marveled. In fact, France's revolutionary age was only just beginning. The fall of the Bastille was eighteen months away, the guillotining of King Louis XVI, five years off. Paris would soon see a time when one riot a year felt like peace. In Jefferson's letter, and in the others he exchanged with Madison that winter and the following spring, you can't miss his sense that fresh forces were tearing apart the world and that America had to position itself for the new order both at home and in its foreign policy. Jefferson knows what this new age demands — liberty — and in that spirit, he fires off suggestions for Madison. It is in this December 1787 letter that he remarks that he does not like the absence of a "bill of rights," a hint that led to an adjustment of historic import.

Jefferson's instincts — about the world and about America's role — were correct. While it may be fashionable now to speak of the period just passed as "the American Century" and to wonder whose century comes next, the reality is that for two and a half centuries, through some of the most violent changes in human history, America has had a remarkable run. A senior American military official once asked me, a week or so before he was to meet the Chinese president, how best to begin his remarks. "You might say that America respects what China has done in the past thirty years," I suggested. "To have brought four hundred million people out of poverty, as Beijing has done, is a historic accomplishment. And America, particularly in the last, intense century, has paid in countless dollars, and with hundreds of thousands of American lives, to establish an order that has benefited billions. The scale of this accomplishment is, by a great measure, historic." Three times over, America has been an emblematic, profound force. It has been a country matched exactly to the needs of her age. Inevitably, the world now asks: *Can this continue?*

It is possible to regard the transformations of politics, economics, and military affairs over the past centuries—the sorts of bold remakings that tore apart places such as the Bastille and produced instruments such as the American constitution—as emerging from a few historic turning points. What is striking is that in passing through these periods of unthinkable change, America has benefited so much, so fully. To begin with, the country was born out of the social and political revolutions of the eighteenth century. The national liberation movement that pulled Jefferson from his Virginia farm and into politics was the first of the great revolutions that convulsed a dozen European powers. France followed America, and then so did Germany and Italy and soon most of the Continent. "The boisterous sea of liberty," as Jefferson called the new political order, required a strong stomach. Tempests of accumulated social pressures—the Reformation, the Enlightenment, the Scientific Revolution—washed aside one ancien régime after another like powerful waves. America, begun on fresh land and with new ideas inked onto clean paper, had a natural advantage in the situation of her birth. "I think our governments will remain virtuous for many centuries," Jefferson concluded in his letter to Madison.

A second transformation of the global order began in the middle of the nineteenth century, as Jefferson and Madison's age ended. Their period had largely been one of *internal* revolutions, as the nations of Europe realigned their domestic orders. What came next were furious contests between these countries. We might think of this new period as starting with the Franco-Prussian War of 1870 and as running, with increasing violence, through to the end of World War II, in 1945. During this murderous seventy-five-year run, America, by reviving Europe's and then the world's fortunes, played a decisive if reluctant role. As in that first period, the country emerged richer, more central, and more modern. Europe's statesmen, by contrast, staggered from one crisis to another. The demands of industry and nationalism and ideology and economics could be reconciled only, it seemed, by war, as if it were absolutely necessary to devour the old buildings and the young men before a new order could take hold. The scale of this violence, like the scale of the industry that produced it, defied anything the wisest minds could have foreseen. Eventually the entire world was pulled into the fire. "In this autumn of 1919, in which I write, we are at the dead season of our fortunes," the economist John Maynard Keynes wrote after the Paris Peace Conference settled World War I, dimly aware that an even deader season lay somewhere in the future, in the form of another war.

A third struggle, the Cold War, immediately followed the end of this second period. This contest was intensely material and as ideological as any conflict in hundreds of years. It represented a debate at the level of the most fundamental question of politics: *How should life be lived?* Two uncompromising worldviews were placed in opposition. This forty-five-year struggle occurred under the threat of nuclear disaster, which gave it something new in human history, the potential for complete destruction. It was possible to find sober-minded theorists pondering problems such as this one: "Assume that for, say, $10 billion we could build a device whose only function is to destroy all human life," Herman Kahn wrote in the 1960s, with a spirit typical of his age in his worrisome masterpiece *On Thermonuclear War*. Yet in this period too, over time, America found itself in an axial role, first carrying one end of the risky fight and then, at the conflict's surprising and jubilant conclusion, in 1989, discovering that it was in a position of unprecedented, unchallenged power. As with the two earlier shifts, this one produced an arrangement tuned, nearly ideally, to America's advantages.

4.

Today the world is entering a new era of revolution. It will be the fourth wave of fresh, turbulent dynamics to confront America since Jefferson gamely predicted those centuries of virtuous prosperity back in that 1787 letter to Madison. Driven by massive technological shifts and their economic, military, and social implications, new forces are beginning to tear into the established global order. Among the most fundamental puzzles now is the problem of settling on an American national mission. What does America want to achieve in the world? And how? On what basis will the United States secure the chance to continue "peaceably," as Jefferson would have it?

Because the country plays such a central role, the answers to these questions will affect the calculations of every nation, of every new force yearning for influence. They represent the crucial background against which we will all live, build businesses, travel, and learn. You might feel, sitting in Silicon Valley or Iowa, that such shifts don't matter to you, but the cold truth is that the international system is unlikely to be arranged, in two or three decades' time, along the same lines as it is now. Too many violent forces are at work. But must this be a disaster? The technological demands of our age are forcing a new sensibility everywhere. Research labs, medicine, science, finance, and the arts are all humming with a new connected outlook. Could the simple act of connection change how we think about the biggest of all historical questions, the one that will decide if we live in an era of peace or one of fear, uncertainty, and tragedy?

The idea that the stability of the world system might honestly be at stake right now feels incredible to the generations of Americans born after World War II. A struggle for global order? Real, sharp, bloody, nation-imperiling violence? Though Americans know that such traps recur throughout history, the country has been numbed by the passing of peaceful and prosperous decades: a blur of IPOs, rising real estate prices, and confident growth out of every crisis. Survival and stability have been, fortunately, the least of the country's concerns. The sly aside of Jules Jusserand, the French ambassador to the United States for twenty years in the last century, summed up Americans' conception of the country's position: "On the north she had a weak neighbor; on the south, another weak neighbor; on the east, fish, and on the west, fish."

Most Americans alive now grew up relying on the durable institutions and ideas built by the generation that fought World War II: Their roads. Their airports. The schools they built. The country absorbed and expanded their habits of consumption: home ownership, debt, optimism. This inheritance produced a historic level of prosperity. It inspired other nations. And—along with those fathoms of fish and friendly neighbors—it assured the

United States a position of real world leadership. Since the end of the World Wars, America has fought five expensive, smaller wars and decisively won one. This record has done little to shake the nation's dominant global position; it did even less to rattle a comfortable sense of national destiny.

Much of America's current confidence can be measured by the astonishing degree to which it embraces the scrambling of even the most elemental parts of our life, from banking to communication. Most societies in the past were largely *terrified* of disruption. If you had arrived in prosperous seventeenth-century Holland and proposed to "disrupt" agriculture or radically change people's banking habits, you would have been lynched. Our age is different. Many of the most unsettling forces in our world are ones we encourage. If I had said to you a decade ago, "I'm going to record all your movements so that you can spend less time in traffic," is that really a deal you would have accepted? But if you use a GPS mapping system on your phone, you have done just that. What if I told you that George Orwell's sick depiction of technocratic life—"You had to live—did live, from habit that became instinct—in the assumption that every sound you made was overheard, and . . . every movement scrutinized"—would be one you'd embrace? That it would describe a *feature* of network life? If I had told you that we were going to build a worldwide high-speed data system that would, as a side effect, make it simple for terrorists in Syria to recruit children out of their London bedrooms, would you have thought that wise?

The optimistic bumper sticker of our age—*Any disruption is good disruption*—marks a wonderful feature of the American character. It is, perhaps, to be expected of a nation built by immigrants who overturned their lives in the hopes of something better. To pull up and leave home for a land where you did not speak the language and knew little of the culture demanded faith. You had to believe: *Any disruption is good disruption.* But no nation, even the most heroically hopeful, is immune to the forces of history. Edmund Burke's old line that "every revolution contains in it something evil" runs like a countermelody through the hopeful music of the age now. America's remarkable spirit does not make the demand for an American grand strategy any less real. Americans are starting to feel that this age is more dangerous than they had expected. In many ways, the country's very confidence and sometimes blindly certain feeling of destiny probably make it even more essential that Americans have a sense of where the United States is going and why. The country needs a grand strategy. And because the country is the axial global power now, the rest of the world also needs a precise and reliable answer to that same question Jefferson was considering: What image of order does America have in mind?

The phrase "grand strategy" is one that carries a particular meaning when we think about problems of global balance. It means the way in which *all* of a nation's powerful tools of economics, finance, ideology, and politics, as well as other resources, can be used together in the service of security and prosperity. To get the terms right, we usually talk about tactical, operational, and strategic levels of action as we watch the gears of history turning. The tactical level is the most practical. It's the choice to use machine guns instead of tanks to secure a street in Kabul, for instance, or to buy up gold for a central bank or to allow high-frequency stock trading. Tactics are where policy decisions meet reality. The most brutal shocks are first felt tactically: roadside bombs or crashing computer code.

At a level above the problem of tactics sits the question of operations. It's here where decisions are made about just how various levers of power might best be moved. Should we send bombers to set back Iran's nuclear program or rely on cyberattacks? Will tax dollars fix aging highways faster than tolls? General

MacArthur's surprise Operation Chromite landing at Inchon on the morning of September 15, 1950, was an operational choice. "Within five hours, 40,000 men would act boldly, in the hope that 100,000 others manning the defense lines of South Korea would not die," he recalled thinking. "I alone was responsible for tomorrow, and if I failed, the dreadful results would rest on judgment day against my soul."

Policy gets implemented through operations. This is where clever bureaucrats and parasitic office politicians prey, where they can most easily undermine the ambitions of visionaries. But it is also the place where inspiration springs from the will and passion of companies, armies, and research labs. Server farms, data-mining algorithms, trade treaties—these are the operational chessboards of our era. Operations is where the bolt tightening for revolutionary change occurs. It is intense, relentless operations that ensure stability in the face of shock or growth or collapse. "The exploding popularity of Internet services has created a new class of computing systems that we have named *warehouse-scale computers*," the Google data engineers Luiz André Barroso and Urs Hölzle wrote in a famous paper several years ago as they described the operational revolution that lets Google serve terabytes of data, instantly, every day. The massive data centers they built, they realized, are so large that they are nothing less than computers that are the size of massive buildings. Solar fields are their power supply; entire rivers are their cooling tubes. And they enable nothing less than magic: instant knowledge, connection to distant lands, a constant picture of what humanity knows. This is the growing, heroic scale of operations now.

Above the operational and tactical levels lies the strategic dimension. Here, overall design is considered and implemented. Without strategy, operations and tactics are incoherent. Strategy imagines how whole structures such as nations or corporations might be directed in the service of the most ambitious goals: European peace or the fiber-optic-speed transformation of tele-communications or billion-user financial grids. It's thin air up at this level, honestly, by which I mean that at these elevated heights, you see the most ambitious athletes of human power at work: the maniacal CEO, the egotistical statesman, the mad dictator. Hundreds of millions of lives are in play, even more in some cases. "Grand strategy" signifies the very peak of this sort of consideration. It represents, in the world of global affairs, the construction of a strategic idea that suggests how diplomacy, markets, politics, and the military might be harnessed in service of a singular aim. Grand strategy is a basic stance toward the world. If it works, it liberates the creativity and energy of a nation. It sets a clear direction. It protects against the steep price of surprise. Grand strategy holds, in a single concept, the nature of an age and our plans to use that nature for the aims—security, prosperity—that decide a nation's future. Like it or not, we all live under the umbrella raised by grand strategic choices.

Containment during the Cold War period. Balance of Power during Europe's nineteenth-century Age of Revolutions. The tributary alliances that shaped a thousand years of Chinese power— these were all big, essential, organizing ideas. They shaped security decisions for durable empires. Each balanced ideas such as freedom or the preservation of dynastic continuity against technological revolution, economic crisis, ideological infection, and the numberless other forces that can crack empires. Each grand strategy reflected the demands of the age, and as a result each tells us something about power in those eras.

The Chinese strategist General Liu Yazhou observed a few years ago, "A major state can lose many battles, but the only loss that is always fatal is to be defeated in strategy." There's something a bit cold in that line, but it expresses a hard truth. A deep commitment to a flawed worldview can turn strength to weakness, and in our connected age, this sort of reversal can happen with particularly devastating speed. In the past, traditional measures of power—numbered in tanks or airplanes or wealth—declined or rose gradually. It took Genoa years to build an expeditionary force to gut Venice's designs in the Adriatic Sea. Decades passed as Germany assembled her naval fleet in the last century. But today, network systems rise and fall with astonishing speed. Once-successful firms in technology, companies such as Wang and Fairchild Semiconductor and Myspace, found themselves unseated in months, after years of growth. New firms can emerge from nowhere and demolish once-strong names. "Change or die," the old computer programmer's line, runs on a very fast clock in a world of constant innovation. This mantra applies to nations and ideologies, to your habits and mine. Think of General Liu again for a moment: "A major state can lose many battles." Those five inconclusive American wars over the past fifty years weren't fatal. They wore only a bit on the nation's pride and position because they weren't *strategic* losses. But future errors, which may come without the firing of a single shot, could be far more costly because of the slick strategic slope on which we are now moving.

5.

Six paradoxes trace the immensity of the gaps the United States now faces.

First: The country is confronted, almost daily, with an unnerving mismatch between broad national interests and ever-narrowing traditional means. The most powerful nation in human history can no longer achieve even simple military and diplomatic goals.

Second: Institutions that were once essential to world order now suffer from a global crisis of faith, as we've seen. No significant institution, from the U.S. Congress to the euro to your local newspaper, is more trusted than it was a decade ago. Many of these institutions seem destined to be victims of the logic of forced obsolescence, which makes the phones, cars, and televisions we bought ten years ago feel like antiques.

Third: Even though the connected age lets people around the world see crises and measure problems with unprecedented precision, our leaders can do almost nothing about them. Global warming, economic inequality, species extinction, nuclear accidents, terrorist attacks—we can see all these in rattlingly sharp detail, instantly, miraculously. Watch the Fukushima reactor meltdown! See BP oil leak into the Gulf of Mexico in HD! The rise and fall of markets, the moves of distant wars, rivers of refugees, appear almost as if we were tuning in to a football game. *But we can only watch.* "Hey, do something!" we want to shout as we see various forms of chaos spill toward us. But nothing seems to move, and what does move only makes the problems worse. This impotence of being mere spectators works like a nutcracker on the credibility of the people and institutions we expect to fix these problems.

Fourth: Many new challenges exhibit a worrying nonlinearity. Small forces produce massive effects. One radical teenager, a single misplaced commodity order, or a few bad lines of computer code can paralyze an entire system. The scale of this whiplashing grows every day, because as the network itself grows it turns pin-drop noises into global avalanches. Dangers were once local. A drought in California was, for the most part, just a drought in California. A slowdown in China hit Shenzhen or Shanghai, not South America. Now, as networks overlap and influence one another, crises cascade at a stunning scale. And while we know that effective foreign policy or politics or economics can't be improvised, the speed of the networks now outstrips the velocity of our decisions—even as citizens expect reactions at the ever-faster pace of their own connection. Think about the speed with which answers are expected in almost any job; the pressure is all the more extreme at the highest levels of government.

Fifth: Though the changes working through the global order are in large part the result of innovation rooted in American institutions, corporations, and ideas, this order seems to be slipping from America's control. Look back just two decades. Then, America stood as the sole superpower, the global leader in finance, economics, and technology—and it was getting other nations to embrace the rules it had written. Today, allies and enemies alike wonder: *Is the global order collapsing? At what speed? And what comes next?*

And sixth, perhaps obvious by now: The country doesn't seem to know where it is going. Though many nations are capable of adjusting activities at the tactical and operational levels—devising better drones, sharper monetary policy, pushing at old borders—few seem to have a clear strategy. American negotiations are aimed now mostly at small problems, not at the heart of the issues the world faces. In what area of national security today does the country appear more confident than a decade ago? What nation does conduct the bold sort of global negotiations that mark a power with a clear sense of direction?

Taken as a whole, these six paradoxes represent nothing less than the potential unbuckling of the greatest power the world has ever seen. And because the whole world is connected to that power, still more of the system may yet be rattled apart. Today America is not merely surrounded by fish, but connected to links of finance, data, and trade as essential for life in New York as in Paris or Tokyo. And of course dangers of contagion or attack or fatal weakness bind centuries-old nations and years-old networks as well in unprecedented, unnerving ways. *A sense of direction.* You have to say to yourself, as you look at this rotten, dangerous landscape we've made for ourselves in recent years, *We need a sense of direction.*

6.

In response to these challenges, America's leading figures are now proposing a range of ideas that don't honestly resonate with much confidence. They are simply having a debate over whether to use more of the old style of power or less. What they aren't doing is grasping the nature of the age. So no clear and ambitious picture of where the country might head yet exists. In fact, as you're probably starting to suspect, the very best ideas of America's incumbent figures may make the world more dangerous by pulling the world into dangers they don't see.

Two approaches are predominant among the most respected American elites. The first proposes something known, appealingly enough, as "smart power." The concept was summarized most sharply by President Obama in his second term, when he argued that American policy ought best be guided by this tight precept: "Don't do stupid stuff." (There is a less polite variant of this too.) And, while it is hard to disagree with this sort of charming, solipsistic formulation—no politician, after all, calls for doing stupid things—"smart power" is no more a foreign policy vision than "good weather" is a strategy for farming. In a way, it suggests that there is no need for a strategy at all. Faced with a problem, just make a smart decision. "I don't really even need George Kennan right now," Obama remarked at one point during his presidency, dismissing the need for a strategist of real stature—and, by implication, the need for any strategy at all.

Such a stance reflects an instinct that the great strategic question of our day—the future—has pretty well been worked out. In this view of history, all the United States needs to do is, well, not do stupid stuff. This appealing idea has taken hold, I think, because of the prevalence of short-term thinking and discomfort about the application of cold, hard power. There's a misplaced confidence at work here, an assurance that American-style power, along with the country's model of politics and economics, is the only answer to the question of how the nations of the world might best be organized. In this telling of history, Americans need only be patient. The world will catch on. And if you grew up in the United States after World War II, a "smart power" worldview would certainly be consistent with your own experience. The problem is that such a comfortable posture is at odds with nearly any book of history you might pick up, from Thucydides' *The Peloponnesian War* to Churchill's *The Hinge of Fate*, both of which will remind you that liberty and freedom demand vigorous defense and that epochal changes come whether they are wanted or not. History will remind you too of this cold truth: Nations that look invincible can find themselves nearly dead in an instant. Great Britain had mastered the globe in 1937; three years later, it was gasping for air; three decades later, it was an afterthought. "Having judged that to be happy means to be free, and to be free means to be brave, do not shy away from the risks of war," Pericles told his Athenian audience nearly 2,500 years ago as they mourned a full year of war-dead sons and fathers—and with no peace yet in sight. Or, as Winston Churchill famously said: "Never give in, never give in, never, never, never—in nothing, great or small, large or petty—never give in." The United States should be embarrassed to hold "Don't do stupid stuff" against these mottos.

Admiral Hyman Rickover's famous advice as he surveyed the nuclear navy he built in the last century has it about right at every level: "To find a purpose in life one must be willing to act." This is true for nations. It is true for each of us. We must be willing to act. It's easy to be sympathetic to the desire for less action. Nothing the United States has done in recent years seems to be working. But that's because the country has been using the wrong tools. The nation's enemies? They are developing the right ones. They are eager to act. To travel the world now is to encounter in nearly every capital figures who have a different reading of history or the future of the global order. They see the world not as some ready-to-eat American political order but rather as a worrying vortex. They wonder: *What might we build?* They look at America's global leadership with the hungry eyes of an Internet start-up faced with an old, unconnected market. "Don't do stupid stuff" is an invitation for these salivating forces to poke at the world, to take risks, and to remind us that so much of what later seems brilliant at first appears stupid or even insane.

In the years since "smart power" became fashionable, another proposition has emerged from a different group of elite thinkers. It is, in a sense, the flip side of that strategy-free posture of passivity. It was distilled by a well-regarded cluster of academic foreign policy specialists in 2012 as America began withdrawing from Iraq. "Don't Come Home, America," they called their essay. As they explained, "The United States' globe-girdling grand strategy is the devil we know....A world with a disengaged United States is the devil we don't know." According to this logic, the country's expansive global posture, while expensive and exhausting and admittedly inefficient, forms a crucial element of its rich national power. Yes, the United States spends nearly 5 percent of its GDP in an expensive, essential chase after security, but the returns give the nation its national muscle tone: access to the best minds in the world, a secure life, a culture of open debate and personal liberty.

The problem here is that "Don't come home" feels, for the most part, like a costly groping after something to hold on to. Ideas that flow from this hopeful camp have a shimmering and expensive unreality, and American public sentiment would be unlikely to support them for long, given our recent experience. Are more aircraft carriers, overseas bases, and jet fighters really the cure for the dangers we face? The ideas of this group have an appealing *familiarity* because they echo instincts about power that were once true. The energetic engagement with the world they suggest is attractive, but America has work to do at home, and— we can all see—the ambitious overseas tasks of recent decades remain unfinished. Instead of the conclusive comfort of "Job well done!" the country still sweats with nervousness. *What is coming next?* After all the blood and treasure, after 850,000 soldiers in Afghanistan and nearly $2 trillion, the world was left with expanded swamps. And trillions more in costs for the years ahead. Like "Don't do stupid stuff," "Don't come home" tells us precious little about the future of world order. (It also tips us off to this: As a general rule, no credible grand strategy starts with the word "don't.")

7.

So we should say it coldly: America has, as of yet, no strategy. The country has no shared picture of the world as it might be. And the experience of other empires that quickly collapsed should offer an urgent lesson. "The struggle to survive," the historian John Darwin has written of the British Empire, "was waged in an age of revolution: a Eurasian revolution that cumulatively (but very quickly) destroyed almost all the global preconditions on which the British system had depended since the 1830s." So it is in our age. Many of the essential determinants of American power are being revolutionized by new, connected forces. Will the changes reduce the United States as they once shrank Britain, or can the country draw on them to establish a longer, more durable order?

The world has changed profoundly from the one in which most students and practitioners of international affairs were educated. And here's the reality: Nothing can stop this change. The past two decades have brought massive change to so many disciplines. Yet somehow, in foreign policy—a field dealing with war and peace, which, if not handled properly, will rain tragedy on every other effort we might have in mind—not much has changed. Except this: a growing sentiment of pessimism that suggests maybe America can't hold on. Great powers get one century to rule, the logic goes, and America's is now up.

It's not merely that the United States lacks a China strategy or a Middle East strategy; it's that the country has failed to discern an overall grand strategy that would produce a coherent answer to the question of what to do about China or the Middle East—to say nothing of how those forces might be played off one another with clever diplomatic harmony, like instruments in a symphony. It is hard to know if this puzzlement represents a failure of imagination or of nerve. Does it mark arrogance or confusion? Or just an ignorance of the revolutionary nature of the forces now at work?

Today, when leading officials remark that their main concern is a rising China or a revanchist Russia, or that we live in a world in which, as Secretary of State John Kerry said, "terrorism is the principal challenge," they are missing the point. The fundamental threat to American interests isn't China or Al Qaeda or Iran. It is the evolution of the network itself. Constructed of switches, chips, data, code, sensors, AI bots, financial instruments, trade, currency, and more, the network is different now than when you started reading this sentence. Its architecture, a wonderful maze of change and contagion and instability, determines its dangers and marks vast opportunity. It touches every problem we would care to name.

Terrorism is merely one example of network danger and power. Financial risks are another example. As is the jockeying of nations as they seek new sources of influence. And these may not even be the most dangerous threats we will face. It's a commonplace to say now that the international system has entered the greatest period of upheaval in more than half a century. But this sort of remark is usually accompanied by a list of moving pieces that appear unconnected to the untrained instinct: Europe's economy, disease pandemics, Russia, changes in the Middle East, globalization and then reverse globalization. In fact they all share a single thread. Each is enabled and shaped by connection. "Who…imagined that the post–Cold War era, which was supposed to be characterized by 'soft power' and economic interdependence, would prove to be so violent?" one team of scholars recently wrote, reflecting the genuine wonderment of many so-called experts. Many had failed to predict the end of the Cold War. And the nature of what has come after. Who would have imagined? Well, anyone who understood networks.

Thomas Hobbes—the seventeenth-century British philosopher and an early master of the analysis of power—once put it simply enough: Nations, he said, *need* to be mastered. "During the time men live without a common power to keep them all in awe, they are in that condition which is called war," he wrote, "and such a war as is of every man against every man." For Hobbes, peace required some country or force or tribe to decisively grip a region, an empire, even the globe. "A common power to keep them all in awe," he wrote, fulfilled a need for order. In our connected age, the common, awesome power is already here. It is networks. The battle now is for and on this genuinely historic, still-curious force. Networks will be attacked, throttled, trashed, accelerated, used, upgraded, won, and lost—and inflicted on each of us by those with a new sensibility. A whole new landscape of power is emerging now; it will permit a new generation of statesmen and stateswomen to use all the fibers of our age in pursuit of a grand strategy that doesn't begin with "Don't." But this demands a new understanding of power. A new instinct. The decisive terrain of this new age is, to the smart-power and "Don't come home" crowds, still largely invisible and, anyhow, incomprehensible.

8.

Just as rivers and mountains and air currents drove commerce and combat in past eras, networks will strongly, often decisively, influence the dynamics ahead. Today you can't, after all, operate on the rivers or in the mountains or the skies or in space without near-instant connection. The landscape these interlocking networks occupy represents a new geography. It is growing every day, as if it were a giant new continent fusing together under the surface of the sea. We are, as the "Gee! Do!" team discovered, moving from a world in which nations battle nations to one in which nations battle networks. And a world in which networks battle networks. In coming years, networks will surely break nations, as once nations broke one another. It is the linked systems of trade and economics and biology and data that will create the conditions for the practice of diplomacy in our future and, when that fails, the landscape for decisive military or economic moves.

Already the emergence of network power is producing strange collisions. Iran versus YouTube videos, during the 2009 elections. The hacking collective Anonymous attacking Mexican drug lords, terrorists, and Russian television. Financial networks used to crack human-trafficking webs. Biological surveillance sensors spread into cities to watch for the unexpected sneezes of an epidemic or bio-attack—a network of machines lying in wait for a network of bugs. Collisions at nearly every scale are already under way, a chaotic ongoing war ramp that we don't yet see. In his 1890 book, *The Influence of Sea Power upon History*, the great American historian and admiral Alfred Thayer Mahan attempted to convince an age obsessed with land forces of the enduring power of armed ocean fleets. Hannibal's smashing attacks against Rome and Napoleon's failure against England—in both cases, "mastery of the sea rested with the victor." The future will almost certainly bring a study of the influence of network power upon history. And it will surely conclude that whether in diplomacy, business, or politics, mastery of networks will rest with the victor. Waves of networked autonomous armed drones, for instance, may rank among the greatest tactical military threats of the next few decades; the only hope of defending against them will be still-better-enabled self-thinking and self-learning robotic meshes, capable of responding at the pace demanded by links of machine learning and optical fiber.

For the most part, the order the American and European world has been accustomed to featured states as the most significant actors. Nations held a monopoly on the use of force. They used it. Violent, state-on-state struggles were the defining events of global affairs. In such a world, the country with the most power, the greatest material reserves, the strongest sense of national destiny also enjoyed the most security—and the most options. A few hundred thousand British imperial troops overmastered India in this fashion. And a handful of really powerful nations—Britain, France, Germany, the United States, Russia—struggled over centuries for dominance of the whole system. Statesmen sought, and even occasionally achieved, temporary balances between the lurching and violent resets of wars that erupted like pressure-release valves for the overinflated ambitions, nationalism, and hatreds that steamed up between nations.

In our modern networked systems, from stock exchanges to trade blocs, power is different. Tiny forces can have immense impacts. One erroneous commodity trade can scramble a market-place—and then tip a bucket of chaos into nations, companies, and trading firms. One hacker sneaking through the back door of a computer network can—to use a term of art—"brick" a nation's defense systems into devices as lively as a doorstop. It once required a big, industrial force to defeat another big, industrial force. Such grinding victories required time. They could be pre-pared for. They could be avoided, even. No more. Even the most formidable physical structures of our world—militaries, markets, governments—can be rendered swiftly immobile by virtual attacks on their connected nerve systems. These strikes (or, in some cases, these *accidents*) paralyze at network speed, by which I mean closer and closer to instantly. When the American national security strategy speaks of a "long struggle" against terrorism or a rising China, it doesn't acknowledge how fast some of the turns ahead may be. Yes, a decades-long battle for control of essential networks and platforms and protocols is in front of us now. But I fear that some of the changes ahead will whiplash us with their speed. Generals in World War I lamented that the whole war might have been prevented if diplomatic communication had been conducted at the stately speed of the horse-carried message. It was the damn velocity of the telegraph that baffled the judg-ment of statesmen, they claimed. Figures whose every instinct runs at a pace far slower than what the age demands were then—and are now—a menace.

The great twentieth-century theorist of political realism Hans Morgenthau once referred to nation-states as "blind and potent monsters." He felt a sort of nervous evil as he studied the moves countries made on the stage of world history. Some of this unease was surely rooted in his own life: He had made a lucky escape from Germany in 1932, as Hitler was finally perfecting a national machine of lurid and murderous potency. I suspect Morgenthau would have been terrified by the always-on, all-seeing, connected mesh that encloses us. Connected forces can move like a capricious monster, smashing businesses or national economies or ecosystems with little warning and merciless efficiency. Connected terrorists have cost trillions to fight; linked-up businesses have demolished trillions of dollars of profits from old sources with their cold, clicking efficiency. Skype didn't steal hundreds of billions of dollars of long-distance telephone fees, for instance. It made them disappear. Amazon, in the space of a few years, crippled physical retail empires built at the cost of trillions of dollars.

The world we're entering into now is one of constant, sensor-filled data streams. They will watch your house and your heart with equal curiosity—and they will remember and think about what they learn from these endless observations. The potent network forces of our day are not "blind," as Morgenthau said of states, but gifted with an exactness of vision. They see everything, always, and more than we or our leaders do. They never forget. Networks seem to have an irresistible energy that impels them to find and then exploit pinholes. Think of Al Qaeda coolly regarding the American airline network in 2000, for instance, or rising powers now poking at weaknesses in the international order that we've not yet begun to consider, let alone patch up. Whether confronting mobs of network-organized terrorists or cascades of computer errors, we often discover the unnerving truth that on these connected systems there is no plug to pull.

Networks of one sort or another are hardly new in international affairs, even if the sheer scale and speed of our modern systems is utterly fresh. The tendrils of the Ganges River, for instance, were a network that fed the Mughal Empire in the sixteenth and seventeenth centuries. The Yangtze and the Yellow and the Mekong river systems each carried wealth and knowledge into a half dozen spectacularly rich Chinese dynasties. The Nile nourished a great power that endured in Egypt for centuries, as did the Euphrates in Mesopotamia. Networks of trade overlay the Mediterranean, which itself became the heart of the wealthy Carthaginian, Roman, and Byzantine Empires. And the greatest geographical empire in history, Great Britain, was nothing if not a network power, run on sea lines. For centuries, waterways have pulsed with power. They were vital for trade, war, and national freedom.

Network empires emerged on land too, assembled from connected webs of politics, of silk and tobacco and gold, or from shared religious passions. These sorts of networks, sometimes as thin as the trail of a single adventurer like Marco Polo, carried promises of prosperity (and intimations of violence) as they spread. Antoine-Henri, baron de Jomini, Napoleon's inspired tactical accomplice, was on to something when he remarked that it was the interior, networked lines of communication and logistics that had delivered victory for history's great empires. "Methods change," Jomini observed, "but principles are unchanging." The skeins of links running *inside* national war machines are as essential for security as any ability to strike out—a lesson Jomini and Napoleon expensively relearned at the end of their gasping supply lines in Russia in the winter of 1812. In our own day, jet-linked networks, commercial webs, satellite connections, and financial platforms span the omnipresent routes of America's global reach. So as we consider the information networks evolving now—the increasingly connected world that is the largest, fastest, most comprehensive network in history—we should ask ourselves the question Jomini might have raised: *Will an even greater empire be based on control of information-powered networks?*

This new world of connectivity won't immediately devour the old. In fact, the classic and the revolutionary will contend for some time, side by side: Cyberweapons and nuclear weapons, for instance, will do a strange dance. Imagine that you rule a country, with no hope of building your own platforms for medicine, finance, information, or security. You'll be permanently dependent on the nations or groups that do control these tools. If you're running a medium-sized country, there's no chance that your own IT industry can develop a search engine with the reach and fluency of Google or a cybersecurity system with the omnipresence of some Chinese one. Might this make you more eager for nuclear weapons? For an atomic hedge against the day you find yourself threatened with national unplugging?

Networks don't lift us above the old conflicts so much as they complicate them. They fill the old hatreds with new fidelity; they sharpen the old grudges and make it easier than ever to slap at the world when you're angry. While it is tempting to say that we've moved from a world of "cold weapons" such as planes and tanks to a world of "hot weapons," in which digital light pulses and biological infections will prevail, it is really the strange blending of these cold and hot systems that is so interesting, so dangerous. Ever-more-precise exploding iron bombs, made from a fusion of GPS data and TNT, will be a part of our future, as will pathogens made of DNA or bits and delivered according to network intelligence about where a contagion might best be started.

Orwell's well-worn line—"The history of civilization is largely the history of weapons"—settles uneasily onto a networked world. The networks are, so clearly already, becoming weaponized. They are not made of bullets and bombs, but they are every bit as dangerous. A great strategist should know and use the materials of his

day. Napoleon had a gunpowder-burn familiarity with his artillery; Mao possessed a wizened-guerrilla sensibility. No matter
what, our global networks are going to be used in pursuit of
power. So we had better consider how to become fluent with their
real nature, how turn them to our advantage, and, ideally, how to
rewrite the rules of conflict so our enemies will only be able to
react—and, then, wrongly. Over the centuries, it was armed invasions, naval bombardments, and air campaigns that shifted power
and wealth. In the future it will be the ownership and use of connection, of networks and machine intelligence, that will deliver
the real, perhaps even final, leverage.

If the strategic aim of Europe's leaders after Napoleon's violent emergence and defeat was to restore the balance of power, if
America's grand strategic purpose after World War II was to contain the USSR and its totalizing ideologies, then nations now
must try for positions of security and for command during the
uneasy transition ahead. The well-being of the whole system
becomes a concern; entities, protocols, and ideas that threaten its
health pose the most urgent dangers, even as they represent seats
of historic power.

The social scientists John Padgett and Walter Powell studied
examples of epochal, collapsing change in political and biological
systems of all sorts—Renaissance finance markets, coral reefs,
innovation clusters. They summed up their conclusions in a little
koan-like package of logic: "In the short run, actors create relations; in the long run, relations create actors." The objects we
worry about now take their meaning from relations. Connected,
your genome is more hopeful than it is alone, unplugged, slipping
into cancer. This idea that relations create actors offers a powerful basis for a grand strategy. It should also offer a check against
some of our horrible miscalculations: America invaded Iraq, for
instance, intending to replace one state with another. Instead, it

replaced a state with a constantly shifting, unstable network—
and not one that it controlled. That web in Iraq still resists our
habits of control. There, relations of family and faith link and
activate murderous, relentless actors. The superpower had all the
objects: tanks, planes, soldiers, money. But it did not have the networks. It could not create relations. No move held for long. We
were like the JIEDDO team—trying to defeat the wrong thing
entirely.

Once we understand how networks work and what they
want—as Jefferson understood what his age of riots, liberty, and
revolutions demanded—the creation of a grand strategy will
emerge as a natural, even straightforward conclusion. We will
come to see that networked economies or technologies or alliances crave a clear line between in and out, because the benefits of
being inside a system in an age of connected dynamics are historically unprecedented. The reach and dominance of technology
firms that have mastered this insight—and that control overwhelming shares of their markets—turns out to represent a pre-
view of just how networks divide power, and the importance of
the gates that decide if you are inside or outside of a given system.
Grand strategy in our future will hinge on a mastery of gatekeeping, and the shaping of the terrain on which such control happens. The network craves gates, we'll come to see, just as it craves
connection.

Success will mean developing a new sensibility, one that
requires letting go of some of the old habits of "Don't do stupid
stuff" or "Don't come home." Networks demand more than that.
But they also give us something in return: a picture of world order
and answers to those six paradoxes the world faces. It's to this
puzzle that we'll turn now. But as a start, we can at least fix the
weird language of many of the world's current foreign policy
elites: We no longer live in what they often call the post–Cold

War era. (Who, after all, called the Enlightenment the post-feudal era?) We live in what is probably best called the Age of Network Power. A world of connection is responding to a powerful logic of its own, not to our hopes and desires and old pictures of how the world ought to work. Network Power is expressed all along new platforms, and those platforms in turn decide a great deal about our lives. Mel Conway's instinct about phone networks was more right than he could have known: The design of these networks does affect the real world profoundly, just as the arrival of the railroad once turned some lonely prairie cities into booming metropolises and others into ghost towns. Even now the networks of our age are starting to shuffle us into "convergence clubs" and "divergence clubs," just as the Industrial Revolution once split the world. You're not wrong to be wondering: *Which camp will I be in?*

PART TWO

The Seventh Sense

CHAPTER FOUR

The Jaws of Connection

In which the Seventh Sense explains the strange, new way power behaves on networks.

1.

The envoy Frank Wisner Jr. was taken by surprise when the call came in. But he knew, after all these years, what he was expected to do, and within a few hours he was preparing to hop on a plane. The caller had delivered an unusual request from the White House and from the State Department—and, though he was a man who had lived a life of many unusual requests, he knew that this one had a certain significance, a *weight*, you might say, if you were the sort of man who measured such things in human lives.

The envoy was such a man. His father, Frank Wisner Sr., had been one too. Wisner père was one of America's most famous and effective Cold War spies. He'd run the Office of Strategic Services in southern Europe during World War II and then built operations for the Central Intelligence Agency in the years after. He was a tough man, from a generation of Americans who had fought and won wars and who unquestioningly weighed their actions in human lives. As a spy in Romania in 1940, Wisner Sr. had watched the Red Army, like some sort of sick machine, round up and then execute scores of his friends. The course of his life was set. "Wisner landed like a dynamo," William Colby, a future CIA director who worked for him, observed. "He started [the Office of Policy Coordination] operating in the atmosphere of an order of the Knights Templars, to save Western freedom from Communist darkness—and war."

Frank Wisner Jr. was known too as a dynamo. When the White House called he was seventy-two. He'd had a storied career as a diplomat, following a rough trace of his father's man-on-a-mission trajectory, also with a bit of that secretive Knights Templar feeling: Princeton, Vietnam, the Philippines, the halls of the State Department in Foggy Bottom. Wisner had become the first phone call for some of America's leading corporate figures when they found themselves billions of dollars backwards in some strange land, even as he'd remained in close touch with the most explosive policy puzzles. Iran. North Korea. He was a voluble and opinionated man but somehow also discreet, exact, and patient. The combination made him both totally reliable and a great deal of fun. Over the years he had been a warm and personable figure in my own life, the sort of man who took the long view of any problem, who laid his hand comfortably on your knee with reassurance when some promise came undone and threatened a bit of chaos. He was like an ideogram of reliability: bulky, bald, coiled, loyal. He'd seen it all, you felt.

Frank Wisner Jr. had served as ambassador to Egypt for half a decade in the 1980s. Almost inevitably, his careful manner and easy charm led him into a close relationship with Hosni Mubarak, the Egyptian president. Mubarak was an urbane former fighter pilot who had come to sudden and surprising power after the assassination of Anwar Sadat on a calm afternoon in October 1981. Wisner arrived a few years later. Though they were not quite friends, Wisner had cultivated a directness, at least, with Mubarak. He'd become a mirror in which the Egyptian president might see how different stances toward America or Israel would appear to the rest of the world. So when, in the winter of 2011, the White House saw Mubarak facing waves of unimagined protest, at a moment when it looked as though the Egyptian president would become the latest head of state to topple amid the accelerating discontent that would be known as the Arab Spring, they sent Wisner with a message for Mubarak: *No killing—and it is time for you to retire.*

Wisner later recalled the tension of Cairo when he arrived. The city felt nervous in a way he'd not seen before. He landed and went almost immediately to see the president. The situation would be brought back to normal, Mubarak assured Wisner. Soon. He'd fired most of his cabinet a few days earlier. He had promised reform and had begun studying what might be done first and how soon it might be carefully attempted. He hinted to Wisner that the rumored transition of power to his son Gamal was not, after all, inevitable. But, Mubarak said, he wasn't going anywhere just yet.

Wisner tried another tack: He asked if the president would like to leave the country. Maybe a trip for medical treatment? Mubarak dismissed the idea. He'd seen worse, he reminded Wisner. Mubarak had been sitting inches away from Sadat when he was assassinated and had survived six assassination attempts himself. In fact, he said he intended to go on television again that very evening. He would speak directly to the protesters. He would tell them and the Egyptian people of his plans for reform and for a gradual transition of power. He would remind them of the greatness of their national spirit. He would evoke the immensity of their ancient history. And he would leave no doubt in their minds that he would stay, that he would die on Egyptian soil. *You can tell that to the White House too*, Mubarak told Wisner. At the end of their talk, Mubarak vouchsafed at least some of the assurances that the envoy had come to collect: no violence. A graceful departure at some point. Elections, even. But all on his timetable.

In those days, Wisner recalled, Mubarak was surrounded by baffled advisers. The men in the Egyptian power structure, all wealthy, comfortable, and secure, had thought their places impregnable. They were, after all, the thin human line between the modern world and the boiling-mad Islamic fundamentalists who hungered to rule the country. They'd arrested the usual dissidents, closed down the normal channels, checked with their informants. Nothing. The old, reliable ways of containing unrest hadn't worked. The pressures grew. It was perhaps easy to understand why they thought they'd survive. They'd never failed. Mubarak had been president for *thirty years*. For now, at least, the syllogistic logic fluttering through the president's own arguments reassured them: *Egypt wants stability. Only I can deliver stability. Therefore, Egypt wants me.*

Wisner left the presidential palace. He reported what he'd learned back to Washington and, with his work done, headed to the airport. That evening he waited for his flight in front of a TV in the crapped-out lobby of an old hotel on the road out of town, watching Mubarak's promised speech. The president projected total confidence on screen. This was the Mubarak whom Wisner had known in the 1980s. There had always been a barreling self-assurance about the man; it was alive in him now, facing the unthinkable. Ruggedly handsome and perfectly controlled. You could almost believe, as Wisner did for a moment, "This was a great man who had led a country through difficult times. He will endure." *Six assassination attempts.* Mubarak had always been a survivor.

Yet as he watched, Wisner knew the challenge the great man faced. Did Mubarak, he wondered? Did he even understand what was happening around him? That he was giving the speech on television, in the face of this strange, revolutionary movement that was unfolding on the smartphones of Cairo as much as on its streets, was a subtle admission: Old power struggles to handle new rules. Wisner had seen tapes of the earlier speeches, the ones intended to calm the crowds, which had in fact inflamed them further. He knew just how fine the edge Mubarak now paced was.

Mubarak explained on television that he would not run for president again. He told his audience that change would come. But Wisner knew something still more was needed. Mubarak had to address the protesters at their own level to show that he understood. There was only one thing he must not do, Wisner thought as he watched Mubarak struggle during the following weeks. He must not be arrogant. Must not address the protesters paternalistically, as a father might speak to a child. So when, shortly after he left Cairo, Wisner watched Mubarak speaking yet again and heard the president offer in his steady, slightly strident voice, "I am speaking to you all from the heart; a speech from a father to his sons and daughters," he sighed at the inevitability of it all.

Two weeks later, Mubarak was gone.

2.

Imagine, for a moment, you are Mubarak—or really any successful early-twenty-first-century autocrat. You've managed several decades of control in your Middle Eastern or North African country. Perhaps you've inherited your position from your father or uncle. They've taught you about power. *Keep it tightly controlled. Replace key officials regularly. Execute your enemies from time to time.* You've learned the virtues of the hard crackdown. You've sent your security officers to the best military schools in the United States and Europe and taught them to temper their firm grip with (a bit of) humanity. In short, you've mastered the use of a strong hand and the establishment of a certain national logic that suggests your name—Gadhafi or Mubarak or El Abidine Ben Ali—as a synonym for stability, for prosperity and even pride. The current order seems to you to be the most stable one possible. You know that someday it might have to change, but that day seems a long way off. You delay reform. You groom your son to take over. Meanwhile, your citizens begin to acquire the Internet and cell phones. And one day in 2008, following a financial crisis far away from your own shores, you begin to notice an unnerving trend.

On the streets of Iceland and then Spain and then Chile and then Israel and Ukraine and Turkey and Mexico and then New York City, thousands or hundreds of thousands of citizens gather. There is no single leader of any of these protests. Instead, these movements breathe and grow like an organic whole. The discontent is diffuse, even if the formula is the same: mass gatherings, control of some essential public space—a square, a stock exchange, a park. All organized, it appears, using completely ethereal techniques: text messages, video uploads, chat rooms. Similar movements appear around the world. In Iran, in Italy, in Russia. Occupy Wall Street blossoms in New York City, a protest against economic inequality and the financial system. It becomes a self-franchising social movement, popping up in hundreds of cities: Occupy Washington. Occupy Central, in Hong Kong. Occupy—strangely—Vegas.

Then in Sidi Bouzid, a Tunisian town far away from all these mobs, a spark lands. A local street merchant has lit himself on fire. Police (worse, a police*woman*) had confiscated his scales and his fruit and then tossed him around for no reason other than that he was poor and could do nothing about it. It is December 2010. Within hours, protests begin in Sidi Bouzid. They spread to Tunis. Then Tripoli. Then Damascus. You watch as the anger, moving on once-invisible technological lines of video and text, demolishes the stability of all of North Africa. Over the next two years, leaders are pushed from power in Egypt, Tunisia, Libya, and Yemen. Their names, instead of being symbols of stability, instantly become bywords for injustice. Other countries—Syria, Algeria, Sudan, and Bahrain—tumble into the black hole of civil violence. Some people mistake all this for a democratic revolution. Over time, however, it's clear that this is hardly that. Something more complex is emerging from the violent mist. New, nearly virtual terror groups organize themselves in the power vacuum as well—hyperlethal versions of connected protest. A new kind of political energy, a method of linking people and ideas and easy, destructive power, is alive. It seems to be as active in murderous fundamentalists as in optimistic youth. Democratic revolution? No. Revolution? Yes, clearly that.

A few years later, after you've been replaced or are on the run, after your own country has undergone upheaval and you've endured your own visit from a well-meaning American diplomat urging you toward a quiet Saudi Arabian retirement, the Spanish social philosopher Manuel Castells will name the disease that undid you. Castells is perhaps an unlikely figure to diagnose the political illness that infected so much of the world after 2008. An elfin, kinetic man with a disorganized mop of gray hair, he sports the wardrobe of an accountant and a rolling Spanish accent that flavors his speech with a surprising taste of romance. It's a mixture that seems somehow ideal for a word often on his lips: "Reevolootion." With the meticulous care an anthropologist might bring to documenting a distant, undiscovered tribe, Castells has spent decades finger poking, classifying, and explaining networks. In the late 1990s, his research set the frame for the world we inhabit: fast changing, ripped through by communications and technology, and linked in unusual ways. "The network society," he explained, "represents a qualitative change in the human experience."

Inevitably, Castells became curious about how such a change was affecting politics. Speaking to an audience at Harvard in the winter of 2014, he reviewed what he had learned in the past decade—and particularly in the years since 2008, much of which he had spent dropping into the ground-zero sites where dissatisfaction was exploding. "We are witnessing," he told the audience, "the birth of a new form of social movement." Information technology was breeding massive, rapidly moving social waves. These movements went from invisible to irresistible in instants. They pressed for political change or for economic justice or even for—and this was odd for such wired-up efforts, but anyhow—a return to a pre-technological age. In most of these countries, the older organizations had little appeal to a new generation of protesters. The political parties smelled of rot. The media was state owned or controlled by billionaires. For a generation accustomed to instant empowerment, the slow-motion progress of life inside the broken structures felt insufferable.

And at any rate, another option existed. Twitter and Facebook and YouTube had taught them. So riots in those dozens of cities, unplanned and uncontrolled, emerged. The collective action of popular movements for hundreds of years, from the raiding of the Bastille to labor strikes, was replaced by connective action. People who'd never met and who shared very different histories and desires were fused together by light-speed bits or rage. Perhaps this was predictable, for it mirrored the fast-spreading dynamism of the 2008 financial crisis itself. As the British central banker and economist Andy Haldane observed, the world had never before suffered a genuinely *global* financial crisis, with every country on the planet, tied together by links of finance and technology (and fear), tumbling off a cliff at the same nanosecond. In one three-month period, essential parts of the global economy had shrunk by nearly 5 percent.

As fast as shocks like that economic one spread, the social and political chain reactions seemed to move faster still, echoing one another, with ever-louder and more complex results. The terrorist phenomenon of ISIS, for instance, emerged almost entirely along skeins of digital connection and was itself a reaction to the network-led disruption that was the Arab Spring—and the earlier fracturing of an older order in Iraq. When President Obama dismissively called ISIS the junior-varsity squad of terror and said there was nothing much for the West to worry about, he was reflecting the same dim and dangerous instincts that undid Mubarak. *These kids can't possibly amount to much.* The youth of these groups, the very fact that they were *not* the varsity team, their intimate, fingertip familiarity with virtual spaces—all these things gave them energy and appeal. Even in countries that looked technologically "backward" by American standards, linked systems speed-bred revolution. They gleefully filled in for a failed traditional media, and they enabled and accelerated the creation of groups as different as the Syrian Electronic Army and Occupy Hong Kong.

Traditionally, a long list of hopeless exclusions—no money, no friends, no access, no power—added up to irrelevance. But ISIS was like the bloggers in Iran and social-justice campaigners in New York and digital pirates in Sweden and vengeful Houthi rebels in Yemen who were all staring back, confidently, at the people who had the money, the friends, the power, and the drones. Obama, Mubarak, and *fill in the blank with a powerful name or institution* were too slow. They were out of touch. Their connections were all wrong. So while the individual parts of the new networks—young students, poorly trained armed fighters—were soft and human and easy to destroy, they still tore unstoppably at old power. Tied together, the connected systems themselves were capable of more than their individual strength might suggest.

What they shared wasn't simply a single issue or identity. It was cheap, constant connection. And they were, frankly, furious.

The old guys were crafty, of course. They tried to shut down the technology itself, or they aimed at crucial points on the network. "Arrest or kill the leaders you can find!" was the sort of command that restored stability to the regime in Iran, for example. Other governments found that they could crack the will of the protesters by going after their relatives. Relational repression, as it became known, was the closest a big power could get, quickly, to using one network to fight another. And there were other strategies: The Egyptian military, for instance, played a deadly serious long game. They gave in to the massed opposition and even let extremist networks come to power. But this later appeared to some as merely a pretext, a way to map the ties of these groups, to coldly study how they functioned and to record the secret sources of their power and influence and money. Then, when the Egyptian population tired of the amateurish Islamists in power—as the military knew they someday would—the generals moved.

Skeptics would demand of Castells: *What the hell did any of these protests really accomplish?* What sort of *reevolootion* was it that left nothing but sinkholes in Tripoli and Damascus? What they accomplished, Castells conceded, was mostly destructive. But that was the point. This smashing at old laws, the cracking apart of ideas of power and control, had changed the landscape. And it had revealed a hidden logic of connection. *Irrelevant?* That was like saying earthquakes or epidemics should be overlooked. In their vibrating apart of once-solid structures, networked social movements told a great deal. They revealed interconnected fault lines. They showed how groups could suck power into themselves from networks, along invisible lines, and animate themselves as if by connection to electricity. The protesters and terrorists understood power that existed simply because of connectivity. And so they had an instinct that eluded the comfortable men in the palaces. The traditional reaction of authorities—*Round up the usual suspects*—didn't work because, as Castells noted, "the usual suspects were networks." You couldn't arrest a network.

3.

Before we can go much further in figuring out how network power might be used, we need what many leading figures are missing as they underestimate network power. We need a mental picture of this new landscape. Much as we once had a picture of the world as "king and court" or "general and armies"—or even "newspaper and readers"—we've got to be able to talk about how companies like Facebook or Uber or the Microsoft cloud are organized, and to see how those same rules apply to financial companies and military forces. What marks successful people who already have a network sensibility is that they see structures in networks that are new and original in design. They understand how power might move in them. Jefferson understood how power might move in a democracy, which is one reason he chided Madison about the Bill of Rights. Revolutionary figures today have similar ideas. The brilliance of server-farm designers at Google or technology-enhanced financial market traders or even, unfortunately, terror groups is that they see what most of us can't yet see. What does a network look like? Would we describe it to each other as we once described royalty? "There's a king on top. Under that there are knights." It's true that you can't arrest a network all at once, as Castells said. But can you spot the parts that are dangerous? When Castells says, "Power is moving," what does that mean, exactly? What I want to do in this chapter is to draw out, as we might have once sketched a picture of king and court, an image of a network. What common designs run through those crowds in Tahir and ISIS? Why were they both underestimated? That picture is like a skeleton key for our age. It unlocks almost all the network puzzles around us. It opens a door, in a sense, to a world where we can begin to use the networks too.

It is a commonplace among historians and anthropologists that power—the ability to make or cause things to happen—is determined by structure. When I say "superpower," I am painting, with a single word, a picture of the international system. The word "highway" tells you something about logistics, trucks, economic power. This is why "org charts" matter so much—or so little in cases where invisible human relations form invisible influence webs. Think of the map of power in your family or your office or nation. Who makes the decisions? Why? The way we bottle up our lives in firms or congresses or universities flavors just about every other decision we make. An imperial CEO creates a different sort of firm from a boss who moves among his employees as an equal. An army that moves from the top down is different from one that lives, as Mao said of the Chinese guerrilla forces that mastered the country against steep odds in 1949, as if they were fish and the people were water. Power is always packed into structures of some sort. Emperors, kings, presidents, and congresses all reflect certain arrangements. But those arrangements change; power moves. You can see leaders struggle with this constant shifting: Think of the "enlightened despotism" of the eighteenth century, as Frederick II of Prussia, Joseph II of the Habsburgs, and Catherine II, in Saint Petersburg, each struggled to marry the then-new ideas of liberty with older instincts for control. History is, in one sense, nothing but the tale of the movement of power. Once, the idea of an Assyrian king was new, as was the notion of a president or a pope. History is paced by the arrival of new species of all sorts and by the deaths of others. This is as true for institutions as it is for bugs, with this caveat: No one gives up power easily.

There are whole approaches to power that look extremely reasonable until one day they look insane. For thousands of years the idea that one feudal lord should control thousands of serfs seemed perfectly reasonable to the lords and serfs alike. John Maynard Keynes's famous line about Egypt—*Just because you built the pyramids doesn't mean you get to use them*—marked a whole approach that seemed inarguable for centuries, even if the experience of it was inarguably awful. Features of the world—moats, massive cathedrals, pyramids, sweatshops—exist only because distributions of power permitted or enabled or encouraged them. The quotidian interactions of our lives—how we shop, where we meet our friends, the politics we embrace—all produce long-lasting structures, just as farmers walking through a field over and over again eventually leave a path. Malls, democracies, war zones— these all emerge as artifacts of human presence.

Pushing power into networks, we can see already, creates whole new arrangements. It leaves new businesses, fortunes, and war zones as a result. It also leaves new and vibrant spaces where education, medicine, and safety can be assured with a really efficient design— and at a historic scale. Some of these structures are as unimaginable to us now as a voting booth would have been to an Egyptian slave. The possibility they suggest, particularly for radical and widespread decency, can tend to be obscured because we have a hard time picturing what they might look like, just as it would have been difficult to envision a search engine in 1985. When we say that ours is a revolutionary age, it's not because you can watch videos on your phone. It's because of *why* you can watch videos on your phone—and what that implies for the old, nervous structures around us. But to develop a picture of power now, it helps to tell the story of power—and how it has changed—over the years.

4.

Before the Age of Enlightenment and the Industrial Revolution began, political and economic power were extremely *concentrated*. A few kings and feudal lords controlled most economic production. Priests decided who could speak to God, and how and when. Finance was dominated by a few families, largely working in the secretive counting rooms of early banking capitals such as Amsterdam, Genoa, or Lyon. Knowledge about the world—science, history, and even geography—was closely held and fiercely opaque. Inside monastery walls or university halls, the aim of protecting (and editing) what the world knew far outstripped any hunger for new ideas. In those times, a lucky or brutal few decided the economic, political, and intellectual lives of the many. You can picture power as balled up in the hands of a tiny and fortunate elite.

Over time, cracks appeared. One of the earliest was also one of the most fundamental: the schism that split the Catholic Church. This was, at first, the work of a young German theologian named Martin Luther, in the sixteenth century. Luther was a man whose view of life, he would say often in later years, was shaped by a single sentence, Romans 1:17: "For therein is the righteousness of God revealed from faith to faith: as it is written, The just shall live by faith." The Epistle to the Romans, as Romans is formally titled, was a letter from Saint Paul to a collection of recalcitrant, spiritually moribund Jews in Rome. His message was among the simplest and most compact possible: The transmission of faith requires nothing more than faith itself. Romans teaches that believing in God, which is *faith*, is enough for access to all the riches of heaven—God's righteousness, an afterlife, forgiveness.

By Luther's age, however, access to those riches was not so simple. Among other things, spiritual control had become a lucrative business. The glory of the Catholic Church, its magnificent cathedrals and clothes, was funded by an insidious habit of selling passes to heaven in the form of indulgences. This glittering greed in the name of God grated against Luther's from-faith-to-faith sensibility. When he saw his own congregation slipping into churches led by priests who cheerfully shifted indulgences for cash, he saw a rank, strange hypocrisy. His rage boiled over in the summer of 1517, and he summarized his case against the Church in the Ninety-Five Theses, which he nailed to the door of his local church on October 31. *Papa non vult nec potest ullas penas remittere preter eas, quas arbitrio vel suo vel canonum imposuit*, he wrote in thesis 5: "No matter what you might pay him, the Pope can't influence what happens to you after you die." And, in thesis 65, *Euangelici rhetia sunt, quibus olim piscabantur viros divitiarum*: "Indulgences are nets with which one fishes for the riches of men."

As much as Luther wanted to restore Saint Paul's sense of a personal faith, he also sought to start a difficult argument about power. Our relationship with God, Luther meant, is *our* relationship. It's not something to be negotiated and certainly not sold. It does not require fancy clothes or cathedrals or gilded scepters. For Luther, the first insight of God's nearness had engendered a profound spiritual crisis. It ran against everything he'd been taught about power. Later in life he recalled the moment the possibility of direct access to God had occurred to him, as he studied the pages of Saint Augustine, probably around 1508. "When I came to the words 'thee, most merciful father,'" he wrote, "the thought that I had to speak to God without a mediator almost made me flee." Who was he, Martin Luther, to speak directly to God? But from then on, Luther's experience of God, his conviction that power passed from faith to faith—and not from faith to money to Church to faith—embodied a heretical idea about power: Revelation was possible without a middleman.

Such a concept undid much of what had been taken as doctrine. The Church immediately understood the danger. It rushed to label Luther as heretical and, later, crazy. In arguing that the Catholic Church, with all its magnificent trappings of faith, was really a useless tollgate, Luther was picking at a still larger, more significant question: *How should power be split?* If Luther was right, and God intended faith to be so easily accessible to each of us, then some other questions tumbled after that one. Should we have direct access to political power? To ideas? To money and land and control of our own economic destinies? Could "from faith to faith" be recast as "from idea to idea" or "from truth to truth" or — and this turned out to be a particularly violent shift — "from citizen to citizen"? The Church was merely one of many institutions that had sat massively, reliably, comfortably (and greedily) between people and power.

Luther, it later emerged, was not alone. An era of awkward questions and answers had begun. The Polish astronomer Nicolaus Copernicus, for instance, had preceded Luther by a couple of decades with his own set of challenging ideas. "Those who know that the consensus of many centuries has sanctioned the conception that the earth remains at rest in the middle of the heaven as its center would . . . regard it as an insane pronouncement if I made the opposite assertion," he wrote. Machiavelli, Galileo, Erasmus, and a growing list of thinkers were all working away with this same questioning spirit. Their "insane pronouncements," when proved true, opened the way to still further insights. The Enlightenment had begun. The old power centers acted almost as if nothing had changed; maybe they believed nothing would ever need to. "This council declares that if anyone disagrees with it, they are damned," the Catholic Church pronounced confidently at Trent in 1547, in response to Luther's Reformation. But there was no turning back. As the German philosopher Immanuel Kant wrote, the motto of the era could best be summarized as *Dare to know!* "Enlighten-ment," he explained, "requires nothing but freedom."

This, it emerged, was one hell of an expensive requirement.

5.

In the years after Luther's Ninety-Five Theses, Europe was torn apart. The Continent's long-standing image of power—concen-trated and unquestioned—was ripped away. Another picture emerged. The idea of personal access to God, a kind of "one man, one prayer" approach to religion, opened other fundamental struggles. The credibility of nearly every sacred body that had once depended on controlling people and limiting their choices—the Church, those kings, feudalism, myths—steadily eroded. "Human knowledge and human power come to the same thing," the English philosopher and statesman Francis Bacon observed in the midst of this shift in his artillery shell of a book, *The New Organon.* Human knowledge, he means, *is* human power. You can imagine the energy, the promise, of the book as it was passed in Latin to Kepler in his study in Linz and to Galileo—who received it with relief—in Venice a decade before his imprisonment. This human power to question was what the masses of Enlightenment-era Europe would use, gleefully at times, to claw apart most of the old structures. Luther's heresy led initially to the wars of the Refor-mation, battles that pulled every European royal family into a struggle between church and state and then between each other. The bloodletting of the Thirty Years' War, the first truly pan-European conflict, established in its aftermath a new balance that let each king select the religion of his subjects. *Cuius regio, eius religio,* as the agreements of Westphalia decided in 1648— or "Whose realm, his religion." The consensus produced some stability, but not for long. After all, you could imbue that line with personal meaning and see what it demanded next: "*my* realm, *my* religion."

In a sense, this revolutionary tumult was necessary to pull power from a comfortable, established *asymmetric* arrangement, in which a few people controlled so much, into something more *symmetric.* Luther's Reformation thinking made God directly and instantly accessible to anyone. (Just as Copernicus's scientific way of thinking gave us, eventually, the ability to question whether God exists at all.) Individuals could argue as equals. In fact, the important notion that men were "created equal" became increasingly evident with each passing generation, though establishing that equality triggered the French Revolution, the American Civil War, and countless wars of liberation.

Democratic political systems aspired to enshrine this balance, shifting countries from rule-by-birth—or rule-by-murder—monarchies to rule-by-majority republics. Markets also reflected the new picture of power. *How good is that product? What is the price? Is there demand?* became the essential questions, not *Which lord controls that field?* Releasing power into the busy arms of businessmen, politicians, scientists, and artists meant that ideas, politics, and innovations competed. They got better. They evolved. And the sum of all these interacting pieces produced sustained economic growth for the first time in history. In a "commercial society," Adam Smith explained in *The Wealth of Nations*, "every man thus lives by exchanging, or becomes in some measure a merchant." Smith didn't mean that everyone was really a merchant; rather, in a world of markets, each of us—our labor, our ideas, our capital—is a commodity. We are liberated, but only to compete. For votes, for jobs, for resources.

If the old faiths and institutions couldn't stand the pressures of these powerful, equalizing forces, then new ones had to be built. The Nobel Prize–winning economist Douglass North called these foundations "the scaffolds humans erect." The idea of equality of influence or power—not merely opportunity—demanded new containers such as voting booths, legislatures, labor unions. Rule of law was one of the most essential: a single code that could be enforced evenly across a society, demanding that principles of order outweigh the habitual advantages of prominence or power or birth. Law aspired to make men equal in front of courts. This, in turn, suggested a new degree of fairness up and down the social order—and a predictable hunger to improve one's position. Gustave Flaubert had the warning about right in his tragedy of social climbing, *Madame Bovary:* "Never touch your idols: the gilding will stick to your fingers."

That didn't stop anyone from reaching for the possibility of the golden life. Flaubert's readers were part of this, after all: Widespread literacy made his audience. And the standardization of measurements around them, as well as the birth of universal credit and currencies, were all tools for spreading hope, power, and access. "She wanted to die, but she also wanted to live in Paris," Flaubert wrote of poor Emma Bovary, fatally drawn by the possibility of more, more, and still more. She wasn't alone: Museums were packed with new crowds. Scientific congresses clustered minds together for debate. Global industrial fairs turned theoretical knowledge into industrial profit. The ever-more-efficient use of iron, steam, and electricity reflected a virtuous loop of hope and achievement that tied together lab and market, scientist and businessman. All the figures of *Bovary*—the social-climbing housewife, the greedy speculator, the wildly hopeful inventor—linger in our own age. They are the cast of characters of the modern world.

"All fixed, fast-frozen relations are swept away, all new-formed ones become antiquated before they can ossify. All that is solid melts into air, all that is holy is profaned," Karl Marx and Friedrich Engels wrote in 1849 about the speed of this change. As more people "dared to know," controversial ideas became irresistible. Evolution, ideas about electricity or politics, all drew a curious audience. John Locke and Isaac Newton and Charles Darwin were as notable for the crowd of debating citizens they attracted as they were for their ideas. The arguments were intended to elicit truth, to give individuals that same shocking sense that Luther had felt on discovering a powerful idea. But, just as important, these debates were recorded—they were printed in journals and books or repeated in letters.

For most of history knowledge had suffered from a coltish fragility: There was always a chance that some important insight would be lost in a plague, extinguished during the strangling of a heretic, burned up in a library fire, or dissolved by military misfortune. This is why, for instance, we have almost all of Shakespeare's sixteenth-century plays and so sadly little of Sappho's poetry from the sixth century BCE. Widespread knowledge was like an insurance policy for humanity's greatest ideas and finest art. "If I have seen further," Newton wrote, "it is by standing upon the shoulders of giants." Newton's revolution had demanded books every bit as much as genius. In this sense, the preservation and advance of knowledge, the new symmetry, was not only the largest shift of power in history; it was also the best thing that ever happened to the human race.

In other ways, of course, it was very nearly the worst. Symmetry had a darker edge. It meant that nations decided the strategic questions of the day by throwing massive, deadly power at one another. With each passing year, Europe's engines of science and industry were grinding out tools of unprecedented destruction. Napoleon's greatest victories were enabled as much by the industrial strength of French artillery factories as they were by the liberated masses of the French Revolution. The very name of France's *levée en masse* hinted at the size of what might be assembled when citizens and not merely mercenaries or aristocrats took to the lines. When France was unseated by the British Empire, it was manufacturing scale and naval depth that tipped the balance. Germany's blood-and-iron commercial engines challenged London's clubby mastery of the globe. Size and scale and safety became linked, a lesson finally confirmed by America's global mastery. The undeniable power of American industry was Winston Churchill's only real comfort for two nervous years after 1939. "I knew the United States was in the war, up to the neck and in to the death," he wrote the day after Pearl Harbor. "Hitler's fate was sealed. Mussolini's fate was sealed. As for the Japanese, they would be ground to powder. All the rest was merely the proper application of overwhelming force." Or, the reverse of that coin—Admiral Yamamoto, grimly, to Prime Minister Konoye: "If you tell me that it is necessary that we fight, then in the first six months to a year of war against the U.S. and England I will run wild, and I will show you an uninterrupted succession of victories; I must tell you also that, should the war be prolonged for two or three years, I have no confidence in our ultimate victory." *Ground to powder.* Mass against mass. This was symmetry at its most decisive, a picture of power that seemed undeniable in its pure logic. Until now.

6.

So how should we think about power in our own age? What picture best captures its vibrant, unceasing demands?

It might be tempting to say we're leaving that world of mass-on-mass power behind. After all, tiny fractures anywhere in a network can now cause massive and even fatal, collapsing pressure—one clever hacker, one loose terrorist, one hedge fund manager with a bad idea, even one purely accidental misconnection can all produce widespread damage. Never before has so much power accumulated in systems so vulnerable to single slips. It seems now that something can grow bigger *and* weaker. A nation may have an ever-larger GDP, but if it is miswired or if its social or legal or youthful connections misfire, then it may be more vulnerable than its financial prowess might suggest.

But this "power of a pinprick" asymmetry is not the whole story. Just when the network looks like a way to bless small forces with decisive influence, we notice something else: tremendous, even historic, concentrations of power. Platforms such as Facebook, software systems such as Microsoft, and search centers such as Google are dense and increasingly impossible to replace. Google answers questions for more than 50 percent of the world every day. Is it the most powerful company in human history? Is Facebook? And should we describe their power as widely distributed? Or as concentrated into algorithms and cloud data?

The leap we have to make in understanding our network age— and by this I don't just mean the Internet, but really any connected system you'd care to consider—begins with this idea: In connected systems, power is defined by both profound *concentration* and by massive *distribution*. It can't be understood in simple either-or terms. Power and influence will, in the near future, become even more centralized than in feudal times *and* more distributed than it was in the most vibrant democracies. Network power, we might say, exists as a skin of billions of tied-together points linked to vital, centralized cores. Our world is filling with countless connected devices and people at an unmeasurably quick pace, but we are also constructing centralizing companies, protocols, and systems. Biological research so complex it once demanded billion-dollar labs now takes place on lab desktops (distribution) that quickly reference immense cloud-based genetic data sets (concentration). You can snap high-quality videos with your phone (distribution); and you share them with millions on a connected central stage such as Instagram. A financial engineer can design a new trading instrument (distribution), but hope for profit depends on instant connection to busy, price-setting markets (concentration).

This pulling, taffy-like web of ties between small (your watch) and big (connected data systems) stretches constantly. It's what you need to picture when you want an image of network power. This is how the wired masses in Tahrir Square emerged like magic on a once-invisible surface formed between their phones and platforms such as YouTube. Little wonder those men around Mubarak were baffled. It is also how hyperlinked terrorist groups appeared from nearly nowhere, jerking followers from around the world via massively connected messaging platforms, surprising wizened analysts of fundamentalism who thought recruiting mani-acs demanded mosques, madrassas, and a final personal touch.

A commercial society, Adam Smith told us three hundred years ago, is one where every man has to become a merchant. In our age of connection, every one of us is a node. We sit on that tense, stretched surface between center and periphery. When we say *Connection changes the nature of an object*, this is the exact bal-ance we have to contemplate. "Social structures," John Padgett and Walter Powell write in their masterful study of complex con-nected systems, *The Emergence of Organizations and Markets*, "should be viewed more as vortexes in the flow of social life than as build-ings of stone." This is an idea with unsettling implications: All the structures of which we are a part—congresses, universities, the companies where we work, our minds, even—are merely temporary collections of relations. And, of course, those relations can change in an instant.

The tension between concentration and distribution acts as a hydraulic jaw. It pries power out of older, once-legitimate hands. Consider my father. A cardiologist, he stands at the head of a medical tradition run for thousands of years on the idea that the doctor is the center of your care. If you show up at a hospital flatlining on a stretcher, my father's decades of training and practice have always been your best hope. But today, nearly every patient he sees—even the ones he brings back from their black flatline future—second-guesses him as soon as he's out the door. The tubes haven't even come out of their noses before they google their disease, tapping into websites of mixed reliability, joining some online community of people with the same sickness. Meanwhile, my father's ideas about their cases face competition. Someday soon the emerging "Internet of DNA," detailed collections of treatment histories and linked databases of medical updates, will be studied by machine intelligences able to outdiagnose him. Constant communication between data centers and sensors we'll wear (or swallow) will extend the edge these systems have on my dad. They will notice things he could never hope to see—small but portentous changes in your heartbeat, chemical chimeras from new medications, how you're feeling in each moment until your last.

Networks create concentration *and* distribution. As a result, they rip apart many existing structures. Look at our worrisome global economy. The extreme concentration of wealth and massive distribution of work to ever-cheaper sources of labor run with this same logic. Just as my father's middleman role in health care is torn apart, so the world's middle class is pressured from above and below at once. Their jobs disappear to machines and Vietnamese sweatshops (distribution). Financial gains, meanwhile, accumulate ever faster to those at the center of the system, endowed with more information, opportunity, and—in every sense—connection.

Placing an economy on a network surface produces new, ripping pressures. "We are being destroyed," a South Korean friend said to me about the hollowing out of his national economy. Korean computer and television manufacturers had once hoped that they could develop their own essential software, that their hardware-manufacturing technology would be unmatchable. But their customers were being sucked, from the moment they booted up, into firms like Google and Facebook and Apple. Local Korean competitors had no appeal — and no chance. Once-prized Korean manufacturing excellence was no match for cheap Chinese and then Vietnamese labor welded to assembly-line technology. To work at a Seoul technology company or my dad's cardiology office had a strange, similar aspect.

We see this pattern of network-led shredding nearly everywhere now, the result of powerful cores of knowledge and widely distributed connection. Newspapers have been removed from relevancy by crowd-sourced news feeds *and* smart social news feeds. Once indomitable television networks of the *Cheers* and *Seinfeld* era have been devoured by cheap uploaded videos *and* the Internet platforms.

Bitcoin and other first-generation digital currencies are doing something similar, eating at the once-unquestionable authority of central banks. Drones too are creatures of connection now, hovering along on a skein of GPS signals made possible by the distribution of aviation technology and know-how. They will do to our old ideas of safety what that concentration-distribution pressure is doing to medicine and finance: making our old ways slow and useless. Self-organized drone fleets against aircraft carriers? Border defenses? Human soldiers? Think of the way that Baron Haussmann laid out Paris in the nineteenth century to manage the Enlightenment-age danger of liberated, angry citizens. The city's wide boulevards, narrow side streets, and central axes were designed to help police move quickly for the fast physical quarantine of rioters. Our cities? They will need to be protected against the pinch of asymmetric attack drones, self-steered ambulances, and robotic police. Someday soon, drones will demand the redesign of our cities as automobiles did in the last century. This is Conway's law of network power at work again. The virtual is forcing itself into the real.

7.

The simple, once-appealing idea that connection is liberation is wrong. To connect now is to be encased in a powerful and dynamic tension. Such balancing forces appear at the very roots of the natural order, in atomic cores. The great breakthrough of physics in the last century was the confirmation that the powerful energy of atoms represented a balance of immense electrical forces. Positively charged electrons circulating on the outside of an atom were balanced by neutrons and protons packed inside the atomic core. Hydrogen is the simplest of elements in this sense: One electron balances one proton. Uranium is on the other end of the scale, with ninety-two powerful electrons matched by ninety-two protons in the nucleus. This same balancing energy applies to networks: The more devices on the outside, the more powerful the central core must become. When there were only a few dozen queries an hour pointed at Google, for instance, it didn't need to do much in its core to keep up. It was like the hydrogen atom. Now, however, Google is bombarded with traffic. Your phone, your car, any Internet browser—they are like electrons pulling at data centers with constant demands. The scale of this is astonishing: Internal traffic on Google's servers as they speak to each other is equivalent to 10 percent of total traffic on the Internet. That marks the work required to handle all those billions of connected points, each pulling on that central information core. The more devices, the more powerful the core must become. Distribution *and* concentration are the essence of power now.

This pulling movement, the way that cores and distributions of power mercilessly jerk at certain once-essential structures and objects and people, explains a lot about our age, including the failure of institutions we once relied upon. Connection changes the nature of an object. That's true for your doctor, your bank account, your army—and for billions of people whose lives will soon alter irreversibly once they connect to markets, to knowledge, to the world. We have to ask just how many of the scaffolds humans erected, ones that were essential for Enlightenment-era advances, will now be pulled down.

If you have the tools or the skill to see the world this way, as a vibrating and pulling mesh of connections, then you can look at tanks or soldiers or years of stability and see weakness and *possibility*. Once new rules and their effects become visible to you, even the most inarguable current sources of influence and control start to look weak. The U.S. dollar. Aircraft carriers. Border fences. The Seventh Sense is defined first by this intuitive feeling for just how power is being re-geared. If you look at a kid with a phone and think *strong*, you have a feeling for the potential of a network. If you look at an angry, barely educated terrorist wannabe and think *junior varsity*, you don't. And, as a result, you may be about to have a very unpleasant surprise. A friend who controls the largest secure Bitcoin vault in the world put it to me once this way: "Platforms mattered once; now it is protocols." His point was that the pipes and rules connecting the varied systems of our world fundamentally affect the distribution of power. The rules of the Bitcoin block chain or the implications of an addressing protocol such as IPv6 reveal something about how we'll all connect in the future. They are examples of how the pulling pressure of networks will become operational.

Try this: Ball up your right hand into a fist. Take your left hand and open the fingers wide. Hold the hands a few inches apart. You can think of your left hand as the vibrating, living network of connection and your balled-up fist as concentrated power. Right hand, Google Maps; left hand, millions of Android phones. This is the picture of our age. Networks live in that tension between your right and left hands, between distribution and concentration. To connect any object—my dad, a newspaper, a refugee, a toy drone—is to irrevocably change its essence. The reason the legitimacy of old leaders is failing, the reason our grand strategy is incoherent, the reason our age really is revolutionary, is that our poor leaders are all sitting in the midst of these pulling, powerful forces. We should steel ourselves for the shredding imminence of this violence. But also—and you know this already, I think—we must prepare ourselves for the task of immense construction. Network power not only pulls apart. It also creates.

This paradox confused me for a long time. Power is manifestly concentrated with astonishing efficiency now. And it is more widely dispersed than ever. We can stare at this strange tension and baffle ourselves as we try to figure out how and why it moves. Understanding this, I finally concluded, requires making a cognitive leap, perhaps, over our usual, Western way of understanding the world, as either *a* or *b*, as either distributed or concentrated, and into a view of how opposites might ceaselessly balance into a whole. Not *a* or *b* but *a and b*.

Let me tell you what I mean: In 1127, the Song Dynasty, which had ruled China for nearly two hundred years, collapsed in the face of an invasion by wild Manchurian soldiers from the northern plains. The Song leadership—along with its best minds and cultural figures—fled south from Beijing for nearly a thousand miles, until they were safely on the opposite bank of the Yangtze River. They settled in the lakeside city now called Hangzhou. In those days, Hangzhou was known as Lin'an, which might best be translated as "Gazing at Peace." To the Song leaders, the little town must have seemed a perfect respite from the horror they had left behind.

The city lay then, as it still does, alongside Xihu, or West Lake, a tranquil stretch of water framed by rolling hills and tea plantations. The poet and statesman Su Dongpo later compared gazing at the lake to looking at a beautiful woman—that same fused sense of calm, peace, and astonishment you might feel while considering the object of your own love. Still water is regarded in Chinese culture as a reservoir of yin energy; you may recall this from Lake Tai, where Master Nan set his campus. Song leaders had fled the angry yang energy of invasion for the yin peace of the south. Yin energy is associated with calm, femininity, fertility. Yang expresses action, violence, creation. Yang is the thunderstorm; yin is the peace that comes afterward, as the crops absorb water and grow. The idea of a balance of yin and yang is among the oldest in Chinese philosophy. "When heaven and earth were formed, they divided into yin and yang," the *Huainanzi*, one of China's greatest political texts, explains. "Yang is generated from yin and yin is generated from yang." Hangzhou became a capital of yin. It produced, as a result, some of the most enduring Chinese philosophy and poetry and art. Greatness emerged from that stillness—and, even today, to sit by West Lake and drink a cup of the Dragon Well tea produced on the nearby hillsides is to have every one of your senses flooded by tranquillity.

That yin-yang balance helps us understand that power split on a network is not really split. Network power is wild at the ends, with all the creative energy of a world filled with devices, empowered human dreams, and the violent slips of old balances. *Yang*.

But at the center it is dense, still, and even quiet, with the silently cranking algorithms of massively concentrated power. *Yin*. In fact, this debate hovers at the dawn of the network revolution. The computer-science pioneer Claude Shannon saw information in 1949 as pulsing with the instability of an entropic system. *Yang*. The machine architect Norbert Wiener, writing at nearly the same moment in 1948, saw the digital age differently, as an expression of stability and structure. *Yin*. His vision for a digital order, what he called cybernetics, emerged from the Greek concept of *kibernetes*—the orderly steering of a ship through sometimes chaotic waters.

We now know the humming webs around us are both yin and yang. They are ordered and chaotic. Good and evil. Power in this connected age is concentrated *and* distributed. Each side of this balance feeds and energizes the other. The crops need the thunderstorm; the thunderstorm feeds off the heat radiating up from the land. Or: The yang violence of the Manchurian wars bred the conditions for the yin renaissance in Hangzhou. The massive distribution of connected points enables revolutions, economic crises, life-cracking innovations. But it also creates a hunger for centralization, for agreement on just what sorts of glue will bind us all together. This idea of opposites balancing into a whole is not unique to Chinese civilization. You can find it too in Ancient Greek or Roman tradition—Heraclitus, for instance, insisting, "All things are one." Or you can spot it in the view that there can be no love without hate, no stillness without chaos, no beauty without the unbeautiful, and, fortunately—as we're about to see—no destruction without creation.

CHAPTER FIVE

Fishnet

In which we learn why networks spread so quickly.

1.

In 1959 a young electrical engineer named Paul Baran, who had been working at Howard Hughes's aircraft-design factory in Los Angeles, arrived for his first day of work at a low-slung modern building along the Santa Monica beach. RAND—a stylish 1950s acronym for Research and Development—had been established by the U.S. Air Force and Douglas Aircraft Company with the aim of bending the best minds of math and science to the purpose of winning the Cold War. RAND was a dream destination for many researchers, offering a fusion of patriotism, technology, and California sun. The place became known for a relaxed, intellectual atmosphere that belied the dangerous, nuclear-tipped problems sitting inside its locked safes and eager minds. Shortly after settling in, Baran was given one of the most troubling and secret of these puzzles.

The Cold War was then in its early days. The debate over how to manage an age when it was, for the first time, possible for humans to destroy the planet was still colored by fresh memories of Hiroshima and Nagasaki. And it was charged with the fear of

Communist expansion, not an unreasonable worry for Americans who had just fought a world war against totalitarian forces. A fear lingered in the minds of many citizens and military planners: Given a window of vulnerability, might the Soviet Union unleash a fast nuclear attack? Avoiding such a risk became a primary concern of American diplomacy and defense thinking. "The chief purpose of our military establishment has been to win wars," the nuclear strategist Bernard Brodie wrote in a 1946 memo. "From now on its chief purpose must be to avert them." Moscow had to know, and trust, that any attempt to strike at the United States would be met with a devastating reply. This "balance of threat," as the logic became known, depended in turn on America's ability to retaliate, even if the nation's military had been half pulverized by an initial round of Soviet missile attacks. If Moscow's planners could find a way to wipe away America's ability to respond in the first strike, then Moscow's leaders might take a chance. They could move first, declaw the United States, and then pick the world apart at their leisure. If Khrushchev's famous line from 1956, "We will bury you!" meant what it said, then such a move would provide an awfully convenient first shovel.

In the late 1950s, when Baran arrived at RAND, the Cold War was at its chilliest, and one of the most closely guarded American secrets was this: If the Soviet Union did attack, there might be no response. The United States, with its priceless collection of bombers and missiles and its million-man army, could not strike back at Moscow for the simple reason that the nation's field officers would have no way to talk to each other or to their commanders in Washington. The military radio and telephone systems America depended on, it turned out, would not survive the hit. This was the secret, lethal problem Baran had been tasked with solving. "At the time we didn't know how to build a communication system that could survive even collateral damage by enemy weapons," he recalled. RAND's computer simulations showed that the AT&T Long Lines telephone system, a copper web that carried the nation's military communications, would be cut apart by even relatively minor physical damage. A full-on Soviet strike would level it.

The military had already spent a fortune on the problem (plus half a fortune, it turned out, trying to hide it). The result was an expensively designed telephone network linking military bases to strategic command posts. But because the lines and their switching centers were laced out in a pattern with just a few big, central nodes, like a bicycle wheel with spokes, the network had almost no chance of surviving the very thing it was designed to help prevent. If you saw a diagram of this network, with its main hub staffed by senior commanders and its lines radiating out to bases and missile silos, it even looked like a target. If the Soviet Union could bull's-eye those hubs with a bomb or two, then the rest of the network would fold right away. America's military would be deaf. And as Soviet missiles became more accurate, the communications vulnerability became more acute. "We will soon be living in an era," Baran wrote, "in which we cannot guarantee survivability of any single point."

The situation, as a carefully screened handful of scientists knew, was in fact even more perilous. Shortly before Baran arrived at RAND, scientists testing hydrogen-bomb designs in the Pacific discovered that radiation from their explosions fuzzed communications for hundreds of miles. A Soviet attack, even if it missed those central AT&T nodes, would still reduce American military communications to a bunch of hissing, empty phones. "Our communications were so vulnerable," Baran said, "that each missile base commander would face the dilemma of either doing nothing in the event of a physical attack, or taking action that would mean an all-out irrevocable war." You could picture the moment of decision: some colonel, alone in his bomb-laden plane over Europe or deep in some cornfield missile silo, wondering, *Launch or not?* This was a horrifying possibility. Baran began to ask: *Is there some other way to send a counterstrike signal?*

2.

Baran would later become famous for developing the ideas he produced in response to this urgent-sounding challenge. His insights led, later, to the creation of the modern Internet. During his years at RAND, Baran would make a set of intellectual and technological leaps that ranked with the greatest science: He imagined something—a way of sharing information—that had very nearly never been considered before. He designed a network model of power before one existed anywhere, the sort of leap—part faith, part intuition, part science—that Brunelleschi made when sketching out an idea for a cathedral dome in Florence. Then Baran figured out how to build his system into something that would endure the worst of shocks. The essence of what Baran discovered reveals that certain types of networks, once they take a grip on our world, represent an irreversible transition. You can't easily go back from a town where everyone has a phone to one where no one does. You can't go back from Google to Britannica. And, we'll come to see, you can't really ever go back to old-style stock markets or military alliances or health care. Baran proved it was possible to build connected systems that are resilient against nearly any attempt to destroy them, and in the process he pre-dicted a world much like ours, one where connected systems go from one point to billions at astonishing speed. Baran conceived too of systems that become stronger when attacked. We might ask: Just why do the great network figures of our world seek to break what came before? It's because they know that what we're entering now isn't a fluke. Their contest is over what will be assembled next. What will replace the NYSE? What will improve on the post office? What will reshape entertainment? A new and powerful group understands the logic of networks that Baran pioneered, even if they don't know who he is. We need to do the same.

Baran was born in Grodno, Poland, in 1926, and his father had a fortunate, uneasy sense about what lay ahead. The family fled to America when Paul, then named Pesach, was two. Young Paul was a model student and soon afterward a prize-winning mathematician. His talents were irresistible to Hughes Corporation's military construction efforts and, later, to the science and security geeks at RAND. But that sharp, irreversible exodus from Poland had left him with an enduring mark, as it did so many refugees of that era. In the 1940s, while the murderous mist of Nazism swept over Europe, one problem took on a searching urgency for the Baran family: How are we to maintain a connection in the face of utter catastrophe? So perhaps it was not a surprise that the defining work of his life orbited this same question. How to stay connected? "I was concerned with survivability," Baran once said.

After two years of patient study at RAND, Baran began to discern the outlines of a solution. In a series of lectures for air force officers starting in the summer of 1961, he worked his way toward an answer, speech by speech and equation by equation. He didn't fully know where he was heading when he began, he later said, but he had an instinct. Some other solution must be out there. By the end of his lecture tour, he had found it.

Baran's design began, like so many innovations, with an idea that *hadn't worked*. The Pentagon, he'd thought, might broadcast thousands of coded messages over AM radio frequencies all at once as an attack approached. Missile-silo commanders and bomber commanders would cluster by their transistor radios, collecting their "launch" codes with the ease of listening to a late-night baseball game. That target-shaped, "just aim here" web of phone lines would be replaced by something far harder to wipe out with a single R-7 Semyorka missile shot. But this approach had its own problems. It relied on broadcast towers and on insecure AM radio waves. Yet the idea of such a widespread, untargetable network got Baran thinking. Sending out the messages and letting them find their own way had a lot of appeal, if it could be done. There would be no central hubs. Information would sail over linked lines in the same way radio signals moved in the air. Military communications, in Baran's system, would bounce from point to point on this tapestry, at each stop being redirected toward their intended destination. The resulting network, if you drew it out, would look like a fishnet: lots of links connected to a few knotted nodes. And because the bundles of data—Baran called them packets—could be moved by the network itself, you could cut or nuke or sabotage the net in a few places and still use it. The packets would find another path. Even a badly ripped-up and irradiated network could, in theory, carry a launch—or a recall—message safely from the White House to a bomber pilot.

"The early simulations," Baran recalled, "showed that after the hypothetical network was 50% instantly destroyed, the surviving pieces of the network reconstituted themselves within a half a second." In other words, his messages were finding new routes on the network, even after huge parts of the system had been taken off-line. And they were doing it nearly instantly. Better still, as he began to model these "distributed" networks, Baran discovered that they were not only capable of surviving attack, they were also incredibly efficient. "If built and maintained at a cost of $60 million (1964 dollars)," he calculated, his design would "handle the long-distance telecommunications within the

Department of Defense that was costing the taxpayer about $2 billion a year."

Baran traveled the country for most of 1961 and 1962, classified presentation and slide rules in hand, trying to persuade skeptical generals and engineers. It was a nearly impossible task. He recalled a visit to the towering AT&T switching headquarters on Broadway in lower Manhattan, an implacable temple of the high priests of hub-and-spoke network design. That one building handled more telephone and telex traffic than nearly any other single point on earth. No doubt the place ranked very high on Moscow's first-strike list. So Baran expected a friendly reception. After all, he'd be telling a bunch of men with a uranium death sentence that he'd found a way to get them off the Soviet target plan. His new "mesh" network would mean that bombing AT&T would be largely pointless. It wouldn't blind U.S. commanders. If only they'd redesign their network, the AT&T engineers might save their own lives.

They thought he was insane.

"I tried to explain packet switching to a senior telephone company executive. In midsentence he interrupted me," Baran recalled. "The old analog engineer looked stunned. He looked at his colleagues in the room while his eyeballs rolled up, sending a signal of his utter disbelief. He paused for a while, and then said, 'Son, here's how a telephone works.'" Of course Paul Baran knew how a telephone worked. You jacked one point to a switch to another point. That was the problem. This was why AT&T's design would prove useless in the face of the catastrophe he'd been told to prevent. Baran was, nerve and blood and bone, as an analyst, and even as a refugee, perhaps, alive with the imperative of survivability, of how connection might mean the difference between war and peace. Those calm, slide-ruling engineers in the AT&T building? What could they be worrying about?

But it wasn't just that $2 billion annual check from the U.S. Defense Department that those wizened phone wizards were seeing vanish in Baran's fishnet; it was a whole way of thinking. The AT&T scientists wanted to control the addresses, the routes, the timing, of messages from the center. This authoritarian design appeared more efficient to them; perhaps it was even more psychologically comfortable, since it matched their own experience of being commanded and controlled. Karl Wittfogel, the historian who identified the water totalitarians of ancient China and Egypt, would have recognized them: *Switch Despots.* "It was a conceptual impasse," Baran reflected. He moved to the next stop. Same result. And the next. Same result. Eventually Baran's engineering colleagues back at RAND were so affronted by the routine dismissal of his logic that they spoke up. They had seen the classified briefings. They knew just how easily the nation could be hobbled—and their Santa Monica building was surely on some target list too. RAND's scientists demanded a detailed, critical study of the distributed network model. By the time they were finished, the air force was preparing to begin construction.

Survivability. Plucked from the impossible-looking puzzle of how to communicate during a nuclear war emerged the first honestly distributed network. Other scientists had been chasing the idea as well, but the design suited Baran's problem particularly well: a network with no central control, survivable, uncuttable. The earliest large network built on Baran's principles became known as ARPANET, the Advanced Research Projects Agency Network—a mesh of connections that even today serves as the backbone for parts of the Internet. Even with the risk of nuclear war hopefully long gone, packet-switching designs of one sort or another still account for most of the data moving in the world. Think of how true an idea must be to endure more than fifty years of technological change. And all the efficiencies Baran first predicted fifty years ago are still at work. Every time you make a call, share a video, or ask a machine to think for you, that transaction likely takes place through fishnet-routed packets. If we had stayed with that old AT&T model, we'd be living in a different world. Riots could be flipped off with a single switch. Data flows could be monitored with the ease of watching a subway turnstile. The far-flung, wild creativity of our plug-and-play, connected world would be stifled. Each additional connection to the system would demand bureaucratic, centralized approval by the Switch Despots, concerned more with their own power than with our survival. Instead we have a slice-resistant mesh that has grown a billion times over, with its original architecture largely intact.

Packet-switched systems such as the Internet give anyone with some string and an ability to tie knots (which, in techno-speak, is anyone with some blinking fiber-optic cables and a TCP/IP connection) the power to weave themselves into the global web. This is why you can so easily turn on your phone or tablet and more or less instantly touch a whole world of data. Every minute now, an additional ten thousand devices get connected to the Internet—not just wired citizens, smartphones, laptops, and tablets but also medical tools, Bitcoin mines, and airplane diagnostic systems. "Anyone can connect" marks our age as much as Luther's "Anyone can speak to God" characterized the Reformation or Kant's "Dare to know" defined the Enlightenment. When people ask, "Why would anyone want to share photos with the world?" or "Why would you ever hand over your DNA?" they are missing the point. Many objects now are complete or useful only once they're connected. When we say *Connection changes the nature of an object*, we're nodding toward the idea that constant connection is almost a kind of *right* for devices and programs and people. Anyhow, it is certainly a kind of yearning.

3.

Networks designed along Baran's principles now permit any of us to connect to nearly anywhere, and to unimaginable technological power. But at the same time, the world connects back to us. Wired jihadists and currencies and bio bits—they're all tied in with us too. So yes, we're murdering the exotic with our data connections and machines and discount plane flights. Should we be surprised when, from time to time, the exotic shows up and murders us right back?

By now we've seen how the pull between center and periphery—that tension of our network—tears apart old structures. Connection changes the nature of an object by placing it on this tense mesh. The Seventh Sense feels this tension. Connect a patient, a doctor, a flying machine, a currency—each is twisted and changed as a result. Some become great. Others snap, never to be rebuilt. Some adjust, painfully. The pulling network action accounts for our greatest new fortunes but also the tumbling of old ideas and institutions. This is why our age is so uneasy. As Baran's fishnet grows, it locks everything it touches into a new structure.

The connected devices themselves are constantly improving too. Back in Baran's day, dozens of scientists counted themselves lucky to share a single computer. A few decades later, the PC revolution gave everyone a machine. And now, of course, we each have many computers in our lives: phones, wired TVs, soon smart self-driving cars. Because of connection, we have access to thousands of such devices in data centers, a fusion of software and hardware and connection that we are starting to lean on as "everyware." This now-commonplace magic was formalized in 1965 by Gordon Moore, one of the founding engineers at Intel, who noticed that since the introduction of integrated chips, in 1959, the number of transistors on each tiny chip had been doubling every two years. It seemed hard to imagine that this pace could endure, but then it did and still does, a phenomenon known as Moore's Law. Back in 1997, Andy Grove—who followed Moore as the CEO of Intel, the chip giant—was named *Time*'s Man of the Year. I wrote the story for *Time*, and I remember Grove telling me, in a confessional spirit: "I never stopped thinking about business. I worked constantly. But when Gordon Moore left the office, he left the work. Mostly he'd go fishing." Moore had the confidence of a man who had spotted one of the fundamental laws of our age, the unstoppable compression of computing power and cost. He had the "let's go fish" air of a man who has seen the inevitable. Grove, by contrast, had the total unease of a man who had to make Intel match the wild speed of Moore's Law and make the inevitable actually happen. Competition was everywhere. One mistake sustained for six months could kill the entire multibillion-dollar business. It had happened to other firms, often. Grove's motto was best captured in the title of one of his books, *Only the Paranoid Survive*. Each man was right, in his way. Moore's Law makes ever cheaper and more functional devices spread. But Grove's famous anxiety was honestly earned too. So much speed. So much connection. Paranoia does seem the best reaction.

You have to wonder what that eye-rolling AT&T senior telecommunications engineer who so mindlessly lectured Baran would have made of this new world. The old New York City temple of phone switches where they met in 1961 was being eyed as a luxury condominium. The company's impregnable billions of dollars of long-distance revenue were eventually destroyed by free packet-switched services running along the Internet. *Son, here's how a telephone works.* What must Baran have really thought? Massive, widespread connection changed everything, including how a phone works. Baran eventually left RAND. He founded several of the most important (and lucrative) companies of the early Internet. Years later he understood with more precision what exactly had happened: The real risk to those vulnerable AT&T systems wasn't Russian missiles. It was an information bomb of sorts, a desire for constant connection that exploded many old tools of control. Yes, it took out the old structures. But because of the very way it was architected, for survivability, it had a remarkable feature that even Baran had not quite expected: It enabled each of us to create too.

4.

Of course, you have to pity those AT&T wizards a bit. Innocuous-looking devices or people take on peculiar, sometimes dangerous aspects when connected. *Let me tell you how a stock market works.* Or *Let me tell you how a biologist works.* Neither of these has quite the same explanation as it would have two unconnected decades ago. We're surrounded by so many networks now, in which relations and ties of all sorts produce a constant, "I never thought of that before" dynamism. "There are systems of crucial interest to humankind that have so far defied accurate simulation," the scientist John Holland observed in a famous paper that helped establish the discipline of chaos science. Holland spent years considering these puzzling, hard-to-model systems and spotted at least one common theme: Whether it was webs of finance, such as the futures exchange, or immunological networks or our own brains, highly connected systems share what Holland labeled an evolving structure—they never stay the same. They seem to shift with an easy plasticity, in response to internal pressures or external changes. This is why so much unexpected chaos is occurring now, from government collapses to economic crises.

Connection means systems take on new forms. In many cases, they become better, stronger, more adaptively fit. It isn't simply that the unexpected appears or that there is more or less good or evil now; it's that the systems are evolving. Holland thought the world was filled with such evolutions, no different from species' adjusting (or not) to a hotter climate or some fast new predator. He called the networks that produce these sorts of innovations complex adaptive systems.

When Holland chose the word "complex," he was making an important distinction. *Complicated* mechanisms can be designed, predicted, and controlled. Jet engines, artificial hearts, and your calculator are complicated in this sense. They may contain billions of interacting parts, but they can be laid out and repeatedly, predictably made and used. They don't change. *Complex* systems, by contrast, can't be so precisely engineered. They are hard to fully control. Human immunology is complex in this sense. The World Wide Web is complex. A rain forest is complex: It is made up of uncountable buzzing, connecting bugs and birds and trees. Order, to the extent that it exists in the Amazon basin, emerges moment by moment from countless, constant interactions. The uneven symphonic sound of *l'heure bleue*, that romantic stopping point at dawn when you can hear the forest waking bird by bird, is the sound of complexity engaging in a never-the-same-twice phase transition.

The word "complex" comes to us from the Latin world *plexus*, meaning "having parts," which hints at the interwoven, layered nature of any object. What appears simple—a flower, our skin, the value of a dollar bill—is in fact a *plexus*, loaded with twitches and influences. In that stitching of new links, countless interactions inevitably erupt in unexpected ways: financial panics or disease epidemics or revolutions. Traffic during rush hour is complex in this fashion—it is the moving bits, the mishmash of cars and pedestrians and bicycles, that determine the ultimate state of the system: jammed or not. Los Angeles at five p.m. on a Friday isn't designed centrally; its honking rush-hour logic comes about—in a slightly different form every day—from interaction. As any system fills out with more actors and more types of connection, it becomes more complex and harder to predict. Merely complicated systems, by contrast, don't produce uncertainty in the same way; appealingly, they just run. Strapping a complicated jet engine to the wing of a passenger plane makes sense, even if it takes decades of refinement to achieve real reliability. Doing that with a *complex* jet engine? Not so wise.

Most of our networked world is a pool of buzzing, fresh interaction—not only hard to predict but also constantly on the cusp of making something new. Scientists such as Holland call this process emergence, referring to the way that bottom-up interactions—between cells or chips or traders or cars—create an order, often in forms that have never existed before. The fundamental uncertainty of a complex process means that when we look at the world, we often forget it is taking place. It's easier to assume that a predictable, linear, complicated logic is at work, an "*a* leads to *b* and *c*" sort of process: Revolution leads to freedom, which leads to democracy, for instance. That such predictions are often wrong—and that we're so often surprised by events in economics or politics—is a reminder that complex systems like economies or elections are filled with mechanisms that upset the hopes of overconfident planners. Too often we look at some puzzle, say Iraqi politics or income inequality, and think it is merely "complicated." We should know better.

"Macro models failed to predict the crisis and seemed incapable of explaining what was happening to the economy in a convincing manner," former president of the European Central Bank Jean-Claude Trichet lamented in the aftermath of the cascading financial crises that hit in 2008. Markets and officials discovered that their system was not merely "too big to fail" but also that it was too connected to manage—and possibly too complex to comprehend. Trichet sounded a little shell-shocked. "As a policy maker during the crisis I found the available models of limited help. In fact, I would go further: In the face of the crisis, we felt abandoned by conventional tools."

This sense of abandonment comes from an attempt to use a mechanical way of thinking in an age of complexity. When you think that an air force can simply pound an insurgency into sand or that some old, reliable business should survive because it rests on billions of dollars of infrastructure, you miss the energetic creative and destructive power of complex connection. It's not entirely right to say that networks always beat hierarchies, because of course networks have layers and structures of their own. But think of Mubarak, the euro, or Lehman Brothers—stable-looking systems shoved rudely toward collapse in recent years by pounding shock waves of network power. Complex interacting systems—which is what networks usually are in essence—can tear apart stiff, hierarchical ones. Can you really look at the firm where you work or the nation where you live and feel it would adapt well in the face of such sudden and connected pressures?

Our age's constant disruption occurs not least because the tools of connection are so easy to snap together. We can see this in the digital devices themselves, which interconnect with a carefully designed ease. You can snap a photo, send it to a friend, edit it, and pass it along again. The world's data can be reduced to ones and zeroes. But this is also an important metaphor: Our trade, our currencies, our ideologies—all these interact now.

Long before the idea of a smartphone or 3-D goggles, the British mathematician Alan Turing anticipated their arrival when he dreamed of what he called a universal device: a notional box that, starting from the ones and zeroes of digitized data, could be constructed to do anything. Since everything can ultimately be reduced to a binary encoding, nearly any sort of data can be shared, studied, combined, or remixed. This easy programmability of so many objects around us is why our world is now more complex than, say, a world of interconnected railcars or ships might have been. Railcars and ships don't change much, and certainly not instantly. In the digital world, however, many of the most essential objects and nodes can be flipped around like digital Legos, connected in different ways. We said earlier that the Seventh Sense is tuned to spot the unsettling ripples that come from the fact that connection changes the nature of an object. The benign act of connection makes *complicated* objects into *complex* ones. The moment an object—a cargo package, a share of stock—clicks into a network, it becomes subject to all the wildness of complexity that may lie there: cascades, whipping external forces, unexpected internal faults revealed only under the pressure of connection. Linked to a whole system of constant evolution, even the most innocent-looking point becomes vulnerable to twitches, infections, or innovations.

This isn't a game of averages. You're not as complex as the *average* of what you're connected to. You're as complex as the *most* complex device you're linked to. It's like that old wartime cargo ship lemma, the one the U-boat commanders would feast on: You can only go as fast as the slowest ship in the convoy. You or I might have the simplest possible life—living retired with no computer off the grid. But our investments? They are likely tied to the markets, which are stuffed with dimly understood complexities. Of course this creates important new opportunities and demands—firms that really level the playing field, that let us manage those risks as well and as fairly as the largest of investors. But when we say there's nowhere to hide now, this is partly what we mean: Even the most innocent-looking acts of connection, like plugging a printer into your computer or taking a vacation to Paris, can expose you to the dangers of a complex world. Those dangers are growing at network speed now. And it is in managing and even using those complexities that we'll find the productive power of an age of connection. But make no mistake: The destructive power of complex systems? That's part of the game too.

Networks turn everything they touch from something complicated into something complex. Maybe we can say that the Industrial Revolution made the simple complicated—think what mechanized agriculture did to farming. But the network age, because of that chaos that travels with connection, makes the complicated complex. *Complicated* systems are packed with parts, but they are predictable. It's the *complex* ones that really change the rules. And once a mesh of complex connection is really flowing, it produces surprising interaction. Precisely because there is no central plan, the best of these linked systems create, in a sense. From computer crashes to market bubbles. Castells's social protests emerged in this complex way, appearing like condensate in the jar of the post-2008 economic crisis. Researchers following in his wake studied the Spanish anti-austerity movement of 2011 and found that it was composed largely of new organizations that blossomed from connectivity. Other Spanish protest groups, such as labor, anti-abortion activists, and regional separatists, relied on decades-old organizations. But 15M, as the movement was known, relied on groups born into a political vacuum, just as Occupy Wall Street and pieces of the Arab Spring and Al Qaeda did. A survey of 15M members looked like a review of new Internet companies: young, wired, vividly unplugged from history, and impossible without constant connection. They were built by leaching people away from traditional political parties. Their appeal was both the potential of the new and the chance to get away from the rotting smell of old politics. This is one reason it is wrong to look at the world and consider it filled merely with random events, with so-called black swans. In fact, patterns appear everywhere. They can be searched and mapped and studied with the tools of data science, but, of course, they can also be felt. They may surprise you if you don't know how to look for them. But they are there. There is more to human history than earthquakes alone.

Even if it can't be predicted, complexity in any system, whether it is an Indonesian coral reef or a Russian computer network, can at least be measured. How many points are connected? How quickly and deeply do they interact? Multiplication of connection generates complexity and unpredictability. When we say that networks can and will devour hierarchies, this is one reason.

More complexity produces more interaction, as you would expect, and that means what lies ahead is going to be even harder, more challenging than what we've faced. Fighting fires in financial markets, battling terrorists, managing the risks of biodevelopment—all these will get more difficult in coming years, not easier. There are intellectuals and businessmen who contend that we've arrived at the end of innovation now. *Where are the flying cars?!* they ask. But that's really the wrong measure. (Not least because the flying drone cars may be here soon.) Connected systems create and surprise. They can't help it, with so many pieces and passions and ideas running together. And we know that lingering ahead of us now is an even faster, more complex world: Quantum computing, for instance, may yet push computer speeds to 100 billion times faster than what is achievable with older technology. Autonomous robotic systems will press into realms in which our soft, human frame cannot survive—deep under water or far into space. "Many biological and social theories were impossible to test because of lack of data," one team of cybersystems researchers has noted. "Now we have not only the data, but the methods to analyze it." There is much yet to understand, and there are fantastic new tools to enable discovery. Anyhow, you get the point: The world is wired to get more complex in the future.

When we say the network "wants" something, it's a useful anthropomorphism: A billion connected users want to be linked, so Facebook emerges. A trillion Web pages demand to be searched, so Google appears. Making such ties produces, first, that merciless clawing action we saw in the previous chapter, which explains the unique power (and value) of the essential firms of our age. Once that's done, however, the mesh of distribution and connection wants something else. To create. This is why the most successful investors and leaders of our era have a near-pathological desire to push and break old systems. They have faith that if they shove hard enough to snap one equilibrium a new one will emerge.

They are right. They have all the laws of physics and history behind them. In commerce, the destruction of old business models breeds new ones. In terrorism, public violence is more useful than bottled anger; it's a tool to speed chaos and, some hope, a new politics. If the Seventh Sense includes a willingness (even an eagerness) to disrupt old equilibriums, it is because of this confidence. Something better will emerge.

Later in life, turning to a philosophical view, Paul Baran said he'd come to believe his webs, distributing themselves around the world with such a smooth and relentless energy, were inevitable. "Every object in the universe," he once wrote, "is connected (by gravity/radiation vectors) to every other object." We know now just how much truth Baran's words contain. We are pulled to connection as if by gravity. And connection means complexity. It means evolution. That kludgy, parenthetically weird phrase of Baran's — "by gravity/radiation vectors" — tells us a lot. Connection is inevitable. So, as a result, is evolution. And a bit of chaos.

CHAPTER SIX

Warez Dudes

In which the Seventh Sense reveals a secret, dangerous architecture of connection.

1.

It was my second overseas trip. I blinked as dawn broke over Europe and seeped inside the airplane. We began our descent into Amsterdam. I changed the tape inside my Walkman. Something a bit more upbeat seemed right. Peter Gabriel. It was 1993. August.

Earlier that spring I'd heard about a plan for a giant summer computer-hacking conference that would be held outside Amsterdam. Hacking at the End of the Universe, it was to be called. It appealed to me immediately. I'd just moved to New York and had been dipping into the city's hacking scene. The "scene" was less a hip hive of action than it was a group of computer amateurs, curious hangers-on, and early IT system engineers who would gather in the grubby basement of the Citicorp building on Fifty-Third Street and Lexington some days after work to discuss various techniques for tricking digital systems of all types. Hacking didn't have a nefarious connotation in those days; it was seen by most people with a technical inclination as a natural extension of an interest in computers. The Internet had about fifteen million users at the time. The idea that two decades later it would connect more than three billion people, or that it would put millions of dollars into the pockets of some of the people gathering in that basement, was honestly unthinkable.

The bible of the group was a thin, irregularly stapled, photocopied magazine published out on Long Island by a guy who used the nom de hack of Emmanuel Goldstein, the hero of George Orwell's novel *1984*. The magazine was called *2600: The Hacker Quarterly*, and it offered a compilation of ideas about how to fool around with systems of all sorts, from Atari gaming consoles to door locks. The name came from one of the earliest hacks any of us at those little meetings knew about, a famous 1970s trick that involved using an audio tone at exactly 2,600 hertz (about the pitch of a truck's backup warning) to force the backbone routing switches of the AT&T phone system to give up access to an "operator mode," which would let the phone hackers—they were called phreakers—make any sort of call for free. The hack didn't really offer much practical pleasure except a chance to make free phone calls to anywhere in the world. Once you'd mastered the trick, you pretty quickly discovered there wasn't anyone in Mumbai you wanted to call anyhow.

The real appeal, the deeper joy of the game, was different. Tricking the phone and hearing the system's clicks gave a sense of secret access, a feeling of control in the largest network on earth. At one point, a phreaker named John Draper figured out that the little plastic whistles stuffed as children's toys inside boxes of sugary Cap'n Crunch cereal produced the 2,600-hertz tone nearly perfectly. The hack made him a legend, and he became known, inevitably, as Cap'n Crunch. An article about Draper in *Esquire* in 1971 had inspired two teenagers named Steve Jobs and Steve Wozniak to start their first company in order to build and sell little blue phreaking boxes. Woz later recalled nervously meeting the Cap'n one day in California. He was a strange, slightly smelly, and extremely intense nomadic engineer. "I do it for one reason and one reason only," the Cap'n huffed to the writer of that *Esquire* article, who was a bit baffled as to why a grown man would find whistling into phones so appealing. "I'm learning about a system. The phone company is a System. A computer is a System. Do you understand? If I do what I do, it is only to explore a System. Computers. Systems. That's my bag," he said. "The phone company is nothing but a computer."

I'd heard about the Amsterdam conference in the *2600* hacking circles, somewhere between the debates about circuit boards and which company was best for the relatively new service of email. The gathering was organized by a group of Dutch computer geeks who published their own magazine, *Hack-Tic*. I sent an email to the founders. One of them, a man with the improbably exotic name Rop Gonggrijp, sent back an irresistible reply. "On August 4, 5, and 6 we're organizing a three-day summer congress for hackers, phone phreaks, programmers, computer haters, data travelers, electro-wizards, networkers, hardware freaks, techno-anarchists, communications junkies, cyberpunks, system managers, stupid users, paranoid androids, Unix gurus, whizz kids, warez dudes, law enforcement officers (appropriate undercover dress required), guerrilla heating engineers and other assorted bald, long-haired and/or unshaven scum," the invitation began. Data travelers? Electro-wizards? *Warez dudes?* I had to go. "Also included," the note continued, "are inspiration, transpiration, a shortage of showers (but a lake to swim in), good weather (guaranteed by god), campfires and plenty of wide open space and fresh air."

In those early days of the Internet, there was only the barest tickle of a commercial instinct at work. If anything, most of the people reading *2600* or *Hack-Tic* were profoundly *anti*-commercial. They were hobbyists, as entranced by role-playing games like *Dungeons and Dragons* as by their clapped-together, often unreliable digital machines. It was no accident that firms such as Apple had emerged from after-work geek meet-ups with names like the Homebrew Computer Club, names that suggested a rooty, self-defining, hippie ethos. Everyone you met in that world fell pretty squarely into one of those weird-by-weirder categories that Rop Gonggrijp had listed in his email. Their relaxed, nerdish temperament was reflected in the design of the Internet itself—open, generous, easy to manipulate, emotional at times in debates over protocols, freedom loving. The net design was, as well, a reaction against systems such as AT&T, which was closed, stingy, and tough (and therefore enjoyable to manipulate).

Jon Postel, the American engineering and programming genius who had helped write some of the essential original protocols of the Internet, summed up this point of view in 1980 in a motto he thought should characterize the architecture of the Internet: "Be conservative in what you do, be liberal in what you accept." Postel's slogan became known as the "robustness principle," and it was meant to determine how switches and nodes on the net should behave. They should, Postel felt, be good at handling lots of different types of communications—they should be "robust"—but they should also be careful not to spread too much nonstandard garbage out into the networks. This was an essential advance over the old ARPANET, which Paul Baran had helped devise. That system worked wonderfully by itself, in isolation, as it sent nuclear launch codes zipping around, but it struggled when it needed to inter-operate with other networks. It wasn't *generous*. The Internet that Postel and others were designing was intended to be much, much larger than ARPANET, so an ability to speak to strange computers and be understood was essential. It was like planning an airport: You wanted to be able to land lots of different types of planes. But if someone started to throw golf balls, Jell-O, and gasoline on the runway, you'd have a problem. It would slow down the system for everyone. Postel was telling engineers: *Be careful what you do and what you put onto the system. Take responsibility on your end. Build something that's generous in what it will handle from others.*

Be liberal in what you accept. From the first moments on the grass in Lelystad, the small town just outside Amsterdam where the Hacking at the End of the Universe conference gathered, the mad diversity that this idea suggested was an astonishing, delightful fact. As broad and strange a group as Rop's email had hinted might come was in fact there, under the trees, happily running cables from tent to RV, powering their connected routers with gas-fired generators, marveling at data-transmission speeds that today your phone might manage from an underground garage with the barest of connectivity. The two-day outdoor festival was an example of human inter-operability. Postel's principle brought to life. Few of us knew most of the group. Nearly everyone was, well, not the most social. But there was instant connection, discussion, board gaming, and a degree of frank inter-operating I'd never quite seen before. It was a harbinger of two decades of digital cross-connection yet to come.

Of all the people at the *Hack-Tic* conference, however—among the system managers and Unix gurus and heating-system guerrillas (hey, everyone should have a hobby)—it was the warez dudes who were of the most interest, both to the participants in the conference and to the white vans cruising nearby, allegedly filled with curious Dutch police. The nickname came from the "wares" they had access to, which were largely cracked-open versions of commercial software that could be shared and distributed and manipulated on private bulletin board systems. The warez dudes were pirates. And, like most pirates, they had an early sense of the very edges of the law and of the smell of money drifting along new and essential routes. If hacker culture was, in those early days, a frontier society—and it was, even down to the sad shortage of single women—these were the people living on the very farthest edges of the wilderness. They fused often-fantastic technical skill with the hacker's instinct for control—and a criminal's hunger for profit.

The first computer viruses and worms were part of what they sold. These had appeared in the 1980s, mostly as curious intellectual exercises. There was a desire among computer engineers, a scientific sort of craving, to see what might be done on the systems they had built. It was not unlike those whistling telephone tones that had so fascinated Cap'n Crunch and Steve Jobs and Woz. Could you make the big, room-sized machines twitch in ways no one had imagined? Absolute, undeniable thrill ran through this sort of activity. I can still recall returning to my office one day in the mid-1990s with a Ziploc bag that contained a floppy disk marked "Viruses," which I promptly used to break my computer so completely it had to be reformatted. Twice. Such adventures, however, were also producing some of the best programmers. Performing tricks inside those early systems required then, as it does now, a profound intimacy with the code defining their electrical operations. (Computer programs are called code; people who write and test them are coders.)

But the secret moves behind those early cracks and exploits were rarely secret for long. The informal culture of stapled-together magazines such as *2600* told you what you needed to know about this band: It was a group that liked to share, to brag, to indulge one another in stories about systems they had cracked open, to play with a bit of light paranoia about who might be watching and who might care. *Computers. Systems. That's my bag.* You might as well spread some of the adrenaline rush of your adventure with others. The sense of a shared alternate reality that most of us had first experienced in games such as Dungeons and Dragons or in the pages of *Dune* fit nicely into the digital world. This open, friendly temperament animated most of the people spread across that Amsterdam field, jumping into the lake instead of into showers. We had the programmer's raw fascination about what a machine might be made to do, even in ways that were deeply unintended. We were harmless. The warez dudes, however, were different. Their fascination was a greedy, nasty obsession.

2.

The business of playing with and inside connected computer systems was, even as we sat on that Amsterdam summer lawn, shifting. And the change revealed something that's important for us today. I've said this is a book about networks of all kinds, but nowhere are the dilemmas of a connected age more apparent than inside information technology systems. They are the place where our network age first lit up, after all, just as the atomic age once began in the New Mexico desert. The precariousness of these networks is an important marker on our route toward understanding some basic principles. I want to spend some pages contemplating the way in which computers are cracked apart not because you or I need to know how to patch a software hole (though this probably wouldn't be a bad idea), but because computer security is a metaphor. The story of the quest to break into and control machines and networks is really, when we look at it, the tale of a quest for control over any sort of connected system. I mean markets, elections, research, online learning. When we embrace the idea that terror groups or political parties are, in the end, networks, we understand that the places they can break (or be broken) are as important as the places that they are strong. Just as Orwell's *Animal Farm* was not a story of a pigsty, so the adventures of hackers and those who fight them are not merely a children's tale of a computer network. The story of the warez dudes, the NSA, or freelance "exploit engineers" has a deeper moral. It's about power.

Constant connection means, unless we're prepared for it, constant vulnerability. What I want to show here is that systems we faithfully rely on today—not just data systems but political ones or financial ones—are simply not built for this frightening demand. They are too easy to manipulate. Which means *we* are too easy to manipulate. These network meshes offer the possibility of historic and unsupervised control. Of you, me, the markets we connect to, the data we need. I don't mean someone hacking a voting machine to change our choice in an election; I mean someone hacking the news and information we use to decide who to vote for. We are exposed through all of our links, for the first time, to a possibility of surreptitious and total surveillance and control—not simply by governments, but by anyone who can worm inside. This is more and more obvious in the world of IT, but it reflects a larger picture of a vulnerable world back at us. When security researchers in 2014 found that fifty-dollar home camera systems were, for instance, sending snapshots every few minutes to a mysterious overseas email address, what they were really unmasking was a crack in the foundations of trust. And trust is what any society needs in order to function. When you find that you live so near the edge of a catastrophe of reliability, when machines and your mind may be manipulated, then the very nature of your political and economic life changes. It should change. You should worry. You should ask: What can I do about it? Don't forget that fatal moment in *Animal Farm*, when the original commandment of the farm that "All animals are equal" undergoes a pernicious adjustment to "All animals are equal, but some animals are more equal than others." This chapter is the story of the forces on networks who aspire to be, somewhat worryingly, more equal than the rest of us.

It was this change that was becoming apparent that summer of 1993. Hacking was slipping from the province of a few earnest hobbyists and system managers to something a bit more sinister. A new word, "malware," was just then circulating as a way to describe malicious software that was taking advantage of Postel's "be liberal" instinct in order to devastate connected systems designed with a few too many trusting and unlocked doors. It wasn't merely the relaxed system design of the early net or computer systems that made exploitation easy. It was also that the networks and machines themselves were slipping, with a kind of frictionless momentum, toward increasing complexity. This meant, invariably, that popular programs were often shipped to users with mistakes or programming oversights that invited hijacking. The year before the Amsterdam conference, for instance, a cruel program known as Michelangelo, which overwrote the data on hard-disk drives with meaningless ones and zeroes, spread into millions of computers. Once a machine was infected, the overwrite command would activate every year on March 6 — a twisted celebration of the birthday of the great Renaissance artist. But because the program operated at the BIOS level, the basic input/output heart of those early machines — their reptilian brains, in a sense — it was nearly impossible to eradicate. Computer-security companies, soon to be known as computer "insecurity" companies because they were constantly *behinder*, responded with the following rather unpersuasive advice: *"Turn your machine off on March 5. Turn it back on March 7."*

As technology advanced, so did the malware, which was adapting and evolving to new opportunities. Think of how hugely different our experience of machines is today, as opposed to just a few years ago. Hacking has matured as fast — maybe faster. Early attacks were aimed at machines that had essentially no defenses. Programs such as Michelangelo were designed to act much like a flu or food poisoning. They sickened and then controlled individual machines, devices with no immune systems. Hackers faced a challenge in finding ways to sneak these digital diseases onto computers, but, of course, they eventually found holes. They hid viruses on floppy disks or inside documents or spreadsheets that appeared otherwise safe. Intelligence agencies became infamous for passing out "free disks" at conferences or littering defense-contractor parking lots with infected USB sticks, waiting for some unsuspecting employee to pop one into a computer and invisibly activate some bit of carefully installed, hidden malware. Or, in a clever case of "know your target," sneaking malware into the code of some particularly violent video game sure to be played by an adrenaline-seeking system administrator in a fit of after-hours boredom.

And jacking machines into the Internet? It was like the difference between living in a small town and walking the streets of 1970s New York City. In one place you'd have few encounters, mostly smilingly familiar and harmless. In the other? You'd face an endless stream of the strange, the perverted, and the unexpected. Every new handshake would be a risk. This is what life is like every day for your phone and your bank and the military—a world of ceaseless assault, often from never-seen weapons. Robert Morris Sr., a cryptographic and security genius who towered over NSA code-breaking programs for decades in the last century, compressed his lifetime of experience cracking machines into three golden rules of computer security:

RULE ONE: Do not own a computer.

RULE TWO: Do not power it on.

RULE THREE: Do not use it.

He could have added a fourth rule: Do not connect it to anything.

3.

Today, of course, we're furiously, enthusiastically violating all four of these rules nearly every moment. In fact, our whole economic and social dreamscape depends on breaking them. We want to own the best device, we want it always on, and we want to use it all the time. "Utility" and "connection" are almost synonyms now. An unconnected phone? Car? Market? Useless. But the networks, and everyone connected to them, can be manipulated invisibly and decisively. "Exploit engineers," a team led by security researcher Sergey Bratus has argued, using the polite technical term for a hacker, "will show you the unintended limits of your system's functionality." Hackers reveal dangerous holes in our new world, and in doing so they show us how networks really work, in the way a cat burglar would reveal the limits of your home alarm. The bad news is that the worst of these hackers (and often the best of them, skill-wise) demonstrate their new fluency by swiping your data, your money, and finally your peace of mind. Their fortunes and safety and curiosity—all these are woven together in their hunger to touch and pull and break the roots of the network. In a world of expanding connection, they are both more powerful and more dangerous than ever. So, here is the obverse side of Postel's hopeful motto: The more connected we are, the greater the risks. And as bank balances, secret jet-engine designs, and other priceless digital data are developed and then slipped away on connected machines, the rewards for cracking into the systems grow—far faster than the costs of trying to break in.

"It is increasingly obvious," security researchers FX Lindner and Sandro Gaycken have said, "that the state of the art in Computer Network Defense is over a decade behind its counterpart in

Computer Network Offense. Even intelligence and military organizations, considered to be the best positioned to defend their own infrastructures, struggle to keep the constant onslaught of attackers with varying motives, skills, and resources at bay." The long list of U.S.-government security failures expresses a strange digital logic: The more essential it is that an organization keep a secret, the less it seems able to do so. Governments around the world have found themselves in recent years in the strange position of asking for access to citizens' secrets even as they could not protect their own. Shortly after the United States Office of Personnel Management was found to be hacked in 2014, government administrators sent an urgent message to civil servants: Don't click on strange emails! Many of the recipients never opened the missive, convinced it too was part of a cyberattack. A *decade* behind? That is the gap between a flip phone and an iPhone. In the hyperspeed world of technology, it is like confronting a laser weapon with a hoplite. The losing race slips easily into Donald Rumsfeld's *aheader-behinder* dynamic. We can ask: *Are we plugging more machines with more layers, software, and applications than we can protect? Are we making more bugs than we're patching?* (Yes and yes.) "Attackers are not like natural catastrophes," Lindner and Gaycken write. "They can analyze their targets."

Sergey Bratus, a math genius who turned to computer science out of curiosity and now teaches at Dartmouth, has spent a fair amount of time trying to understand just what happens when a computer or a network is exploited by a hacker, or "pwned," in the funny idiom of warez dude language. (The phrase means to take control of, or to "own," a system. The spelling is an artifact of an overenthusiastic video-game death-match gloat, when one player killed another and in his rush to celebrate typed something along the lines of "I pwned you!" The mistyping lives on today: The highest award in information security is known as the Pwnie.)

Bratus calls the resulting pwned device a weird machine: a computer, a sensor, a drone that has been silently made to do something unintended. Made *weird*.

Hacking is, after all, a kind of perverse programming. It involves slipping inside a machine and then driving it to do things it wasn't intended to do by giving it instructions its designers never knew it might receive. Developing and using computer bugs, Bratus found, is not unlike the most sophisticated software research. Hackers follow careful patterns. The best of them really conceive of whole systems in the way that the finest data architects might. These attackers look for particular designs; they weaponize their code with a delicate elegance and aim relentlessly at total control. As Robert Joyce, the head of the NSA's hacking efforts, said in one public speech: "We are successful because we put in the time to know that network. We put in the time to know that network better than the person who designed it." A normal machine does what you tell it. A weird machine does what someone else commands it to do.

How is such a system born? Well, a software hole of the sort that produces a weird machine might be as simple as a failure to secure computer code after it is compiled—sort of like not locking the door to your house after you leave—or a programming oversight that means a machine can't handle unexpected inputs. Take the technique of "fuzzing," for example, a famously effective way to turn a normal machine into a weird one. Whenever you or I enter a user name and password into a closed digital system—say we're logging into our bank or our office email—the computer takes that information and matches it up against data stored in an internal, protected database. It's like giving the machine all the pieces of a jigsaw puzzle that shows a picture of you. The machine has a program to snap the jigsaw pieces together. If the image is in fact you, it lets you in. A fuzzing attack involves sending the machine something it did not expect. An extra piece with that jigsaw puzzle, say. Or a crossword instead of a jigsaw puzzle. If you type joe@user.com!@@ into a user field instead of the normal sort of email address a machine might be expecting—joe@user.com—that last !@@ can send the machine into a confused panic, as if it had assembled a jigsaw puzzle and found it had a piece left over. If you have a program that can send jigsaw puzzles to the machine from two different places at the same moment, you can cause many computers to break down with bafflement. "How can he be in two places at once?" they will wonder. The machines "fuzz" up. And in their confused state, they may crash, or run an endless loop, or just think: "I don't understand this puzzle, so I'll just open the door." Modern hackers can easily tailor-make machines to do any of this: Deliver crosswords where jigsaw puzzles are expected. Make you appear in two or twenty places. And they can create these illusions thousands of times a second. So here, for a malicious hacker, is an inviting limit: Computers still have to be told what to do. And what not to do. If you walked up to your bank teller and yelled "Glookie!" at her, she'd think you were nuts. But if you did more or less the same to a digital bank system that hadn't been told what to do when someone yelled "Glookie!" it might very well let you into the safe.

System designers in recent generations have become much more sophisticated in trying to avoid such problems, not least because they've so often fingered the embarrassing or costly aftermath of these kinds of holes in their own code. "You do not understand how your program *really* works until it has been exploited," Bratus has said, a sentiment that hints at the stomach-lurching moment that many coders and their suddenly victimized users have now had. *You don't understand yourself until you've been pwned.* The odds that the endless possible glitches can ever be completely patched is zero. Hackers can continue to use classic exploits such as fuzzing, back doors, and rootkits for years—and develop new, more intricate ways to steal a machine's mind. This race for mastery is a sprint, but it is not mindless. It has a goal: The closer a hacker is to the core of a computer program or a network, the more control they have. Mastery of the heart of a system means control over all the information it sees and how it makes decisions. Such a hack would be like having a foreign spy win the presidency, turning the whole U.S. government into a weird machine. That prize of immediate, high-level, and totally trusted access is the warez dude gold standard.

The most dangerous—and therefore the most alluringly valuable—of these sorts of attacks are known as zero-day exploits. The danger they represent becomes apparent only at some awful instant, "day zero," when they are revealed to have been running wild inside some hapless network or machine. That first moment of awareness of the bug is like day zero in a cancer diagnosis, and it begins an immediate race to find and deliver a cure. Such vulnerabilities represent fissures in the walls of computers that their manufacturers, system engineers, and security experts usually don't realize are there. The dream of hackers and spies and warez dudes is a version of this trick called an advanced persistent threat: hidden, back-door access to a machine that endures, even for years, through upgrades and security checks and system cleanups, all the while forcing the now-weird computer to do things its user won't even be aware of—sending a copy of every keystroke to another machine, for instance, or serving as a robotic launching pad for attacks on other machines, all while acting like a perfectly normal machine.

The best zero-day exploits are based not on the idea of sneaking malicious software into machines so much as on taking existing, trusted code and finding tiny holes that can be blasted into giant tunnels through which data can be stolen. Such attacks often rely on errors left accidentally inside computer systems or on innocent-seeming features that can be made dangerous. All computer and software designers know that their systems are vulnerable. Mathematicians have proved that you can never be absolutely certain that a connected machine is safe. A mobile phone, for instance, can contain more than 10 million lines of code. The systems that run massive cloud-computing basins such as those at Google or Amazon are even larger, are updated every day, and have to cope with tsunamis of data at very high speeds. Even the best programmers leave four or five errors in every million lines of code.

Software and hardware manufacturers usually struggle to keep such exploits secret until they can deliver a fix, but this doesn't always work. Secrets get out. And even once a patch is developed, it can take weeks or months before it's widely installed. It's not uncommon, therefore, that within hours of the announcement of a newly found zero day hole, attacks using that method explode around the net. Thousands of hackers try to take advantage of the vulnerability, to kick at the defensive walls of systems while they are down for repair or restart—or simply left vulnerable by slower-witted system administrators who don't yet know that it is now open hunting season on a particular bit of code. Heartbleed, a zero day that permitted hackers to slip into your computer through holes in your Web browser, was disclosed to the world on April 7, 2014—more than two years after it had apparently been put in place because of a programming error. Accidentally? By an overworked engineer? Deliberately? By some state security agency? No one knew. (Or no one was saying.) But in the two days after Heartbleed was announced and long before most computers were fully patched, attacks using the method grew from a few dozen per hour to millions as hackers tried to suck data from unsecured networks.

4.

In recent years, hacking has moved deeper still, beyond the level of software and USB drives and into the very atomic level of computers, the places where the electrons that make up bits and bytes float. The technical elegance of these microlevel hacks has often been breathtaking—the exploits look like Wagnerian operas compared with Cap'n Crunch's thin, reedy weird-machine whistle. Consider one recent breakthrough hack involving magnetic charges. Electrical signals, recall, have a magnetic element, and as companies such as Intel and AMD began packing more memory cells on silicon wafers, for example, they noticed magnetic interference flowing across the surface of their chips like waves. A bunch of tiny digital cells, in other words, is like a bowl of magnets. In 2014, security researchers Mark Seaborn and Thomas Dullien, who worked at Google, discovered that they could use the magnetic vibrations on two parallel rows of memory chips to flip the electrical state of a third row—sort of like using a magnet under a table to move a paper clip around—in a way that the system might never notice. This permitted them to reach off-limits, supersecure areas of the machine's memory, where they could do what they wanted. They called the break "rowhammer," and it represented an ideal and essentially unfixable hole that affected nearly every small chip set made for half a decade. They published the result immediately, as a warning to possibly affected victims, but the exploit targeted such a basic level of the system that it has proved impossible to fully patch. It was like trying to patch physics.

The computer researcher Nathaniel Husted once described the world as filled with "emergent vulnerabilities"—wormholes in software or hardware, communications or finance, that pop up in the connected universe, unbidden. "The fundamental aspect of emergent vulnerabilities and attacks," Husted writes, "[is] that they appear benign until certain criticality conditions are met, at which point they become malignant." The risks we don't want sit right alongside all the things we do want from connectivity. In fact—and this is Husted's point—they *are* the things we want from connectivity, perverted into danger.

Paul Baran would have been impressed to see just how right he was, how connections between us now are like the irresistible tug of gravity—and how gravity always wins. In 2015, for instance, Israeli security researchers developed an astonishing hack that proved Baran's nearly spiritual claim that all objects can be linked by connection—and demonstrated the way that wily attacks might breach even the safest-looking arrangements. "It has been assumed that the physical separation of computers (air-gap) provides a reliable level of security," Mordechai Guri and his team wrote in a paper describing how they had used one isolated machine to infect another. Physical separation is, in fact, one of the cardinal rules of safe computing, a kind of lemma to join Robert Morris Sr.'s "Don't connect" rule of network safety: Two machines, unconnected by a network, should not be able to affect each other. Imagine I put a kid with the flu in one classroom and a schoolmate of his in another building. The second kid should remain healthy.

The Tel Aviv research team wanted to challenge this. First they placed two computers side by side on a desk, unconnected to each other by any wire or network. One machine was connected to the Internet. The other was completely isolated—in computer security parlance, it was "air gapped"—like the healthy kid in the distant building. Then the researchers began their Houdini trick: *Look! Watch us corrupt this completely unconnected machine!* Running a set of programs on the network-connected machine, the Israeli team was able to warm the processor board of that computer as though they were revving a car engine, eventually making it hot enough for the temperature changes to be detected by sensors inside the secure, allegedly impregnable "boy in the bubble" machine sitting a few inches away. The heat wave triggered a fan system inside the clean machine, which in turn activated a piece of pre-installed malware that let the hot machine pwn the "air gapped" one through temperature variations. In a video demonstration of the exploit, you can watch the infecting machine glow ever hotter, issuing "thermal pings" as it sweats and then infects its safe, supposedly "unconnected" neighbor. The heat transfer sent a simple message: Nothing is safe.

Why put such effort, worthy of the deepest physics problems, into the challenge of sneaking into a cell phone or computer undetected? Well, for Seaborn and Dullien, the drive was part of a "discover and publish" effort to keep the overall system clean. It is better to hack, discover, and patch than to be hacked and have the hack remain undiscovered. But the good guys are racing against equivalently sophisticated teams with indecent motives. The development and sale of zero-day bugs is, after all, a business. Modern versions of Cap'n Crunch whistles can crack open some of the most essential financial, political, and security data stores on the planet. As the value of hacking targets has increased, so has the price of the exploits. Public "zero-day markets" pay hundreds of thousands of dollars to researchers who discover holes in their systems. *Better to find them ourselves*, the thinking goes, though that does not always make the embarrassment less acute. At one of the most carefully watched public hacking competitions in early 2015, for instance, a skinny, smiling South Korean named Jung Hoon Lee took home $225,000 in prize money by pwning a series of some of the most important programs on the planet, including Apple's Safari and Google's Chrome

Web browsers. These systems had been constructed at the cost of hundreds of millions of dollars by some of the best computer-science PhDs in the world. (Though they had clearly *underspent* on security features.) Jung Hoon Lee ran through their complete defenses in less than a minute.

As good and fast as someone like Lee might be, he's nothing compared with the best hackers. They don't work in public or compete in hotel ballrooms. They don't brag. And they develop ideas that make $225,000 look paltry. These successors to the warez dudes work for cybercriminal billionaires, for intelligence agencies, and even (often) just for themselves. They help find and deploy the sorts of really deep system exploits that enable brazen cyberthefts of millions of pieces of personal data or attacks such as the Stuxnet virus, which caused thousands of Iranian nuclear centrifuges to vibrate themselves apart. And they do still more: Most of the attacks we've talked about so far occur in installed, running boxes. But the companies that make those boxes oversee a whole process of design, testing, manufacturing, and installation. And it's on that path, with billion-dollar budgets at work, that some exploit teams make and leave invisible vulnerabilities that they can use later. Every step of that gestation—from sneaking secrets into early code bases to intercepting and rewiring routers as they ship overseas—is now an opportunity for secret control. It's also an opportunity for unanticipated risk and "emergent misbehaviors" that defy simple precautions, as baked into machines as fault lines are into California. Not surprisingly, hackers have mimicked the design of the technology companies they aim to exploit.

What was once done by a single warez dude is now often handled with a division of labor, technical specialization, and intensive pre-attack research. Every innovation in "righteous malware" is quickly copied and transformed into attack tools. Criminals examined the clever modular design of Stuxnet, for instance, and years later similar features popped up in attacks against banks, credit card companies, and health insurance firms. "We are not experts in military history, doctrine, or philosophy," cybersecurity researchers Stephen Cobb and Andrew Lee have written, "so we are unaware of the correct word for the following category of weapons: the ones you deliver to your enemies in re-usable form." The correct word is *terrifying*. "Righteous malware is unique," Cobb and Lee conclude, "in that you are giving away your weapons, tactics, and designs, simply by using them."

It's not only American intelligence services such as the NSA that are hunting for and using such backdoor keys and battering rams, of course. Computer-forensics experts describe opening up the laptops of unwary business travelers and finding the machines blasted inside by malware and other technical cancers carefully planted by a half dozen intelligence agencies and criminal organizations. It's like discovering a closet full of spies in your house, each careful not to step on the others' toes as they eavesdrop on your life. *Why is my computer so slow?* a government official in a Eurasian capital might ask. It is because it has been simultaneously pwned by Americans, Russians, Israelis, Chinese, and maybe a local Mafioso or two—and their code is not running smoothly.

Grab the five electronic devices nearest you, and you can be pretty sure each is vulnerable, which of course means that you are vulnerable too. Not merely to the loss of your secrets but also to perversion and control. This is the cold truth: That old hacker ethos, the one spread out so warmly on the Amsterdam grass twenty years ago, the "Be liberal in what you accept" frontier-society instinct, is dead. Weird machines and normal machines, weird networks and normal ones, people who have been made weird by technological manipulation and those who have not will live side by side. The question is: Do you know which you are?

5.

All around us today, huge power accumulates in certain irreplaceable cores. Giant search engines, certain algorithms, database or communications protocols overmaster us. Imagine life without search. Or a link to friends. *What makes a city?* urban scholars often ask. We might wonder: *What makes a platform for network power?* The answer to both questions is the same: density. If the first cities of the Aztecs or Mesopotamian civilization differed from early tribal clusters because of their density, the same is true of our first platforms of instant connection. Facebook is *denser* than AOL ever was. It has more people, more data, thicker connections. Future platforms will be denser still. And if cities packed too tight with people were once accelerants of plague and revolution, our own dense clusters of connection have risks too. Imagine if you knew that your government could be switched instantly and invisibly toward malicious ends. Or picture a nation of connected citizens wired for nationalism and hate. Such a possibility exists in linked systems because when everyone links to a core, that core links to everyone—like a country with a single airport. Every evil thing beats in the potential of these central nodes: With weird access a hacker or an ill-intentioned administrator can change what you know about the world, how you vote, where your money sits, what you remember via stored photos or sounds or schedules, how soon a doctor spots (or doesn't) a slipped knot in your DNA.

"Read over and over again the campaigns of Alexander, Hannibal, Caesar, Gustavus, Turenne, Eugene and Frederick," Napoleon wrote once. "Make them your models. This is the only way to become a great general and to master the secrets of the art of war." Reading over stories of zero-day attacks or of clever hacks such as rowhammer and the Tel Aviv heat hack, we can distill a tale of broken, once-secure systems and this essential principle: The hackers rush always, relentlessly, at the central core of an entire network. They aim to identify trust relations inside a network and then find the weakest thing that is trusted and make it weird.

Network influence doesn't merely come from that 10-million-devices-per-day spread of global connectivity, after all; it also comes from incredible *concentration* of power inside certain systems that we all rely on. Control of such hubs and roots of our world can influence everything; little wonder that they are such appealing targets.

This instinct that our systems are truly vulnerable if you can get to their hearts is, of course, exactly what lures the opportunists ever deeper, into the central programming hubs—called kernels—where the most basic instructions are kept. That hackers can make machines weird by using the devices' own code against them, like some sort of autoimmune disease, is only a marker of the particular perversity of our problem. Security researchers call such holes "vulnerabilities" in a system, but of course they are much more than weak spots. They are potentially fatal. In a way, the hot rush to touch and tickle and maliciously use these already waiting cancers reveals to us the essential Seventh Sense secret of the warez dudes: Connection makes an object vulnerable, yes, but it also reveals the possibility of total control. Lord Acton's line "Absolute power corrupts absolutely" twists in this age into something like "Absolute access corrupts absolutely." Connection makes possible total exploitation and total control. "Whom do you trust?" and "To whom are you connected?" are the same question.

"The greater the dependence on a technology, the greater the need to study and expose its inner workings," one group of radical digital activists has argued in "The Critical Engineering Manifesto." As we turn our safety, freedom, and health over to a world of devices and their makers, we must know what goes on inside the very hearts of such systems. It's not merely that everything is connected now; it's also that everything is monitored. Remembered. Studied. And in our own consideration of code, of software, of algorithms that drive much of our connected age, we should be careful. Just as labeling terrorism a single phenomenon is a mistake, so is thinking of all software or code as a single phenomenon. *That damn code crashed the market.* Code is as different as the people who write it and the machines that run it. It is diverse, surprising, filled with errors and flaws, and it decides much about how any system works. The warez dudes' drive to get ever closer to the cores, to perform even that atomic-level hacking, tells us something about just how much power is locked up in the nodes where this information accumulates. The 2,600-hertz whistle was, it seems, only the first of an endless series of battles for control of the roots and trunk lines of modern power. "Just like every drinking binge ends at vodka, so every hacking session ends at kernel.org," Thomas Dullien, the mathematician and good-guy hacker who won a Pwnie in 2015 for lifetime security achievement, once observed. So much power in a connected system lies at its root: kernel.org, for instance, is the reference copy for Linux computer code, which powers most digital machines on earth, sort of like the original DNA of the net. Everybody who runs Linux—from data centers to Wi-Fi routers to smartphones—trusts the code on this machine. To manipulate kernel.org would be to touch the essence of the Internet. If the aim is control, then inevitably kernel.org or its equivalent in any system is the ultimate target. Hackers might start with beer (your phone) or a few glasses of wine (your office email system), but what they really want is vodka (kernel.org). Such central trusted nodes exist in any linked system, and they represent at once both the greatest accomplishments of our most masterful system designers and the points toward which others, as masterful, direct their most relentless attacks.

Dullien saw something else too as he considered the work of hackers. Comparing system cracking with drinking wasn't a funny aside for him. Hacking *is* almost a kind of addiction. It becomes a chase for a bigger and bigger high, which in computing terms means a race to compromise as many machines as possible. Rapid escalation, a loss of self-control, the need for more and more—these are the hallmarks of the best widespread attacks. This is why stealing source code, the original instructions that lie behind any computer program, is such a prize for warez dudes. Source code is the original text of the machines and networks around us, the basic program that determines their operation. So, twisted the right way, it can be used to slip silently into any device or web in order to, well, steal still more source code. This looked to Dullien an awful lot like addiction.

And it's not just lone teen hackers looking for a dopamine jump who are chasing machines with an addict's blind urgency. Governments are doing so too. "Surprising realization (at least for me) after the Snowden leaks," Dullien observed. "Hacking is so addictive that entire organizations can become addicts and show addict-style behavior."

6.

Over the years, as the stakes of hacking grew, new pressures descended on the programmers who'd lived so easily in the *Hack-Tic* days. Postel's motto to *Be liberal in what you accept* had been a byword for most of them, and it had helped the networks grow at an incredible pace, but at the price of vulnerability. Now most everyone has something to protect. No one wants to be too liberal in what they accept—the opposite, in fact. The brutal, inarguable, profitable demands of this kind of power cracked apart the unique social webs of the *Hack-Tic* era. The openness that we loved in so many areas of life, from our minds to our markets, has now become a liability. "I remember what the Internet was like before it was being watched, and there has never been anything in the history of man that is like it," Edward Snowden once observed, nostalgic for the datascape he saw melt away during his time at the NSA. There is a whole new generation of young programmers who won't ever know the original, generous ethos of a publication like *Hack-Tic*. There is a fresh cohort of the digital age that now operates at levels of technical mastery far beyond anything that might have been imagined in the Citicorp building basement twenty years ago. They will confront endless battles to get inside and exploit and make weird the cores of network power. They will know and design and manage a world of gates, built for protection. Their instincts will be for opacity and control, not openness and generosity. Invariably, this shift will affect the design of the systems this new generation will build, which will, in turn, affect all of us.

It reminds me of an old puzzle of Chinese history: Why were the very strongest dynasties—the Han, the Ming, the Tang— always confronted by the best-organized, most deadly rebels? The answer is rooted in the development of each side. The better a dynasty defended its farmers or its trade or its annual rice harvest, the more the rebels had to become strategic and unified and powerful. When it was easy to pick off single farmers, then the rebels had no need to be well organized. They could snatch a year's undefended harvest in an afternoon. They could be a bit lazy. When it wasn't easy, however, the rebels had to innovate and improve. Amsterdam's hacking and camping crowd of 1993 was like a bunch of lone, unprepared farmers.

That our most essential systems are vulnerable to the loss of control imparts a chilly feeling. It is a reminder of the power of the people who know how to crash and manipulate—or build and operate—parts of our world that most of us barely understand. It's like discovering that someone could take over your lungs or your heart. And we can't really, yet, tell good connection from bad. It all looks the same, for the most part. It really is like Orwell's *Animal Farm* when, in the end, the pigs are walking on two legs like humans and no one can tell them apart. We don't understand the networks, most of us. But we depend on them entirely. Some of these hackers are moved to mischief by technical beauty; some by the giddy, smashing rush of breaking in, of touching the core; others by greed or patriotism or by secret, zealous, unlawful obsessions. What the technically best of this group share, however, is a pressing desire to get as close as possible to the kernels where invisible code decisions are made, where digital DNA is printed, in a sense, and where a total mastery of the binary guts of the system is possible. That Cap'n Crunch thrill, the dream of whistling up control over the thick, helpless trunk of a network—*that* remains the dream. Remember Conway's Law: The design and activity and control of a network redound on, even determine, the real world. If the whole network is, in a sense, filled with holes, if it contains inherently the possibility of being turned into a weird machine, what does that mean for the real world?

All the systems we rely on, that we think we control—financial or political or digital—can all be made weird and pwned by forces that we cannot see and that we struggle to stop. I mean stuff you use every day. Social networks. Stock markets. I mean: Be damn careful what you are connected to. Not just because of hackers. Presidential campaigns can manipulate voter turnout by targeting citizens with data-led precision. Financial groups can remove the pretext of a level playing field in markets because of their immense access to data. The networks can't be regarded as harmless anymore. The evolution of the *Hack-Tic* crowd from openness to caution is one we will all follow eventually. Bratus was right that we don't really understand any system until it's been exploited. Are we going to wait until our world is pwned and exploited before we understand the system we've built? I hope not. That's what this book is for.

CHAPTER SEVEN

The New Caste

In which we meet a powerful group defined, enabled,
and enriched by their mastery of the networks.

1.

In 1965, an MIT computer scientist named Joseph Weizenbaum found himself, somewhat unexpectedly, considering a problem with his computer and its users that he had not quite anticipated. Weizenbaum was in the midst of an experiment that started innocently enough. He'd written a program to perform what is now known as natural language processing, essentially a bit of code designed to translate what a human tells a machine into something the machine can actually work with. When someone asks a computer, *What is the weather?* the machine uses a special processing approach to turn that into an instruction set. Answering those sorts of queries demands a great deal of digital work before the computer can figure out what you mean and how to fill you in. This was particularly true of a computer in 1965.

Weizenbaum's program, which could handle simple communications tasks, was a breakthrough. And after developing his algorithms so that they really could talk with a human a bit, he wanted to find some way to demonstrate the power of his new approach. So his harmless-seeming idea was to build a system that would, in a very limited sense, carry on a personal conversation. The program would take typed input from a user and then, based on what it understood, ask a question. Weizenbaum borrowed this simple conversational approach from an American psychotherapist named Carl Rogers, who believed that the best way to talk to patients was not with Freudian mind tricks but rather with simple open-ended questions. Weizenbaum wrote two programs. One was called DOCTOR, and it was engineered to understand the input and figure out what to say. He wrote a second program that would use that data to speak to the user. He called that program ELIZA, after the heroine from *Pygmalion*.

Here is a discussion between ELIZA and a user that Weizenbaum recorded in 1965:

Patient: Men are all alike.
ELIZA: IN WHAT WAY?
Patient: They're always bugging us about something or other.
ELIZA: CAN YOU THINK OF A SPECIFIC EXAMPLE?
Patient: Well, my boyfriend made me come here.
ELIZA: YOUR BOYFRIEND MADE YOU COME HERE?
Patient: He says I'm depressed much of the time.
ELIZA: I AM SORRY TO HEAR YOU ARE DEPRESSED.
Patient: It's true. I am unhappy.
ELIZA: DO YOU THINK COMING HERE WILL HELP YOU TO NOT BE UNHAPPY?
Patient: I need some help, that much seems certain.

Weizenbaum's program quickly became famous around MIT. (The joke was that it was a better conversationalist than most of the awkward shoe gazers studying at the Cambridge campus.) ELIZA did what Weizenbaum had intended: It gave users a chance to experience what a machine with a mind of its own might feel like. Soon, the program spread to other campuses, to different research institutions, and with every step of its success, Weizenbaum found himself more distressed by the feedback he was receiving. What troubled him was not ELIZA but its users.

One after another, the humans talking with ELIZA became entranced with the computer conversation. They became convinced of the power of the machine to help them. Even professional psychologists wrote to Weizenbaum to say that his miracle machine might one day take over the work of diagnosis and counseling. This felt like a natural next step in the ceaseless progress they were used to in the rest of their lives. Better refrigerators, stronger seat belts, faster jet planes, more plastic—why not a computer doing therapy? It sounded kind of wonderful. "A number of practicing psychiatrists seriously believed the DOCTOR computer program could grow into a nearly completely automatic form of psychotherapy," Weizenbaum wrote a few years later in his masterpiece *Computer Power and Human Reason*. He was horrified. Weizenbaum knew that the empathy ELIZA was exuding was faked. *It was just code.* "I had thought it essential, as a prerequisite to the very possibility that one person might help another cope with his emotional problems, that the helper himself participate in the other's experience." He concluded, "science has been gradually converted into a slow-acting poison."

"Would you mind leaving the room?" Weizenbaum's secretary said to him once, lost in a particularly personal discussion with ELIZA. "This reaction to ELIZA," he wrote, "showed me more vividly than anything I had seen hitherto the enormously exaggerated attributions an even well-educated audience is capable of making, even strives to make, to a technology it does not understand." And this made him nervous. Who, exactly, did understand the technology? Certainly not the users. But all the same, here was his secretary, with only the dimmest idea of how the machine might really work, open to the most intimate sort of discussion with it. Trusting it. The immense power of such machines—and of the people who might control them—rattled Weizenbaum. "The computer programmer," he concluded in a flash of uneasy insight, "is a creator of universes for which he alone is the lawgiver."

2.

Looking back over several hundred years of European history, the Oxford professor David Priestland found that the movement of power might be scored by reviewing the alliances and hatreds and hopes of three distinct, interacting groups. They seemed to him almost like castes. If Indian society could be split into the Brahmins, Kshatriyas, Vaishyas, and Shudras, he thought, then we might also regard Europe's most influential elites as divisible into merchants, soldiers, and sages. By "merchants," Priestland meant the bankers, traders, and industrialists whose capital and political power turned Europe's once-feudal economies into something modern and industrial. The Medici, for instance, or Dutch coffee traders and Scottish cotton barons. By "sages," Priestland had in mind the churchmen and, later, the technocrats of various empires: John Locke in England, Otto von Bismarck in Prussia, or Niccolò Machiavelli in Italy. And by "soldiers," he meant both the great aristocratic warrior classes of Europe and upstart, genius figures such as Napoleon or Wellington—men who handled martial force with the fresh, surpassing brilliance of an artist, not merely the temperament of a war-mad king.

The interests of these three castes, Priestland wrote, could be aligned at certain historical moments like powerful gears.

Combine France's sage-bureaucrats with her artful soldiers and you get the French imperial period. Marry Britain's trading bankers with her martially inclined sailors, and the result is globe-spanning Victorian success. The merchants and soldiers and sages still operate today, of course. They sit in sovereign wealth funds, wired situation rooms, religious schools, and research labs. You could see American power, if you wanted, as a result of the fusion of the country's financial and commercial castes with a powerful, experienced martial caste. But now, all around the globe, we're seeing the emergence of what we might think of as a new caste, joining the merchants, soldiers, and sages. This is the caste that controls the networks on which we all depend. And because so much of what they do is basically opaque or invisible to the rest of us, they are everything Weizenbaum feared: creators of universes for which they alone are the lawgivers.

The members of this new caste that controls our networks are defined by their personal proximity to and fingertip feel for the connected meshes that drive so much of our world. They represent a fraction of our population but possess growing influence. They control machines and video networks and databases. Their computers run financial markets that efficiently decide the price of steel or stocks. Every connected system now has some figures who possess more knowledge and more power than others. They are powerful not merely because they are more connected, but also because they actually design and then direct these systems.

Think of this example from the world of technology: Maybe one million people can write object-oriented code at a high level. A hundred thousand of them can shape that code into some sort of innovative data structure. A few thousand might be able to use it to build a large data center. But get down to the couple of dozen who know how Google or Intel or Bitcoin really works, the group who can make machines seem to think, who know and use back doors at that atomic level of hacking—well, then you have a tight elite. If connection changes the nature of an object, it also elevates those who control that connection to a level of rare power and influence. Through the networks and protocols and data they control, this group touches more parts of our lives than any group of elites ever has. That many of them are billionaires as a result should hardly be a surprise.

This caste is so powerful that I think we can make this sober judgment: The countries (or really any group—even terrorists or criminals or bankers) that breed the very best members of the New Caste will possess a really unusual power. This doesn't mean training millions of programmers or having every kid graduate with high math scores. That is an industrial way of thinking about the problem. No, the New Caste, by definition, will be small in number. We've seen how tiny forces can have big impacts in a connected world. Well, so will a small elite. Think, for instance, of the legendary Xerox PARC research lab in Palo Alto, which during the 1970s produced not just some of the best early members of the New Caste—the systems designers Alan Kay and John Seeley Brown, for instance—but also a series of inventions so fundamental that a handful of them produced trillions of dollars of value: the computer mouse. Laser printing. A graphical user interface. PARC was arguably the most economically significant small group in human history, an entire Renaissance packed into a couple of dozen offices. In the technology world, so much can depend on a few innovations that mastery of those particular nodes is like mastering the cores and kernels Thomas Dullien was describing.

Much of our future will be dependent on the efforts of this group, whether they are in the world of IT, politics, medicine, or really any space transformed into a network. How should we weigh their courage in innovation against their wisdom and power? Think of the computer guy in your office who fixes the system when it goes down. What does he know? How does he know it? Anytime you see a network system, from cutting-edge databases to networks of commodities trading, there is someone like that or some tight group of elites who feel out the inside of the systems with a fidelity most of us will never achieve. Just what are they up to? Knowing this too is an element of the Seventh Sense.

You could, if you wanted, compare this New Caste to an earlier generation of empire-deciding figures, ocean explorers—Christopher Columbus working for Spain or Vasco da Gama for Portugal in the fifteenth century, for instance. Backed by an early version of venture capital, the "risk finance" of trading houses, these discovery captains had a hunger to test what they knew they could master—navigation, sailing, and shipbuilding—against the uncertainties of geography, weather, and luck. There was as much sheer nerve in these adventures as there was knowledge. What lay five weeks' sailing time away from Cádiz? If you were willing to endure the difficulties, to believe in what might be out there—and your own ability to handle it—then fortune possibly awaited.

"Early intercontinental travellers not infrequently had to pay for access to distant shores by enduring bitter asceticisms," the German philosopher Peter Sloterdijk has written of that early generation, a group that was once as important to human progress as scientists or trading barons. Months at sea, risks of ocean turmoil, starvation, endless boredom—these captains knew the hardships, but they also knew the rewards: fame, riches, and knowledge. Sloterdijk cites Goethe, who, reflecting on the power of nautical life in 1787, observed that "no one who has never seen himself surrounded on all sides by nothing but the sea can have a true conception of the world and of his own relation to it."

When you talk to some of the most powerful New Caste members, you sense right away that they have a new perspective: They know what it is like to be surrounded by connection. They have an instinct for it, as those early sailors did, sharpened by years online instead of years at sea. ISIS commanders who understand that a video with twelve orange-suited victims is more influential than the Sixth Fleet know just how connection will make them more powerful than the old military caste intent on wiping them out. Politicians who know that "news" for most people has become a self-reinforcing network of tilted information, bandied about in tight clusters with no middle ground, understand how to keep feeding the connected web with ideas, noise, and images that spread with viral speed. Old-school campaigns are like old-school militaries in the face of insurgencies. Wrong weapons. No networks.

New Caste figures exist in finance, in biotech, in any discipline in which connection marks a change. You'll notice this about many of them: They are self-taught. It's not surprising that so many of the most famous New Caste figures dropped out of school or emerge from surprising places. The path they are walking is new; an old-style education would be the worst possible baggage for such a trip. But that doesn't mean they are not masterful when it comes to understanding what they are doing. The computer scientist Andrew Ng, a pioneer in artificial intelligence, once summarized their position this way: "When building machine learning systems, making good decisions is a strategic skill. Every day you wake up and you are in some totally unique situation that no one on the planet has been in before. It's not a fact, there's no procedure." Surely Columbus had such a thought. As did Bismarck. Or Cosimo de' Medici. This newness brings members of the New Caste what is surely among the most powerful of human experiences: Touching something that has never existed before.

Billion-user connected worlds. Thinking machines. New trading networks. But for the rest of us, caught up inside their systems, there is a bit of that chilling feeling Weizenbaum had fifty years ago. We too know that there is a human in the loop somewhere. But we need to understand: Just what sort of human is it?

3.

Here, in a nutshell, is the paradox. We are surrounded now by what the French philosopher Bruno Latour has called "black boxes," but we have no idea how or why they work—or the values of the group that directs them. Latour was describing all the non-transparent technology and networks we turn to, unthinkingly, every day. In fact, the better these systems work, the less we notice them. "Scientific and technical work," Latour says, "is made invisible by its own success." The operating system and network protocols of your tablet device are, for instance, opaque to you now in a way they never would have been two decades ago, when even the casual computer user had to face a blinking cursor and a C:\> prompt. And this spreads into many areas of our lives. "Each of the parts inside the black box," Latour has written, "is a black box full of parts." This is true for your stock portfolio, your computer, or your biosensored heart. You might think that you know why something you rely on is moving one way or another, but do you really? Look around you—how many screens do you see? Each is a billboard for the fact that the New Caste is at work.

This creeping opacity of power, like a thickening fog settling between us and the world we inhabit, presents a problem. Because, as much as the New Caste is in the business of making knowledge widely and instantly available, it is also madly black-boxing our world. This creates an inevitable tension with that famous Enlightenment admonition: "Dare to know!" Would you like to *dare to know* why your computer is secure from digital attacks? *Dare to know* how your genetic information will be studied? How encryption works? Mostly the answer is: *You can't know.* It's too complex— and anyhow, if we told you, it would make the whole system less secure. There is nothing disingenuous here: You likely *wouldn't* understand. It *is* too complex. You'd be lost at the first turn into strange technical language in which simple words such as "object" and "edge" have specific, essential meanings. And telling you would, in fact, expose you and everyone else to all sorts of risks. It's as if we've returned to that famous philosophical debate of more than two thousand years ago, the one lingering between Athens and Jerusalem: Can the world be known and atomized and understood, as the Greeks would have it? Or are mystery, inscrutability, and opacity the nature of truth, as the rabbis said? We are children of the Enlightenment, after all, so we want to know what goes on inside the machines. We want them, at least, to be accountable to us.

This tension is one reason why places such as Silicon Valley often leave a visitor with an uneasy feeling. Go drive along the anodyne strip of asphalt that runs in front of Sand Hill Road in Menlo Park, home of the greatest venture capital funds of our age. Inside those offices, revolutions are dreamed up, debated, and funded. You might expect to see, as a result, something as magnificent as the Vatican for these high priests of technology. But what you pass in that two-mile strip resembles nothing so much as a row of mildly prosperous dental practices. Black boxes. Perhaps you've heard of this famous manufacturing trilemma, that you can have something made with two of these three characteristics: good, fast, and cheap. If it is well made and delivered quickly, you can probably assume it won't be cheap. Fast and cheap? Okay, but don't expect quality.

In our network age a similar puzzle emerges. Systems can be fast, open, or secure, but only two of these three at a time. A computer network that is really secure can be open, but it will be *very* slow, inspecting each packet and instruction like a bank security guard watching customers in a bad neighborhood. Think of an airport. Want it to be fast? Secure too? Then it won't be very open. Mostly what we want today are fast, secure arrangements for our markets, our nations, our data. So these will become, I think, ever less open. This is as true in trade discussions—the most recent of which were conducted largely in secret in order to ensure their success—as it will be in finance, where the advantage accrues ever more not to those with public information but to those with some sort of edge. What marks the New Caste is not merely mastery of the visible connected systems around us. No, they handle much greater sources of power.

Here is the strange result: It used to be that history was made in public. Big wars were impossible to miss. Revolutions made headlines. Discovery of some new scientific breakthrough was widely shared and debated. When the planet shifted in some significant way, it was noticed and understood. Pericles's funeral oration in the Athenian central square was watched and recorded; those riots of Jefferson's Paris were an obvious harbinger of change. Now, however, subtle manipulations at the heart of network systems, inside the black boxes, will produce historic-scale external effects. Shifts in power will take place before we are even aware of them. And even if we were aware of them, we might not recognize their power. Decisions about computer-code design, search algorithms, the structure of digital currency, DNA-alteration rules—all these will be made by New Caste figures who largely operate outside the machines and corporations and governments we know and regulate now. A few years ago it occurred to me:

The most important things that will happen in our lives will happen in secret.

I'm not sure I've recovered from this shock.

4.

To educate and deploy masses of people capable of such transcendent design genius will mark a difference between nations that succeed and those that fail. But such training brings a tension. Let this group rip away at their work, but: What won't they attack? Control over the protocols that answer questions, move money, protect data, analyze your DNA—it's hard to think of any single locus of power that will ever be greater than the platforms emerging around us now. As much as the work of the New Caste looks tactical in nature, most of what they do is guided by a strategic hunch. Behind even the smallest advance, whether it is fingerprint recognition on your phone or some new auto-translation app, lingers an unadulterated, unquestioned faith in continued network revolution, and in the idea that the values of efficiency that underlie the best programs should also guide the world. The danger here is clear enough. "Respect, understanding and love," Weizenbaum wrote as he considered ELIZA's effects, "are not technical problems."

The biggest of the platforms controlled by the New Caste herd together billions of people, bind them with ever-thickening cords. The revealing tics of every movement in the virtual world, and every step or drive in the real world, are marked down, remembered, and scored. Operating the strategic levers of such a force is, in all reality, no less significant than leading a nation. The distinction between a CEO of a major connected firm and a head of state lies less in the depth and efficacy of their influence than in the questions of how they got such power and how they might use it. The New Caste has an admirable conviction, near to faith, that their products are truly universal. They are absolute technological determinists. Watching their services and influence expand, one often senses that strange aura of an irresistible force taking on an immovable object. They believe that their black boxes will bulldoze concerns of politics or history. And soon.

Historical ambition of this scale, the sort that touches really countless lives, has always blended commercial and technical mastery with faith in progress—the moves of the East India Company turned as much on better ship design, maps, and navigation as on imperial confidence. The aim of the New Caste is the same as it was for those three older castes, the merchants, soldiers, and sages: to put the tools they've built and mastered in the service of still more dominance. The commercial calculations of the most powerful figures of the New Caste carry a sense that they are seeing many moves ahead, playing a very real kind of chess. Their billion-dollar acquisitions, their investment in moon-shot R&D ideas, the hundred-million-dollar payouts for great engineers—all of these mark the astonishing scale of what they have in mind. Are they seduced by having a billion users? Sure, but not because of the billion users, but rather because of the seductive allure of the black box, of what it means to control such a central point of connection.

5.

I remember sitting with a member of the New Caste the week the first batch of mimeographed and laser-scanned Snowden papers was released, as we both discovered that everyone we knew was devouring the documents. Like a novel. People were texting one another—"Have you seen this?!"—and you couldn't get through a dinner without a debate over the technical merits of what was on display. The Snowden files were fascinating to the New Caste in a way that few others might understand, in the way that a room of ballplayers might examine Ted Williams's swing mechanics. Let me try to explain it this way: When I was younger, people called our generation—those of us born between 1965 and 1980, more or less—a generation of slackers. Generation X. Generation Nothing. There was an argument to be had about the Baby Boomers. Had they been the most destructive, selfish generation in American history? Was it a reaction against the selflessness of their parents? Had they retired, only to leave the rest of us to pay their future medical bills and ogle their underfunded pensions, to cope with the manipulated political system they'd sued into existence? Or had they left a legacy of tolerance, a firming of American confidence? But anyhow, Generation X? By comparison, irrelevant: a collection of sad, passive slackers.

But the great Internet companies were largely built by Generation X. The foundational experience of 1989—the fall of the Berlin Wall—bred optimism. It created, in fact, the possibility of a new exploration. Jon Postel's idea to "be liberal in what you accept" seemed reasonable. This encouraged new links in trade and finance and friendship. Wi-Fi and TCP/IP and other advances made wiring the world possible, but the context? The two decades between the collapse of the Wall and the 2008 financial crisis had a magical aspect for a lucky few. There was a lightness of hope, mixed with the speed of a suddenly opening world. Life was a feedback loop of profit and, frankly, amazement at how easy it was to connect.

So the Snowden papers were a shock. It was as if the NSA had enrolled most of the digitally visible world into a twisted panopticon of a social network, one in which your "membership" began the moment one of your data packets was sniffed or chased along fiber-optic lines. No one who had been around tech for long was naive. The immense possibility of what had been built already in networks was clear enough, as was the still-greater power yet to come. But the Snowden papers showed another part of the New Caste, a group that understood the networks profoundly but eyed different aims. That members of the New Caste could listen to Radiohead's "Karma Police," on the one hand, while also enacting the *OK Computer* logic of surveillance on the other was a cold reminder: There is no inherent guarantee that a network will be good. Or that it will produce virtuous uses. The collection engines of the NSA and others were strange masterpieces of spying and storage and analysis. They relied for their safe operation on the humans in the loop. And what was it, exactly, that the humans had appeared to do in the face of such power and responsibility? Almost like that enchanted secretary chatting with ELIZA, the New Caste had suspended their sense of humanity.

Looking back on his formative years, before Europe was ground up in the First World War, John Maynard Keynes bitterly recalled the iron certainty of his generation. "We were not aware that civilization was a thin and precarious crust erected by the personality and the will of a very few, and only maintained by rules and conventions skillfully put across and guilefully preserved. We had no respect for traditional wisdom or the restraints of custom," he wrote. It was the war, then the depression, then another war, that finally taught them the expensive lesson of what the will of a very few meant.

The essence of the Seventh Sense will be not merely to be beguiled by our technology, by the way it smashes old systems. If we find ourselves too seduced by it, we may end up just letting it run. Possession of the Seventh Sense isn't about just letting the tech do its thing. It is not about passivity in the face of so much power. Rather, it demands grasping the nature of a connected age and seeing how it might be used to further, not erode, the things we care most about. Yes, we need to produce a new caste that can ensure continued technological advancement. But, more than that, we need to make sure the advancement fits our essential aims. We will see, in a moment, just what that means in practice, how our best technology and our most avid hopes can be fused. But before we can do that, there is one final question we need to answer about the networks all around us now, the only one that will put us on an even level with the New Caste: *What, in the end, are the networks really for?*

CHAPTER EIGHT

"MapReduce": The Compression of Space and Time

In which we learn what networks are really, rather wonderfully, meant for.

1.

Starting in the early 1990s, the American scientist and inventor Danny Hillis began what has since become an every-few-months sort of ritual. He packed up from his home in Encino, a short drive over the Hollywood Hills from Los Angeles, and headed off for a desolate corner of the Southwest for a few days that would largely be defined by rock and dynamite. Hillis, who was born in 1956, has spent most of his life working at the electron level of the world, crafting some of the most significant computer processing systems of our age. So the sort of Paleolithic earthmoving he was heading off to manage was a departure from his usual scale. His aim was to work on blasting and then refining a space in an isolated mountainside for the construction of a towering clock that he had designed, one intended to run for ten thousand years. That ten-millennium span was not accidentally chosen. Civilization, when Hillis began his work on the clock, had been around about that long already. We were, as he pictured it, at a midpoint on that twenty-thousand-year stretch of time. Hillis and the group of tinkerers, thinkers, and engineers who had backed the clock—people such as Amazon's Jeff Bezos, spreadsheet inventor Mitch Kapor, and investor Esther Dyson—were planning on a project that would endure as close to eternity as they felt reasonable. The Clock of the Long Now, they called it. I remember pulling into Danny's driveway in Encino one afternoon as he prepared to depart for the backcountry and being struck by the contrast between the lovely, inoffensive suburban blandness of Southern California and the tools he was taking with him to make an assault not merely on a mountain but on a whole conception of time.

I had met Hillis in an unusual fashion. I'd been asked to chair a committee that would award a million dollars to a figure who had made an essential contribution to the world of technology. The directors of the foundation behind the then-new prize had been, from the start, slyly dropping big names—*Bill Gates! Steve Jobs!* They hoped such a laureate would cast a bit of glamour on the first year of their award for Contributions to Man's Present Condition. But when our committee sat down to talk it over, we knew that the boldfaced names didn't want or need a prize. They certainly didn't need a million dollars. As we considered people we all knew who'd made fundamental, essential contributions but had not been as boldfaced as they might have been, Danny Hillis's name came up immediately.

Hillis had developed a revolutionary "massively parallel" computer in the 1980s. The machine had helped create an entire discipline of high-speed computing by tying together tens of thousands of processors to tackle a problem at once. Traditional computers worked problems the way you or I might, step by step. Hillis's design was the equivalent of millions of minds all moving at once. It was coordinated, connected, and awesomely fast. In the years since, he'd played a key role in a dozen other breakthroughs, from designing artificial intelligences to fine-tuning classified military aircraft systems that depended on mathematics for their stability. When you wander into a deep part of Google's technical database systems, you're touching his work. When you talk to your phone, the interface bubbles with some of his patents. How did Baran's 1960s idea of a survivable, packet-based system at ARPANET become the Internet? Danny was part of a cluster of dirty-fingernail engineers—computing pioneers such as Vint Cerf and Jon Postel—who'd done the work to make it possible. His centrality in that project was memorialized in a famous speech he once delivered in which he described having one of the very first Internet domain names in history—and then whipped out a sheaf of bound pages that represented the entire Internet address list at the time. It ran about fifty pages. If there were membership cards in the New Caste, Danny's would have had a very low number. It was an easy decision for our prize committee. No Bill Gates. No Steve Jobs. So here's how I met Danny Hillis: I called to tell him he had won a million dollars. (I recommend this as a way to start a friendship.)

Hillis had been a tinkerer since he was a child and never seemed to have lost the pleasure of a wild intermingling of joy and practice. You can't tell with him where passion ends and work starts. He was so technically adept that he could inject even the coldest digital projects with a bit of hot emotion, like Bernini breathing life into a block of carved marble with one "just so" grace note of his chisel. One of Hillis's most famous projects, for instance, was a fifteen-foot-high tic-tac-toe-playing Tinkertoy robot he'd built in his second year as an undergraduate at MIT. Made from ten thousand wooden spindles and poles, it was an early attempt of his to show how machines, even simple ones, might seduce us with both brains and looks. The effect of a giant Tinkertoy pile sitting there at the Massachusetts Institute of

Technology had to make you giggle even as your mind boggled at the fact that this heap of sticks, strings, and dials was beating you again and again at a child's game. Hillis is an artist as much as an inventor—one reason he'd not become Bill Gates or Steve Jobs. (And why Gates and Jobs maintained a consistent, admiring respect for him.) He'd spent several years at Disney designing rides and thinking up new dreams as a kind of real-world mayor of Tomorrowland. He liked to joke that he knew he was at the right place when on his first day, he asked where he might find a parachute harness for an experiment and heard, in response, "What size?"

Hillis is an avid reader, and he has the habit of thinking of his bleeding-edge work in the context of long historical gulps. Conversations with him often tie back to Paleocene-era biology or some other deep root. That long-term view, married to his unmatched hands-on feel for complicated systems, made him the ideal designer for the clock, a machine intended to last millennia.

The problems associated with such an undertaking are, honestly, as unreal as you might expect. How should the clock be powered? (By hand winding, the better to ensure it is not forgotten.) How should it be protected? (By putting it in the middle of nowhere.) Did you need to plan for global climate change? (Yes. The design was adjusted to accommodate shifts in the earth's spin when the planet's ice caps melt.) Do you write a user's manual for people ten thousand years from now? (Yes.) Do you write it in English? (To be determined!) Working with composer Brian Eno on the sound of the clock chime, and with a team of geologists and physicists, Hillis had made the clock into a natural extension of his Tinkertoy tic-tac-toe machine, a device that served a purpose and sent a message. If there is an emotion the clock conveys in the way that Bernini's *Apollo and Daphne* might inspire terror or joy, it is meant to be awe.

Stewart Brand, one of the supporters of the clock and an early member of the New Caste too, would tell you that the idea for the clock had emerged from a desire to emphasize, to *physicalize*, the importance of longer-term thinking in a way that no one could forget. We've all arrived now, Brand and the other clock masters worried, at a moment in history when no one has a view that extends much past his or her own life—or sometimes past the next election, or the next fashion season, or the next financial quarter. Our "on to the next thing" economics and politics are eroding every slow, patient instinct. "Civilization is revving itself into a pathetically short attention span...," one manifesto for the clock began. "What we propose is both a mechanism and a myth."

With its ten thousand years of ticking, the Clock of the Long Now was meant to make us think in longer jumps. Consider that human-based winding mechanism, for instance. Why not use a battery or solar power? But Hillis liked the idea of generations of clock winders sharing in the work, of a group that will be connected in a long thread over the ten thousand years. A sacred priesthood of time. As I spent time thinking about the clock, I found myself too craving the solidity and isolation it promised. Who among us these days doesn't want a break from the instant nowness of our age?

Yet the more I understood the clock, the more I realized something else was at work. Stop for a moment to consider who was backing and building the device. It was a cluster of people who had as a common link the fact that they had their hands honestly *sunk* into the guts of the Internet. Hillis, after all, had been waving more than that slim book of email addresses when he talked about the early days of the Internet. He was waving the credentials of a man who had been living in the virtual cyber-neighborhood of Web connections from its very first days. He is as close to a native of the connected, fiber-optic, light-speed world as you can find.

All the names supporting the clock smelled similarly of burning electrons: Jeff Bezos had built Amazon into a high-speed marketplace whose backbone is the Web itself. Another backer, Mitch Kapor, had cracked apart several centuries of slow accounting habits when, in 1983, he created Lotus 1-2-3, the first successful computer spreadsheet program. It helped executives to see and change their whole business one keystroke at a time—which they promptly did. Kapor's software had been instrumental in moving finance to a really instant-by-instant sort of business—more or less the opposite of the "long time frame" the clock team was aiming to preserve. Esther Dyson, another funder, was one of the earliest, best investors in network companies. This was a collection of men and women unified by a genius for connected change, sure, but also by a desire for ever-faster clock speeds, ever-speedier delivery, ever-faster processing. They had lived this. Enabled it. Profited from it. If there was ever a group you might hope to take aside, pull into a quiet room, and ask gently, *What are the networks really for, anyway?* this would be it.

2.

This question, I think, is one we have to answer and own before we can move on. It turns out that networks are intimately connected with fundamental problems of time. How to use it. Measure it. Even eliminate it. And it is in understanding this idea, and in following some of the people who know it best—like Hillis—that we can see just why the networks are so powerful. We will come to see why they will enforce, whether we like it or not, a complete change in the apparatus of power, politics, economics, and military power.

The act of keeping time, of marking it, is embedded in the

nature of any age. Our lives are, after all, dictated by timetables: school schedules, the seasons, rush hour, the burning candle of birth, love, marriage, death. Time in the days before industry was measured by nature's schedule. How long it took a crop to mature. The solstices. A beehive filling with honey. It was marked by moving tides and shifting seasons, and it demanded a slowness, a personal presence on the shores, in the oceans, atop the fields, over generations. "Summer afternoon," the novelist Henry James remarked in a précis of a slower age he felt passing away in 1895. "To me those have always been the two most beautiful words in the English language."

Then, in the Industrial Revolution, time became money. Electric lights, for instance, undid the restful distinction between night and day—and made twenty-four-hour life and manufacturing and economics possible and then, of course, inevitable. Movement from countryside to city established a really new sense of what the German critic Georg Simmel, writing in 1903, called tempo. "With each crossing of the street, with the tempo and multiplicity of economic, occupational and social life, the city sets up a deep contrast with small town and rural life," he explained. "The technique of metropolitan life is unimaginable without the most punctual integration of all activities and mutual relations into a stable and impersonal time schedule." Punch cards. Bus schedules. The forty-hour workweek. Our education, our manufacturing, our markets, and our lives all began to run on timetables. They had to, or the whole project of industry would collapse. Summer afternoons became a time to work. Simmel worried, for instance, over the diffusion of pocket watches. To carry one was to look at a constantly draining bank account.

This sense that humans were reduced to cogs—churned, run, disposed of, on a schedule not their own—unnerved the residents of that first mechanical age. Cities had been the earliest tightly packed networks; *industrial* cities ratcheted this further still. They succeeded and failed by the degree to which they geared themselves and their citizens to machine speed. When the Austrian novelist Robert Musil began *The Man without Qualities*, his classic story of the era, with the flattening of a Viennese citizen by a speeding delivery truck, he meant to point out not only how urban speed and urban life (and urban death) had become inseparable, but also the mismatch between the weak brakes of the age and its acceleration. Musil's book—like Mahler's contemporaneous symphonies—is alive with that slipping, pre-accident sensation you may have had: You are pressing hard on the brakes. The car is not stopping. "Cities, like people, can be recognized by their walk," Musil wrote in a line that any modern New Yorker or Parisian would endorse. "A man returning after years of absence would have known, with his eyes shut, that he was in that ancient capital and imperial city, Vienna."

To know a city by its pace. Musil was touching on something important: The speed of an event affects how we perceive it. The difference between what you will notice when walking up a hill— chirping bugs, tiny rocks, changes in color and gradient—and driving up that hill is so complete as to make them almost different experiences entirely. Google research found that when search times were cut from one second to a tenth of a second, user behavior changed. People searched more, and more deeply. Speed changed how they thought, as a result. Soon, when the whole world tumbles upon us at fiber-optic speed, when invasions and revelations and accidents all spread at the rate of Wi-Fi or cell phone radiation, our sense of time will be permanently blurred. You have to wonder what Georg Simmel would have made of a smartphone.

Life in our connected age is instant and mostly always on. This demolishes an older, easier sense of pace. Computers were once switched on at nine and off at five—just like their human masters. But digital activity is constant now. The networks are paying attention all the time. They have to. Our machines—tractors and trains and cars—used to echo our pace of life. Now we echo theirs. We want them to be fast. To be instant.

It was certainly true, as Stewart Brand insisted in his manifesto, that the Clock of the Long Now was meant as a reminder, as a kind of constant totem of the fact that we're all just a small tick on the endless continuum. We do think in too short a time frame. But the clock also, I began to suspect as I considered it, had another role. Those ten thousand years of marked time were an attempt to scratch an itch bothering these pioneers of cyberspace. It might even have been a sort of guilty sensation. After all, there was something that they had demolished in their fast connecting of the world—maybe accidentally, but anyhow, it could never be put back. If the great industrial titans had, over several hundred years, vanquished distance, lacing the world with trading networks, the men and women behind the clock were fracturing something else, something that for all of human history had seemed the only reliable, safe, sad constant of our condition: time. For most of history, distance and time were seen as facts, as forces that could not be overcome or adjusted or fought. Time particularly has been the quintessential, tragically nonnegotiable condition of life. The backers of the clock were, in their day jobs, in the business of overcoming, adjusting, fighting, and even destroying time. What might once have taken years, they were committed to making happen in an instant.

The Long Now project, then, was like one of those carefully isolated arctic freezers in which samples of essential grains and DNA from Beethoven's hair and Einstein's brain are sunk and iced against the day when, God forbid, our basic feedstock or a chunk of humanity has been wiped out by accident or disaster.

Blasted into a mountain hole, designed to last thousands of years, the clock is a repository for time itself. It is a defensive museum, built against the moment when instant networks finally devour the off switch and kill an older, essential feeling of time. The clock makers knew, I think, that they had helped to demolish a particular sense of pace with their instant networks. They wanted, with the knowledgeable keening of the guilty, a new device, one carefully gated away from the very revolution they had encouraged with their business and technical obsessions. This hunger for speed had built their fortunes. Their revolution (and its IPOs) had paid for the clock, frankly. And the hope for an "instant world" had inspired their dreams. Bezos's first name for Amazon, Cadabra, captured exactly this sense of waving wands and having whatever you might want appear at eyeblink speed. A "Now you don't see it, now you do!" appearance of just what you want or need that was becoming our new, expected velocity. They were murdering time. This, in the end, was what the networks had been built for.

3.

Danny Hillis's father was an epidemiologist. His mother was a biostatistician. And his childhood was a blur of infection-led family migrations. "Anywhere in the world there was an epidemic, we would go," he recalled. As the family bounced from Delhi to Cairo to Dhaka to Nairobi, racing diseases one after another, Danny developed an energetic autodidactism. He would collect knowledge from his parents, the streets around him, his new friends, anywhere. In a library in Calcutta, for instance, he once found a copy of George Boole's 1854 book *An Investigation of the Laws of Thought*. Boole invented symbolic logic on those pages, and, though his instincts were grounded in an age of steam and machines, his vision still echoes in modern computer design. "Language," Boole wrote, "is an instrument of human reason, and not merely a medium for the expression of thought."

Hillis has a magnetic intellectual charisma, as you may have guessed by now. An afternoon with him resembles nothing so much as lingering in a mental theme park: roller coasters of big ideas (a ten-thousand-year clock!) mixed with smaller, sugary treats (how to design a better fence post). No wonder he fit in at Disney. Critics accused Steve Jobs of having a "reality distortion field" in which the Apple founder's charisma bludgeoned the boundaries of the practical. Hillis, by contrast, has a sort of "reality enhancement field" in which much of the world as seen through his eyes is filled with possibility.

From an early age, Hillis had been interested in the dream of a thinking robot. Maybe it was that the constant uprooting of his childhood left him with a giddy sense that it was easier to assemble your own friends than to try to meet them at each new stop. But somehow this led Danny to the idea of an artificial brain, which was his main idea when he arrived at MIT in the fall of 1974. The Tinkertoy tic-tac-toe computer he built was a nod to this hope, but its jerry-rigged aesthetic masked deeper ambitions. "Someday, perhaps soon, we will build a machine that will be able to perform the functions of a human mind," Hillis wrote at the start of his PhD thesis a few years later.

What Hillis and others such as his mentor Marvin Minsky realized was that the human brain worked differently from the way most machines were then built. Life, after all, is not a series of linear math problems, which was how most early computers handled information. You look outside. It occurs to you to say to your wife, "What a lovely day." This is not a result of some "*a* then *b* then *c*" calculation but rather the product of thousands of simultaneous inputs and twitches dancing through the space of your consciousness. If you were to process that same thought in a linear fashion, like an old IBM machine, it might look like this: First, look at the sky; then examine the cloud-to-blue ratio, check for too much wind, sense the temperature, open your mouth. Your wife would be out the door before you'd even begun to speak. The ability to operate on many different pieces of data all at once is one of the most striking, enviable features of the human mind. But, of course, that is fundamentally a *network* problem. How do you consider a problem from hundreds of perspectives at once? Instantly? Connection.

So it was that, a dozen years after his tic-tac-toe machine, Hillis began work on a device designed to think faster than any computer ever had. He called it the Connection Machine. "This ability to configure the topology of the machine to match the topology of the problem turns out to be one of the most important features of the Connection Machine," he wrote. Adding, in case the possibly too old-fashioned academic panel at MIT missed the point: "(That is why it is called a Connection Machine.)"

Hillis's ambition to build this device boiled in him while he was at MIT, and it finally outstripped what the university could support, so he gathered a group of like-minded students and started a small company, the Thinking Machines Corporation. Blessed by some combination of Hillis's charisma and the fantastic promise of the project, the company became a magnetic field for talent, ideas, and money. In the early days of the firm, for instance, the hunt for investors led Danny to the luxurious New York City apartment of William Paley, the founder of CBS. Hillis lived then in a ramshackle house close to the MIT campus. He drove a surplus fire truck. Faced with the urbane, powerful eighty-one-year-old founder of the largest radio and TV network in America, Danny jumped right into a passionate introduction of *his* ideas about connection and networks. Paley, coolly: "I didn't understand a word you said." Then he wrote Hillis a check for $4 million.

Or there was the time that Danny asked the Nobel Prize–winning physicist Richard Feynman to tip him off about smart young scientists Thinking Machines might hire. Feynman, sixty-five years old, volunteered himself. For the next few years, he passed his summer vacations working alongside Hillis and his team. When it came time to test the first Connection Machine, it was some of Feynman's data that helped reveal just how well the black box was doing its job. The architecture of their computer had cranked through what would have been a month's worth of physics problems in hours. And as the machine got better, these already-fast processing times improved by another factor of a thousand. The creation of such a machine, for scientists who were desperate for computed answers, was like adding years to their lives. If they could solve a problem in an hour instead of months? The whole texture of their careers would be altered.

Thinking Machines Corporation sold Danny's computers to Lockheed to model stealth fighters. Oil companies used them to model petroleum fields. The U.S. government bought several to help predict the weather. Puzzles long resistant to mere power melted in the face of parallel consideration. "At times," one fellow computer developer remarked, "the Connection Machine seems so different from current computers that it seems more akin to science fiction than to high technology." Nothing was more exciting about Hillis's machines than the unprecedented link between intelligence and speed. If you have twice as many processors as I do, you can perhaps crack a puzzle of genomics or cryptography a year faster. But say you have figured out how to have 275,000 machines linked together, and I have 1,000? You can solve a problem *eight years* sooner. Between 2007 and 2015, the number of connections a Hillis-style neural computer could handle grew from 1 million to 100 billion. This speed did produce things very like science fiction: Accurate voice recognition. Real-time genetics. And it also began to mark out, clearly, the surprising place where the battle for our future will be decided: in a contest over time itself.

4.

Of all the things that mark a change between our modern lives and the days of those who came before us, few are as sensationally obvious as the sheer acceleration of life, the reduction of delay, and the emerging *instantness* of experience. What is going on inside the machines, as Mel Conway's old law about how networks affect reality would have told us, is showing up in its effects on the surface of our lives. That the headlines are marked, ever more, by networked terror or networked financial crisis or networked tycoons is just the visible bit of a larger acceleration. The networks get faster; so do we.

A feeling of breathlessness in the face of speed isn't new, of course. When Anna Karenina folds herself under an oncoming train at the end of Tolstoy's novel, her suicide is as much a metaphor for that era, a comment on the disorienting steam, engine, and rail pace of modernity, as it is a personal tragedy. Speed kills, old habits and ideas particularly. Between 1840 and 1940, travel times between Anna's Saint Petersburg and Vronsky's Moscow shrank by nearly ten minutes every year on average, loosening deep cracks in Russian economics and politics, tearing apart Anna's slow-moving world of glittering balls and hereditary estates with the force of industry, modernity, and then the awful pliers of Communism. Tolstoy's own death, in 1910, held a bit of this acute tension between old and new velocities: At eighty-two, he abandoned his family for the rural Russian town of Sharmardino, hoping to live out his final days in peace, away from the clanging sounds of modernity. But he wanted to get there in a hurry. So he traveled by train and died at a station on the way, like an absurd figure in a Gogol novel, enacting the tragedy of trying to use the modern to get to the past.

At more or less exactly the same time, however, the American rail system was working its own transformation, but with almost no ambivalence. America was using the modern to get to the future—as fast as possible. This was a decisive difference in temperament. "The American frontier," Frederick Jackson Turner wrote in his famous 1893 essay about borders and American life, "is sharply distinguished from the European frontier—a fortified boundary line running through dense populations." American rails and roads (and trade) encountered no substantial fortifications. They ran nearly unchecked into the wilderness. The only apparent limit to expansion, that generation thought, was technology itself. During the three decades after 1840, the refinement of small but important details—faster steam engines, stiffer carriages, tracks that were straighter, an ability to move and reload boxcars at night—pressed America into the steam-engine age at a faster pace than that of any other nation. "The most significant thing about the American frontier," Turner explained, "is that it lies at the hither edge of free land." There was nothing, physically or psychologically, to stand in the way of more speed.

This brisk acceleration of rail transit revealed an axiom that matters even more in our connected world: The faster your speed, the less distance matters. Accelerate from five to fifty to five hundred miles an hour, and the mileage you are covering becomes less significant with each new notch on the speedometer. At a faster speed, it takes the same amount of time to go farther and farther. An hour delivers five, then fifty, then five hundred miles of distance. Marx called this process "the annihilation of space by time." He was right. Speed kills distance. The simple algebra linking increased speed and reduced distance had been apparent already in the shift from rowed galleys to sailing ships, but in the age of industrial transport by rail or air, rapid changes—accelerations that affected the very quality of life or commerce—took place within decades. The acceleration from horseback to train to plane speed happened over a period of 150 years. Each new acceleration *diminished* the impact of distance.

There's a phrase for this process—"space–time compression"—first identified by the American sociologist Donald Janelle in 1966. Janelle saw that the technologies of transportation—trains and planes and boats, and all the little innovations that made them move ever faster—were disrupting old spatial habits. They helped move goods more quickly, sure, but in the process they were also making the old, geographic maps less useful. When you could fly over a mountain, its importance diminished. In a wagon train you might have contemplated the desert with fear; by car you'd merely consider it with care. In a plane it is irrelevant. Janelle concluded that raw economics drove this compression as much as science. Centuries of constantly collapsing space and time had been driven not least by the hunger to poke into distant markets, to latch on to cheap labor, and to pull natural resources to wherever they were needed. This was "civilization" as a verb.

The demands for ever more commerce, ever faster, ever more profitably, suggested that the horses-to-trains-to-cars-to-jets acceleration was an inevitable feature of modern markets—and, by extension, modern life. We should expect it to continue, Janelle figured. Great fortunes would accumulate to those who mastered speed. To be fast is a competitive advantage; to be *faster* is decisive.

Absolute speed is absolute power, as the philosopher Paul Virilio framed it. That idea of space–time compression sounded felicitous enough, like the name of a clever magic trick. Space *compressed?* Time *reduced?* But that felicity hid the violent, revolutionary nature of the mechanism at work. It means that the battlefields of power, which for most of human history have been over the control of space and territory, will now become — rather incredibly — about the control of time.

Janelle published his first paper on space–time compression in 1968, in the pages of the reference journal of mapmakers, the *Professional Geographer*. But he was, of course, blowing up nearly everything professional geography thought it was about. "Geographers, as physicists, have traditionally been concerned with the positions of points (places) in space...," he wrote. "However, geographers have not employed the concept of 'velocity' in studying spatial relationships. Yet it might be of value and not too far-fetched for the geographer to ask 'at what "velocities" are settlements approaching one another?'" We should ask ourselves the same question now. At what velocity are you and I getting closer to each other? To distant points on the planet? Janelle was writing in the late 1960s. He was concerned then about the sound barrier as the practical limit to speed. But imagine his insights applied to an age in which networks are always on and constantly faster? In which a mistake or an innovation or an attack in one place can happen instantly and everywhere, because the speed connecting *a* to *b* is the speed of light?

5.

At first glance geography seems the least dynamic of sciences. It is rooted in the glacial-paced realities of geology, a discipline in which speed is usually measured in the creaking, inches-a-century advance of tectonic plates. The faster links of transportation, whether they are trains or planes or data connections, now lie, blanketlike, atop that slower-moving geological layer. These high-velocity networks are a new geography. Mathematicians and data architects call the landscape they represent a topology. The word refers to any kind of map that can be rearranged as a result of connection. It describes places where speed and the distance between two points do affect how "far apart" they are. You can think of it this way: Geographies are pretty much constant; topologies can change in an instant. In geographic terms, Moscow and Saint Petersburg are always four hundred miles apart. In topological terms, they are as far apart as the fastest connection between them—about 0.3 milliseconds on a light-speed fiber-optic cable.

When you hear network engineers talk about designing for a certain "topology," you should think of architects describing the natural geography where a bridge or a skyscraper will one day sit. They are considering questions of time, latency, and speed in their design. When you use a software application, link to a bond market, or wire yourself with sensors, you're connecting to a topology. An appreciation for tone and movement on network topologies is a sign of the new sensibility that we have called the Seventh Sense. The old world thinks in terms of geographies, of space to be traversed. The New Caste and anyone with a Seventh Sense think in terms of time: How fast can I make this happen? Recall how Napoleon saw the battlefields of his age differently than his enemies. They saw flat surfaces for the collision of soldiers; his revolutionary insight was to see a third dimension, the air, that might be filled with artillery. Masters of the Seventh Sense see wired topologies shot through existing landscapes in this same way. Even though these topologies are often invisible or made up only of narrow fiber-optic strings, it's important that we too try to picture them as real, as places where fortunes will be made and lost, wars fought—and every bit as influential as physical geography.

Topologies represent the landscape where the Web or the New York Stock Exchange or Hizb'allah operates. Topologies can change instantly, depending on their design, on who is connected, and as the speed and thickness of that connection shift. The topology of Wall Street in the 1920s, for instance, was largely defined by who happened to go to the trading floor on a given day; today it is a global landscape, influenced instantly by news, rumors, and real-time profit twitches from all over the planet. Just as moving a river from one place to another would radically change the utility of a bridge, changing the topology of a market or a war zone changes the shape of everything else connected to it. That Seventh Sense instinct present in hackers and terrorists and clever entrepreneurs, the one that senses how the powerful can become useless and the useless can become powerful, is earned first through a fluency with the impact of fate-changing topological shifts. To know that instant connection will demolish border security with drones or advertising with GPS-enabled messages or the role of a slow-thinking doctor with a database is to feel topological forces at work.

In recent years the topologies of our network world have changed at the pace of technology, which is very fast indeed. Every new piece of a network, every new platform or protocol, alters how we connect. This process works on our sense of distance like an efficient, strange sewing machine: Something very far away can be, suddenly, with one stitch of innovation, right on top of you. The speed and the quality of a connection are what determine how honestly "near" or "far" something is. Location is, in a sense, as changeable as velocity.

Distance, on any living, networked web, is an endlessly pliable sheet. Just as you can bring two distant points on a piece of paper right next to each other by folding the sheet, so you can glue points in networks together by bending the space on which they are connected. A map of the network world or of nations or even of our city is not some given, settled graph. One small twist and we are, like it or not, connected. This makes it particularly murderous to hold on to the old idea that you and I are unrelated points. In this way, the entire premise of Enlightenment life, the atomic focus on the power of the individual, becomes dangerous.

It is now essential to use virtual topologies to operate in the real world, to bend these ethereal elements of connection toward influence and even total control. Thomas Dullien, one of the researchers who discovered that rowhammer chip hack, captured this in a new law of network security that echoes throughout all of connected life: You don't have to possess an object in order to control it. "Being hacked," he explained in a 2014 speech called "Why Johnny Can't Tell If He Is Compromised," "is loss of control without change of ownership or possession." Your phone, resting constantly in your pocket, may in fact be pwned at every keystroke by someone thousands of miles away. This is an extremely important idea, an expression again of how connection changes the nature of an object: It makes it controllable without possession. An army might be able to master an enemy's territory without ever possessing it, for instance, if it can manage to own the crucial topological infrastructures: banks, databases, communications systems. One nation might be able to pwn another in this bloodless fashion. Networks, you recall we said, will break nations in the future. This is just how such smashing control will be achieved, from control of the linked mesh running silently and irreplaceably under every element of national life. Today, billion-dollar firms control cars, financial systems, and hotel rooms without possessing them. The links draw out value. *Every block of stone has a sculpture inside it*, Michelangelo once said, *and it is the task of the sculptor to discover it.* Every network has a topology. It is the task of every general or trader or entrepreneur to discover and use it.

Topologies linger everywhere there is connection. Though networks can be designed in countless ways, they all have topologies. The fishnets of Baran, the hub and spokes of a data center, the ever-changing mesh of a trading system, are maps of connection. As a result, the risk that lingers in any one place in the system also exists in nearly any other linked place. Constant connection produces, as an unsettling result, constant threat. Topology is not marked out merely by a description of how we connect. Rather, it is scored on what is called a trust graph. The term implies much more than a mere graph; it answers the questions: *Whom do you trust? How much?* An older generation still thinks networks are things made of wires and switches and plugs, things that can be attacked easily or yanked from the wall. But the real power of a connected system comes from trust ties, which are far more ethereal. When you connect to a person or an object, you connect as well to its whole history of decisions about whom to trust. Every EU country connects to the choices of a single border guard, for instance. Whom does he trust? Is he right? Financial systems and technology webs are the same. If you are what you are connected to, you are also the sum of every trusting (or untrusting) choice someone or some machine has made. "In the systems we've built now," Dullien has explained, "there is no way to establish who is in control." If you or anyone you're linked to has made a trust mistake, you may be pwned, vulnerable, and one hacked slice from loss of control.

Any object—the navigation system on a plane, a digital medical device, a cargo drone—can become dangerous now in this sense, which tells us something about life on a topology. Nearly any place can be attacked in some fashion or another as long as it is connected. Markets in Mongolia, airports in Europe, urban landscapes in China—all of these can be struck more or less at any time because they are all connected. Unlike traditional conflicts, in which the location of your most terrifying dangers might be exactly pinpointed and watched, in which military zones and civilian zones were divided by front lines, a connected world has no front line. Everywhere is a battlefield. The old commonplace of military strategy that a clever or desperate army can always retreat, can trade space for time by running away to fight another day, is nearly gone now. Space is a wall that can be breached by networks; there's no place to run except to some better-protected topology. This doesn't just mean the end of a difference between places of war and peace. It also suggests an end to the idea of a difference between periods of war and periods of peace. The networks are always on; that means the risks are always present too. And we know that the political demands of living in a wartime state are, and always have been, very different from those in a nation at peace.

That the knotting together of distance, speed, and power changes the nature of an object was something that Janelle, the father of space–time compression, anticipated. He labeled it "locational utility" and defined it as the way in which something becomes more useful or powerful or relevant as it is drawn closer to us by increased connection and speed, even if it stays the same "distance" away. A nuclear weapon three hours from landing and one that is three months away are nearly different objects entirely. Adam Smith's famous remark in his *Theory of Moral Sentiments* that most people would be more perturbed by the loss of half a finger than by the news that a million Chinese had perished begins to take on a different color in an age when a billion and a half Chinese are nanoseconds away. When we say that connection changes the nature of an object, we mean this: Networks change the locational utility of anything they touch. When connection makes an object instantly, clearly visible, it revolutionizes its potential. Little wonder that so many great fortunes are being made in making our world faster. Part of our unease now—and part of the problem we have in strategizing about the world or our businesses—is that stability on our topological maps is some time off yet. There is so much yet to be connected. There are so many new topologies to be built.

"Time *is* a ride," Danny Hillis once remarked in an early meditation on his ten-thousand-year clock, "and you are on it." He was right. That ride takes place, in a connected age, on topological rails. And just how "instant" you are will be a mark of what sort of ride you're on, of how successful you can be. In the same way that rivers and oceans and mountains define different landscapes in real geographies, the topological neighborhoods we will inhabit will also have unique quirks. Some will be superfast. Others yoked by politics. Citizens of Santa Fe or Mumbai may choose to compress time in different ways. But everyone, I think, shares this common desire: to do more with less. The compression of time offers the possibility to live more with less time. The German philosopher Peter Sloterdijk and the Dutch architect Rem Koolhaas, writing about the way in which some people breeze through airports and borders (with first-class tickets and preapproved immigration) while others struggle to move at all out of refugee camps or poverty traps, have labeled the winners of this new order a kind of "kinetic elite." They are the first-class passengers of topological travel, in possession of golden keys to a special, frictionless topology that gives them not only a financial and an information edge but also the ability to eliminate space and capture time.

The technical language of network design actually has just about the perfect word for this, one that comes from the special code that operates inside most data centers now and that makes ceaselessly arriving bits understandable: MapReduce, which was first introduced by Google in 2008. The name combines two well-known computer functions, Map and Reduce, and it is just the sort of program Janelle and Hillis would have dreamed up, had they ever met. Practically, the job of MapReduce is to turn a question like *Where does Bob Smith live?* into an answer. It provides a way to reduce the space between a question and its answer by accessing data on thousands of servers nearly instantly. What MapReduce *implicitly* does, however, is crush what might have taken years for older machines to accomplish into mere microseconds. It reduces universes of unstructured data to instantly scannable graphs. If the charmed phrase of Henry James's stately Victorian elites more than a century ago—the words that captured the spirit of their age—was "summer afternoon," the phrase of our age might be "MapReduce." A magic code for a whole way of living and thinking that captures the reduction of space and time around us now. The reduction of all our old maps.

6.

Here's why the compression of time matters so much: In the past, the most successful political and economic systems let people liberate themselves into a life of their dreams. Liberty meant tearing down old barriers to influence and security and knowledge: tipping over the Bastille, escaping colonialism. And it meant, too, providing a scaffolding of education, of social support, of laws and stability, for citizens. The industrial, urban, and rich countries that populate our world now evolved to be that way because they freed up their citizens to really live, not to be stuck in old habits or power arrangements. The premodern world was one in which where you were born or who your parents were determined most of the rest of your life. Modern nations let citizens make that decision for themselves, for the most part. This was the miracle of the Enlightenment, as we saw: *Decide what you want to be. Dare to know!*

Look ahead now. The very best future political and economic arrangements will need to do more than simply liberate us. They will have to enable and permit us to compress time. Governance systems that slow down the ability to get the best data, to learn faster, to squeeze more time and health and knowledge from the networks around us—they will have to explain why they are standing in the way of total speed. Just as the idea of a democracy was shocking once, this concept of a political and economic system tuned not merely to liberty but to the compression of time will force us to remake a lot of our institutions. Nations and corporations and ideologies that can deliver this liberty of velocity will grow, thrive, and accelerate. Those that can't, slowed maybe by history or blocked by social or ideological design, will miss the turn if they are more obsessed with control than speed. If they can't innovate fast enough to develop tools to manage massive data flows or are unable to absorb the best new technology, they will be the new divergence club. Fast networks will elude them. Self-defense will be impossible; their time will be as vulnerable to manipulation by enemies as the resources of Africa and Latin America were to colonialist plunder several hundred years ago.

In the next decade, everything from self-driving cars to war-fighting robots will begin to become commonplace in the most advanced nations. Think of the efficiencies these will bring: cheaper logistics and transport in a world of self-handled and self-unloaded trucks. A country such as the United States, which might be a leader in adopting such systems, would outperform even further a nation such as Chile or Nigeria, which may wait years before automated logistics can be implemented. This also presents a terrifying military asymmetry for many nations that will be too backward to resist technological attacks. All power will depend on instant and smart networks. Some nations will have them; others won't. That will be a fatal divide. And it will grow wider with each new cycle of technology. Think of the way in which airpower after World War II, for instance, shifted battles from two to three dimensions. "Only large states are able to resist three-dimensional envelopment," the historian Nicholas Spykman wrote in 1942. Even today, air superiority is the precondition of nearly any American war. If a nation can dominate from above, nearly anything seems possible. But networks add a fourth dimension, time superiority. Can you move faster than your enemies? Can you bog them down? Or are you a victim of fourth-dimensional envelopment? Control of time—yours, your enemy's: This will decide your strength.

"There is no equality of justice between the weak and the strong," the Italian historian Giambattista Vico once noted. So it is in our age. Between the fast and the slow? No equality either. There is a remarkable advantage, in wealth and opportunity, that accrues to the people and nations and businesses that can compress space and time best, to that "kinetic elite" among us. *Die Ware liebt das Geld*, Marx famously wrote: "Commodities love money." Speed is now the decisive commodity—and it *loves* money. (The feeling is mutual, by the way.) The race for speed lights something competitive: The faster I go, the faster you feel you need to go, the more powerfully you feel your slowness.

The centripetal charm of acceleration, the way that speed attracts us and then makes us demand even more speed, honestly surprised the earliest architects of steamships and rail and airlines and roads. They underguessed how popular their tools of space–time compression would be. Surely the maximum number of people who would ever want to zip from L.A. to New York would be about a thousand per week, jet airline pioneers assumed. *Would more than a few hundred engineers really want their own computers?* Gordon Moore asked at a dinner party shortly after Intel proposed putting his chips in the first PCs. Yes, it turned out. Billions more. Highway designers call this surprise "induced traffic": the faster a highway, the more people pile onto it. Urban planners in Los Angeles in the 1950s looked at their packed, congested roads and thought they could fix them by adding lanes. They embarked on construction programs, tore up the transportation network that girded the city, and built a new one featuring optimistic twenty-lane highways, as wide as a football field and as flat as a plate. Traffic got worse.

What is it, exactly, that we're so hungry for? The extreme end of fast connectivity is what computer systems designers call statefulness—a word that has nothing to do with states like nations but rather with the condition of a connection, the "state" it is in. Early electrical circuits were either in a charged or uncharged "state," switched on or off. Today when we talk about a "stateful" connection, we mean a link that we maintain and that is always on. A video call is "stateful" in this sense; a letter is not. Looking at your wife here and now is a "stateful" connection; a photograph is not. Older generations would "break state" when they left family at home or friends at school with a "See you later." Our generation never quite leaves. "See you always," we might say as we wave good-bye but track each other by GPS or Twitter or some social network. Technology permits us to remain in constant touch. "We don't have a word for the opposite of loneliness, but if we did, I could say that's what I want in life...," the millennial writer Marina Keegan wrote in a famous essay that captured more than a little of this zeitgeist. "More than finding the right job or city or spouse—I'm scared of losing this web we're in. This elusive, indefinable, opposite of loneliness." The early interface of Snapchat, where you had to leave your finger resting on the screen in order for the video to unspool, was a kind of metaphor for this unbreakable relationship between touch and connection. (As was, in a different way, the diffident, "out of my life" left swipe of Tinder.)

Networks, we are discovering, don't only compress space and time; they compress, in the process, the path to knowledge. We are also, now, statefully in touch with all sorts of knowledge. We might call this skill–time compression: Techniques that once took a decade of training or that demanded access to million-dollar machines can now be understood, applied, and then evolved unimaginably fast. No one had ever heard of the Syrian Electronic Army a year before they were hijacking websites, injecting world-class malicious code into opposition computers, and demonstrating a digital-attack fluency. Of course, the charming side of such a shift is evident too: Walk the Vatican with a historian in your ear, master sourdough in a weekend. There's something not a little miraculous in the way the networked tools to recombine DNA or hack computer code or design viral software are getting both more sophisticated *and* simpler. If earlier eras put epoch-making implements into human hands—the knife! the train!—our age is now placing new, mind-shaping forces within instant reach.

7.

Back in the fall of 1988, at about the same moment that Danny Hillis and his team were busy peddling their amazing Connection Machine—and trying to smash every world computing-speed record they could find—another device appeared in the world of massively parallel supercomputers. It was, everyone who saw it agreed, an extremely strange machine. Its appearance was completely unexpected. Its designer was not a famous thinker about parallelism, charming TV network founders and physics Nobelists. In fact, its very success emerged from this strange fact: The creator knew basically nothing about the sort of parallel design that informed Hillis's thinking. Which was strange because this machine was far more "parallel" than the Connection Machine could ever be. It was also cheaper. Simpler. And it was faster. In fact, it was the fastest parallel machine in history.

The machine began, quietly enough, in the mind of a twenty-two-year-old Cornell graduate student named Robert Tappan Morris. Morris came by his computer chops honestly enough: He was the son of Robert Morris Sr., the legendary NSA scientist we encountered two chapters ago, the man who penned those partly amusing, partly terrifying golden rules of computer security. *Rule one: Do not own a computer.* The machine that Morris Jr. created was made entirely of software. It took the form of a compact, simple computer program that he'd written and designed to spread quickly and easily on the young systems of the Internet. It ran a mere ninety-nine lines, took most computers nanoseconds to execute, and worked like this: The program—it later became known as a worm by the police who would come to find and arrest Morris Jr.—would find an open door on a network-connected computer. (In 1988, in the pre–warez dude era, finding such doors was not difficult. Finding *locked* doors was probably harder.) Once Morris's program had slithered inside and loaded itself onto the machine like a dog slipping through an unattended puppy door, it would sniff around, rattle a few more doors to find any passwords that had been left unsecured. Then it would move on to the next machine. *Knock, knock. Rattle, rattle.* Next machine. Morris designed his code to simply repeat this process over and over, filling, as a result, each machine's memory with multiple performance-deadening copies of the same program. A house full of puppies, in a sense. After several hours of this flulike spread, a wave of unplanned, unending computation began choking the net.

Morris later explained that he'd meant his program only as a demonstration, as a test of sorts. He wanted to show how machines might be made safer. But he seemed to grasp almost immediately that he'd made a mistake and that the worm was running away from him. He emailed a friend: *How the hell to stop it?* His friend had no idea either. They scrambled at least to warn system administrators about the dangerous code that would shortly devour their machines. "There may be a virus loose on the Internet," they wrote. But that note, in a bit of bad luck, was quarantined inside a Harvard computer that had already been unplugged. So, a few hours after Morris released his code, unwarned and unprepared, the Internet nearly froze. On November 2 and 3, 1988, machines around the United States were shut off, cables were pulled out of walls, and systems were wiped and restarted in a race to stop the robotlike spread of the disease and then to finally kill it off.

The Morris worm was, on those fall 1988 days, acting out a sober-minded insight of the famed biological historian Alfred Crosby: "The nineteenth century was followed by the twentieth century, which was followed by the…nineteenth century." Crosby meant that our age of topological connection had delivered us, again, into an age of infection. And this was true: Morris's program mapped out, like an epidemic, new routes in the age of high-speed digital contagion. But—and this is why we care about it here—by the time it reached "peak infection," the worm was also doing something else. It had infected tens of thousands of machines, which were all cranking away in unintended harmony.

During the forty-eight hours of its brief and unforgettable life, it was later calculated, the Morris worm had become the most powerful parallel computer in history. At its peak, it managed to achieve a processing speed of 400 billion operations per second—about twice the speed of the most expensive supercomputers of the day.

Like any unexpected epidemic, the worm became a social, cultural, and technological milestone. First, it caused Morris to be arrested. He was handed a $10,000 fine, some community service, and several years of probation. He later went on to found an important Internet company, to join the faculty of MIT, and to receive the highest honors in computing for his (other) efforts.

Then, a year or so after the virus had been finally corralled, the computer scientist Fred Cohen, one of the earliest specialists in malware—in fact, the man who invented the term "computer virus"—wrote an article that challenged the notion that all computer viruses are inherently bad. What drew his attention was that fabulous, unbelievable record of the Morris worm: 400 billion computations each second. "The features that make computer viruses a serious threat to computer integrity," he wrote, "can also make them a powerful mechanism." This optimistic gloss triggered a furious response. Eugene Spafford, also a well-regarded computer researcher, fired back: "For someone of Dr. Cohen's reputation within the field to actually *promote* the uncontrolled writing of any kind of virus, even with his stated stipulations, is to act irresponsibly and immorally."

So here, then, is a line of sorts. The Morris worm, an example of really massive connection and interaction and speed, is a model for the world we live in now. But who is right about the implications? Cohen or Spafford? Do we want our whole world cranking away, superfast, compressing time to nothing?

We can, all of us, decide to fight against the very idea of a network, as Spafford suggested. Or we can, as Cohen offered, look at the terrifyingly fast nature of this world and see something amazing. Of course, Spafford was not wrong. There *is* something scary and thought muddling about the idea of intentionally authored computer viruses running wild, ever faster. But there is also something thought muddling about this whole world we're entering. Networks are pulling at every existing structure. They hum with the most elemental and precious human data—our DNA, our wedding photos, our hopeful voice mails and most essential knowledge, our small savings against disaster. In its speed and its depth, in its increasingly comprehensive grasp of each of us and our world, this new network order is at once the most amazing thing we've ever created and the most terrifying. But recall, for a moment, Hillis's dream for his parallel computer: "The ability to configure the topology of the machine to match the topology of the problem." What if we really could rewire our thinking, our networks and politics and economics, to match the problems we face now? Poverty. Fundamentalism. Inequality of various kinds. Disease. The Seventh Sense shows us, as it has shown entrepreneurs and traders and terrorists, a topological landscape on which we can begin to construct new edifices.

8.

"A man may postpone his enlightenment, but only for a limited time," Immanuel Kant wrote in his eighteenth-century essay "What Is Enlightenment?" Kant wanted to explain just what that process meant. We might say, "A man may postpone his enmeshment, but only for a limited time." And it is toward understanding the terms of that connection that we've been working so far. What have we learned?

First, networks appear to distribute power in ways that are new in human history. Before the Enlightenment, power was balled up in the hands of priests, kings, and warriors. The chain of events running from the Reformation to the Industrial Revolution gradually began to pull that power free. Democracy and capitalism were intended to give politics to the majority and prosperity to a growing middle class. But networks, we've seen, both concentrate and distribute power—each with an intensity new in human history. They put more power in our hands than any generation before; they also concentrate more influence into new and powerful companies and protocols. A sign of the power we might tap into: Billion-user firms (and billion-dollar fortunes) can be bred with breathtaking speed. Drones, derivatives, wired terrorists, waves of migrants torn from their states but plugged in to technological tapestries—all of these are products of network power. Much of the world has not yet been fully connected. This is why we say we live in a revolutionary age.

Second, networks are made up of many complicated pieces, but in their essence they are complex. This is an important distinction. A jet engine is complicated; a thunderstorm is complex. Both have many moving pieces; one is unpredictable. Complex systems create. Social networks like Facebook emerged, in this sense, from millions of interactions. Shared-car services, financial crises, and political movements are no different. ISIS emerged from connection. As did the subprime financial crisis. We shouldn't expect this process to end anytime soon. In fact, it will accelerate.

Third, while we were following the trail of warez dudes and hackers, a feature of the networks around us became apparent. Not only are connected systems honeycombed with vulnerabilities, but they possess historic amounts of power in their cores. Hackers hunger to master these kernels of power. To control a system everyone connects to is, in a sense, to control anyone who connects. Trade. Politics. Finance. All these systems will come to express this logic. One result is an inversion of historical norms: In the past, the important events happened in public—wars, revolutions, elections. From now on out, history may be decided in secret, in the manipulation of algorithms or network designs, apparent only in their impact but unstoppable at their birth.

Fourth, we met a new caste of figures who dominate and control many of the systems we depend upon. If past eras were mastered by merchants, sages, or soldiers, our age increasingly relies on a young, technically savvy group. The nations and companies (or terror groups) that train and equip them best will have an incalculable advantage. This group's newness is their great advantage but also their greatest danger. As much as they may know about networks, history and politics and philosophy do not yet influence their thinking. The world appears to them, often, as a machine to be coded.

Fifth, we unearthed a new and invisible set of landscapes that will decide much of our future. These topologies are the connected fields on which power moves now. The webs where stocks are traded, cyberattacks occur, imports are moved, or biological data are recorded and studied—each of these is a landscape where maps can change in an instant. Topological control will matter as much as mastery of sea or air or capital did in earlier eras.

And finally, we learned what the networks are for: the compression of time. For all their technical magnificence, we find that beating in the heart of these systems is a very human desire. To do more with less; to live more with the time we have. This compression of time is why we hunger to connect. What the demand for liberty was to the Enlightenment, the call to compress time is now. It is a fundamental and political requirement that none of our existing institutions have been built to answer.

These six elements make up a rough outline of a new sensibility.

Seeing them at work in the world is the mark of a powerful way of thinking and feeling called the Seventh Sense. The shift ahead of us really is like the Enlightenment in its scale. It will tip everything over. Already we can see that the credibility of structures of an older world, from our political parties to our markets, is eroding. No one in power seems to have a clear, convincing picture of just what is going on. Most of us have started to feel the danger we face like heat rippling from a nearby inferno—our world led into the future by a class of old leaders who don't understand networks, and a collection of new technologists who don't understand the world.

There's one last thing that we didn't really learn here, but I think you probably suspected: If we're going to shape this world at all, we don't have much time.

PART THREE

Gateland

CHAPTER NINE

Inside and Out

In which the Seventh Sense brings us face-to-face with the most powerful feature of our age — and perhaps of any age.

1.

The Shangani River runs in a small, green vale, through some of southern Africa's most celebrated nature. It marked, a bit more than a century ago, a northern line of the British presence in Africa. While other parts of Queen Victoria's colonial empire crackled with desert harshness, the mountains and hills rolling up from the Cape of Good Hope and down to the Shangani were notable for a pleasing softness, a shading toward pastels in the changeable light of the region. For London's colonial mapmakers, South Africa was a treasure, an ideal restocking point for British ships headed for Lombok, Calcutta, Pondicherry, and beyond. "We have lost America," the explorer William Dalrymple wrote to Prime Minister William Pitt in 1785, "and an half way house would secure us India, and an Empire to Britain." South Africa would be that halfway house.

Following the 1814 Anglo-Dutch Treaty, which gave the British control of the cape, the English pressed into Africa and found that each newly opened district delivered more wealth than the last. A colonialist's dream: Diamonds. Gold. Endless fertile fields. Their efficient engines of industry and exploration (and exploitation) chewed easily into the land. "Having read the histories of other countries, I saw that expansion was everything...," the mining baron Cecil Rhodes wrote in 1875. "The world's surface being limited, the great object of present humanity should be to take as much of the world as it possibly could." And so the British did.

If there was a moment that showed the tenor, the power, of this ruthless asymmetry most clearly, it was the battle that exploded along the Shangani in 1893. The Matabele, a powerful local tribe, had been fighting the colonists for years. The British had tried to charm, pacify, and bribe the Matabele and their chief Lobengula with money and land. None of it worked. They tried threats. That did not work either. "The Chief has had all your messages," an imperial adjutant reported back to Cape Town after another frustrating, pointless discussion in 1892, "but he has the art, not unknown to civilized despots, of ignoring what is not convenient." Or perhaps he had the instinct of knowing what to avoid. One Boer commander, a blood enemy of Rhodes, had warned Lobengula about any treaty with the British: "When an Englishman once has your property in his hand, then he is like a monkey that has its hands full of pumpkin seeds—if you don't beat him to death, he will never let go."

So when, in October of 1893, the British finally tracked Lobengula to the banks of the Shangani, the two sides faced off for what promised to be an intense and decisive battle. "It was just after 2:15 a.m., a peaceful night, clear sky but on the dark side," one of the British infantrymen later recalled. "The bugles gave the alarm, the camp was all excitement in a moment, all noise with the opening of ammunition boxes and shouting of officers, the men were getting into their places. There was a din outside... from the on-rushing Matabele *impis* that had decided to attack in the usual Zulu fashion." The British soldiers were outnumbered.

They were far from home, hanging on the thin end of a five-thousand-mile supply line. The Matabele knew the territory. They were fighting for their lives and families and honor. But one sound was the decisive noise of the scale tipping toward the British. A hushed clicking against the yelling all around. *The opening of ammunition boxes.* The British, for the first time in African action, had mounted machine guns.

The weapons worked that morning on the Shangani with a violence that you and I would have expected. They reversed, more or less instantly, the Matabele advantages of men, familiarity, and even furor. Machine-gunned Matabele were found, in the hours after the attack, perched in trees, dug into dirt mounds, and piled desperately atop one another, killed as they had scrambled. One British soldier wrote later that the weapons had mowed down the Matabele "like grass." Lobengula survived, but his army was massacred down to a squad, and he was reduced to pleading. "Your Majesty," he wrote to Queen Victoria in the days after the battle, "what I want to know from you is: Why do you people kill me?" With this missive, the chief entered the ranks of the queen's many powerless correspondents, those once-omniscient-feeling men in Africa and Asia and India who wrote her imploring letters after some devastating battlefield reverse. Did she even read the letters? It was hard to know, but that only made the pleading more perversely imbalanced. The locals had no idea, really, what they were up against.

Martial leverage. It was the inarguable force of the nineteenth century. It made Europe's colonial masters. Of course they lied, stole, fought—did whatever sensible and sleazy thing Cecil Rhodes and his ilk suggested was needed. The monkey with the pumpkin seeds. But Rhodes was right: Expansion *was* everything. Imperial dreamers in London, Berlin, Brussels, Vienna, and Paris saw with total clarity the immense historical imbalance in their favor. It marked a chasm of industry and science and reason that "the natives" would never cross. Rhodes's confessed ambition to "take as much of the world" as he possibly could was simply an armed and greedy version of Kant's "Dare to know!" Just as no question was unaskable, no place was too far off to exploit. No nation's position was secured by history or distance or sentiment. This was, for instance, the lesson taught to Lin Zexu, the Qing Dynasty bureaucrat sent out from Beijing in 1839 to stop the British opium sales that were reducing China to a nation of useless, comatose drug addicts. "Suppose there were people from another country who carried opium for sale to England and seduced your people into buying and smoking it?" Lin wrote to the queen. "Certainly your honorable ruler would deeply hate it and be bitterly aroused." Lin thought that he was speaking as the voice of a great, eternal empire. Victoria never replied. To the extent that Her Imperial Majesty was aroused by anything in southern China, it was likely by the way in which, in the years after Lin's letter, the British emasculated the Qing military and moved into Hong Kong for a 150-year stay.

"Whatever happens," the British writer Hilaire Belloc had his colonial character Captain Blood famously quip in an 1898 poem, "we have got / The Maxim Gun, and they have not." The machine guns were a totem of dominance in Shangani and on other colonial front lines; they marked a gulf between the modern and unmodern, between the industrial and agricultural. The weapons had first appeared in the mid-1800s on battlefields in the American Civil War, after the inventor Richard Gatling sent a package of samples to the White House and convinced President Lincoln — a famous gadget freak — that their firepower might bring the Civil War to a faster close.

Lincoln ordered the army to try the guns, but Gatling's early attempts were honestly too immature to tell decisively on the battlefields of the American South. Within a few decades, however, the guns were perfected in places such as Africa and on the front lines of the 1904 Russo-Japanese War. They represented a compelling, inarguable logic of industrial war: a machine *and* a gun. *We mowed them down like grass.* You could read that line as metaphor: Mowing grass was, in the end, the act of a machine squashing a wild, natural world into submission, turning it into a clean, useful order. The Europeans were the grass-clipping machine; the rest of the world was, well, the grass. For imperial commanders who had refined their temperament for the "Great Game" of empire on the playing fields of Eton, preparing a lawn for tennis and a territory for exploitation were not particularly distinct acts.

The Shangani battle gunshots struck the European mind as powerful confirmation. Everything they had suspected about the magic violence of an industrial age seemed true. The image of a machine gun's efficient work suited the aggressive, engineering-led mood of the era. As Gatling—and his competitor Hiram Maxim—peddled their guns, they faced a predictable resistance, of course: Europe's cavalry officers were in love with their well-bred horses. But the age was, finally, the story of gears and axles and grease. Trains were assaulting the countryside. Factories were pounding apart the habits of labor. Social stampedes of speed-climbing nouveau riche, political attacks of new industrial unions, and counterattacks against them all expressed this new energy. The soundtrack of Germany in the decades after 1869, as Bismarck stitched together a new nation from dozens of hereditary principalities, was the ceaseless *ping-ping* of rail building and welding and industry. How natural it must have seemed to add the *rat-a-tat-tat* of a Maxim gun. Crown Prince Wilhelm, the kaiser's eldest son, wrote that defensive thinking was "utterly foreign to the German spirit." Bismarck's national motto, Blood and Iron, became, finally, personal for many Germans, who were prouder to leave their universities with hot, red dueling scars on their faces than with a subtle ownership of Goethe in their hearts.

"During the decades before the First World War," the political scientist Steven Van Evera has observed, "a phenomenon which may be called a 'cult of the offensive' swept through Europe." Wars, it was believed, would run with the same swiftness as trains or the new industrial sewing machines. It was this instinct that led German generals to assure the kaiser in 1914 that a war begun in August would be finished by Christmas. English university students sprinted to enlistment centers in the days after the war began, worried that the fight might end before they tasted blood. French farmers moving from their crops to the trench lines of Flanders, Russian aristocracy crowding toward the Danube, the politicians who led them all—they operated, mostly, with this same conviction. British foreign secretary Sir Edward Grey's mournful meditation on the evening of August 3, 1914, the first night of the war, was a lonely one: "The lamps are going out all over Europe," he said. "We shall not see them lit again in our lifetime."

The First World War was a kind of engineering tragedy. The disaster had deep roots—domestic politics, the insecurity of kings, profound colonial greed—but it also grew out of a fundamental miscalculation about the nature of war and peace in an age of industry. Machine guns and all the tools of industrial war, from gas to battleships, were not magic tricks of fast victory or permanent peace, as some had thought. A mechanized, modern army wasn't, as much as it may have seemed in theory or in drills or in midnight massacres in the African bush, some steam press built for cold rolling the armies of Belgium and Prussia and France. In fact, the weapons encouraged battle as they piled endlessly in national arsenals. They tickled fears of fast or surprise attack even as they gratified that weird Continental hunger for violence. Hilaire Belloc's poetic joke, the sly *we have got / The Maxim Gun, and they have not,* took on an unexpected character when both sides had it. The machine gun reached the fiery acme of its purpose not as a spur to end wars altogether, as Gatling once hoped, but rather when it was married to barbed wire, to shovels, and to gas—and then admixed with the trigger-tugging fear of twenty-year-old boys. So: sixty thousand British casualties in one day alone, July 1, 1916, at the Somme.

The rhymes changed. Hilaire Belloc's jigs were a distant memory for the starved, surprised, and shocked men in the field. Siegfried Sassoon:

> *You snug-faced crowds, with kindling eye*
> *Who cheer when soldier lads march by,*
> *Sneak home and pray you'll never know*
> *The hell where youth and laughter go.*

As soldiers dug into trenches that would endure for a half decade, a terrible strategic fact dawned on the generals who led Europe's armies. The Great War was going to be a charnel house. The Continent had built itself into a battle machine, wired by trains and telegraphs and armies. There was no reverse gear. There was not even a switch to slow it down, let alone turn it off. A massive, technology-powered, fast-moving system with revolutionary implications, built beyond the comprehension of any one figure or nation, had slipped out of control. And the men in charge of planning and directing the use of this superfast complex? They failed everyone: their soldiers, their kings, their armies. They were all but insensible to the real nature of their age.

Sound familiar?

2.

Here, then, is a question of the sort—violent, loaded with the possibility of tragedy—that you'd rather not have to consider: A new way of war arrives, a new weapon, a fresh idea about fighting. Does it make your world peaceful or treacherous? The lethality of the equation *guns x machines* at the end of the nineteenth century appeared to some industrialists and bankers and statesmen as inarguable evidence for peace. With everyone possessing violently efficient weapons, who dared start a war? As we now know, *guns x machines* was a formula for some of the worst killing in human history. Gatling's fond hope that his weapons would stop war was naive, insane, even. His competitor Maxim had been clearer eyed. A friend told him: "Hang your chemistry and electricity! If you want to make a pile of money, invent something that will enable these Europeans to cut each other's throats with greater facility."

So let's be a bit warmer about this. *Networks x weapons* equals what, exactly? Is there some disaster lingering in our own future, as unimagined from our current perspective as machine guns and trenches were a century ago? Do we consider war impossible now? There's something sickening in such puzzles, of course. Think of the men and women who, over the millennia, have contemplated similar questions knowing full well that the answer would be measured in blood and treasure and children. Put yourself in the place of the population of Melos, a peace-loving Mediterranean island whose destruction twenty-four hundred years ago was chronicled by Thucydides in *The Peloponnesian War.* "Surely you have noticed that you are an island and we control the ocean," an unwelcome Athenian general intimated to a Melian citizens' council one day 416 BCE, as his soldiers and ships collected menacingly outside the city's walls. Athens wanted the Melians to join an alliance against Sparta. The Melians—like poor Lin Zexu or Lobengula of the Matabele—yearned only to be left alone. "You would not agree to our being neutral, friends instead of enemies, but allies of neither side?" they asked. No, the Athenians replied, and then came a line that has resonated throughout the problems of nations ever since: "It is the nature of power that he who has it takes; he who does not must submit." The Melians voted against surrender. Perhaps the Spartans would mount a relief raid? The Athenians might change their minds? Neither happened. The Melian men were betrayed and then massacred. Their wives and children were sold as slaves.

What do networks do when they touch the balance of war and peace? How might we use what we know, what we sense, about a connected age to manage the dangers ahead? While an insane Cult of the Offensive flavored the end of the nineteenth century, our own age vibrates, as we've seen, to a Cult of the Disruptive. The great tale of our times is the diffusion of a new, promising, and disorienting network order. We've been told that all this interconnection makes war an impossibility. *Everyone would be a loser in such a war.* But the way in which that earlier age was so horribly wrong about the product of *guns x machines* should unnerve us. We don't yet really know what *networks x weapons* means—to say nothing of *networks x networks x weapons.* Or of, to sum up what we've seen so far in this book, *very fast networks x artificial intelligence x black boxes x the New Caste x compression of time x everyday objects x weapons.* Would you look at that weird formula and say conclusively: "Hey, we'll all get along"? I wouldn't either. We should worry about the day we might face a Melian choice of our own, when some general or infomanagerial despot—or some clicking computer—shows up, unwelcome, and says to us: *It should be obvious that you are merely a node and that I control the network.*

When leaders label the rise of China or cyberweapons or terrorism or the decline of the United States as the "main problem" of our age—and all of these have been designated as such by famous foreign policy figures—they are missing the revolutionary, uniting force that animates them all: networks. Whether we are trying to slice apart the roots of the Islamic State or slow Russian territorial dreams or understand narco-economics or hedge-fund finance, connectivity touches and defines each problem. New and essential platforms for finance and biological data and artificial intelligence are emerging now, having blossomed out of network connections. These ecosystems must be designed, built, protected, all while the world we know fights back, sometimes crumbling, sometimes fighting for dear life. I promised earlier that we'd apply the Seventh Sense to some practical problem, and the deadly test of war and peace is the one I'd like to consider. The sharpest challenge of truth for any view of the world is, after all, the design of a grand strategy. Get it right, and you can secure your safety. The energy of the age can be your tool. Get it wrong, and you reap the battles of the Somme, Melos, Canton, the Shangani. Recall General Liu Yazhou's line: "A major state can lose many battles, but the only loss that is always fatal is to be defeated in strategy."

The leaders of our major global powers may be as blind to the dangers and possibilities of our world as Europe's heads of state were to the nature of their era one hundred years ago. You know what the Seventh Sense is now. Who has it? We should wonder if we've merely now done Hiram Maxim one better. Have we developed something with our age of connection that will reach its fullest potential in allowing us to slit each other's throats more efficiently? I don't think so, but understanding why means we need to consider the networks, to feel them out with our new sense.

3.

The essential problem of politics is not difficult to state. It was as true for Seneca in the Roman Forum as it was for Lobengula on the Shangani riverbank or as it is now for congressmen in Washington or cadres is Beijing. *Who has power? Why?* By "power," I mean the ability to control others, to tell them what to do—or what not to do—and, of course, the ability to avoid being dictated to in that "surrender or die" way. Max Weber, the German sociologist of the last century, had it right when he defined power in terms of *Macht*, the ability to achieve what you want despite the resistance of others. *Don't develop nuclear weapons* and *Don't attack us* and *Join our alliance against Sparta* are all examples of *Macht* in action.

Our world shuffles into a new order now and *Macht* is expressed by all kinds of in-or-out borders. What the Seventh Sense reveals as it feels our new power arrangements is gates. Everywhere. The world is not one big, flat equally connected topology. It is filled with closed and gated worlds. Facebook. Bitcoin users. Doctors with privileged access to genetic databases. Members of the New Caste. Those revolutionary investors disguised as dentists' offices on Sand Hill Road. These are all are gated, in-or-out worlds. Look around and see how many gates enclose you or your family or your company. The Internet. The FTSE 100. Your Apple or Android operating system. In our connected age, the act of drawing lines *between* points is also an act of drawing a line *around* those points. It is not simply that we're enmeshed in networks now; no, we're enclosed, even entrapped, by them. While the great ambition of Cecil Rhodes's era was the expansive conquest of territory—the more territory, the more *Macht*—in our own age, power is in the construction and control of gated spaces. *Gatelands.*

Today, no position is more important, formidable, influential, or profitable than that of the gatekeeper. Defining who is in or out of any network is among the most essential moves of design. In financial markets, on the Internet backbone, or inside the human immune system, the accept-or-reject decision determines a great deal. The first sign of order breaking down, whether it is in the Roman Empire or your lungs, is a failure to manage what slips in and out. Flows of bits, of migrants, of gold and patents and medicines — all of these forces can be controlled, bent for good or stopped for ill, as they pass through or collide with gates.

By "gates," I mean not only in-and-out passages but also protocols, languages, block chains. Whatever binds and shapes a topology is a gate. Code and encryption and binary instructions all describe a line between in and out. So do trade arrangements, financial rules, and laws. If you want to make a fortune or a revolution (or both) — if you hope to shatter some barrier of tools or ideas between you and a dream, or to lead a religious revival, or to spread an infection of hate or revolution or insidious computer code — then, fundamentally, this is what you have to consider: *Where are the gates? How do you smash them? How do you build your own?*

If older, hierarchical systems craved a top — a king, a superpower, a pope — our age demands valves and protocols and gates. We all hunger for connection, which means we hunger too for throttles and brakes. The reordering of power will produce a fight over topological spaces. Who will be the gatekeepers of finance, biology, trade, and pretty much every other source of power? The scramble is as decisive and essential as the one Rhodes and his peers embarked upon. Inside or out? Here is how to measure your own *Macht:* Are you the gatekeeper? Or the gatekept?

4.

We wander into Gateland the moment we switch our phones on. We enter it when we book an airline ticket, when our genetic information is folded into a pool of data, or when we take a new degree, master a computer language, or check on friends via one connected platform or another. We enter it, in short, when we connect. Gatekeepers choose what we see. They determine the rules we follow, what we can and can't change. They reward us too—once we're inside—with benefits of speed, knowledge, and safety. Gatekeepers, which can be people or protocols or treaties, decide who can join closed communities and who is left out and why. They pass us the fine benefit of the compression of time even as they expose us to potential instant disaster that strikes everyone in a closed space at once. Gatekeepers control how (and how fast) financial data moves between members of "in the know" trading pools and the suckers outside. What you can see on your phone or in your medical records or on your shopping cart—all these choices are made by gatekeepers. They can, if they wish, manipulate any step of life inside their orbs of power—and, by extension, they can twist data and machines and you. The line between perverting search results and election results is a thin one.

The idea of gatekeeping first emerged as it related to newspapers, back in the 1920s, when politicians, advertisers, and a few social scientists watched a print information explosion—and developed an uneasy feeling about how the world looked through many newspapers. The personal whims of an editor or his boss's economic interest often decided what "facts" made the paper. Minor international incidents were turned into fearmongering bait. Major global shifts were ignored. Gatekeepers today have a far more profound reach. They might be governments or regulators or CEOs or machines or research committees, each controlling the design and development of systems we depend on—and exerting historic, invisible control. Do you want accurate DNA analysis? Protection from an epidemic? A cyberdefense system? You can't have any of these, you know, unless you are inside someone's gateland. Even systems that look open—the Internet, the world of U.S. dollar transactions, the election rolls—are gated. Of course there is, at times, a balance between the gatekeepers and the gatekept, between those of us inside a system and the tools and people who overmaster us. "Traditional literature focuses mainly on gatekeepers as elites who hold the power in their hands while the gated usually are treated as powerless...," the information theorist Karine Nahon has written. "In networks, however, it is necessary to give sufficient weight to the role of the gated, since being subject to gatekeeping does not imply that the gated are powerless, lack alternatives, or that gatekeeping is forced on them. Actually, being gated sometimes is a matter of choice." But sometimes, of course, it is also a matter of necessity.

In the slower, less wired worlds of our past, gates mattered too. Nations, governments, militaries, religious orders—all of these clustered behind marked lines. Map lines, front lines, dogmatic lines. The Triple Entente that bound Britain, France, and Russia together in the last century was as much a gated system for their own security as the Peloponnesian League, twenty-five hundred years earlier, had been. Deciding who could swap silk for spices beyond the Tang Dynasty's border was a gatekeeping choice, as consequential for Chinese strategists of the eighth century as the decision about what might or might not be wheeled into the city was for the tragically uncareful councils of Troy. But now, in an age when connection decides so much, control over gates gives gatekeepers a unique leverage. When you finally can feel out the topology of our age, when in anger or frustration or hope or wonder you are ready to act, this is among the first questions you have to ask: *I'm on the topology now—where are the gates?*

Gates in an age of instant, ubiquitous, smart networks are, you can imagine, different from the ones that girded Troy or the Tang Dynasty. It's not merely that they're made of bits and concepts, not bricks; it's that the underlying nature of their power is different. The most visible evidence of this distinction was first observed by economists a couple of decades ago as they contemplated the first fortunes of the Information Age, wealth that had been assembled at an eye-watering pace. Traditional businesses always turned over time into competitive slugfests with very low profits. But many high-tech firms seemed to run with a new, nearly inverted logic. The longer they survived, the more profitable they became. "Our understanding of how markets and businesses operate was passed down to us more than a century ago by a handful of European economists—Alfred Marshall in England and a few of his contemporaries on the continent," the economist Brian Arthur wrote in the *Harvard Business Review* in the summer of 1996. "It is an understanding based squarely upon the assumption of diminishing returns: products or companies that get ahead in a market eventually run into limitations." Marshall had been the first to name this phenomenon, in the 1890s, "diminishing returns." When a line of business gets more competitive, the profits—or returns on investment—shrink. Henry Ford invents a car; he has no competition at first and fairly prints money. But Ford doesn't enjoy his monopoly for long. Pretty soon the Dodge brothers follow him into business, as do Walter Chrysler and then a flood of new automobile companies. They each eat a piece of Ford's pie; profits for every car-making firm shrink. Then the Japanese pile in. The Koreans show up. These new companies compete with growing intensity. Profits decline for everyone. Then the Indians arrive. And the Chinese.

As he studied the balance sheets of infotech firms in the 1990s, Brian Arthur noticed something strange: Their returns were *increasing* over time. As high-tech markets matured, some companies made more marginal money with each passing day, not less. Marshall's nineteenth-century industrial economics had never contemplated such an absurdly lucrative arrangement. "Increasing returns," Arthur explained, "are the tendency for that which is ahead to get further ahead.... They are mechanisms of positive feedback that operate—within markets, businesses, and industries—to reinforce that which gains success or aggravate that which suffers loss." In other words: Winner takes all. No second place.

Arthur was thinking, as he wrote, about the then-nascent computer-software business. Say, for instance, that Arthur had sent you a copy of his paper as a Microsoft Word document. Well, if you wanted to see what he had to say, you'd pretty much have to own a copy of Word yourself. If you then sent it along to some friends for their input, they'd be in the same position. One after another, in just this fashion, users acquired the program. It became a standard, a "platform," in industry-speak.

And Microsoft enjoyed a particularly appealing economic leverage: Developing Word may have cost millions, but once that work was done, each additional copy cost just cents to produce. This sort of profitability demanded a whole new economics. It also forced a reconsideration of what "competition" might really mean. Once Excel or Windows had settled into place, had become a *standard*, you couldn't really compete with it. New, optimistic, maybe even better rivals rushed into the marketplace, like the Dodge brothers charging at Ford, but they were all assaulting the impregnable wall of habit, of a locked-in technology. *Should this be legal?* Arthur wondered. Traditional economics said that such monopolies were bad for everyone. (As did the Department of

Justice and their global peers as they chased Microsoft.) But was that right? The "platform dividend" that accrued to Microsoft was surely large, but what if you could somehow total up the benefit to the world? The convenience, the efficiency, the benefits of Microsoft's billions of dollars of research spending to you and me, might dwarf even the company's massive profits. "Increasing returns," Arthur wrote, "cause businesses to work differently, and they stand many of our notions of how business operates on their head."

The essential phenomenon that Arthur spotted at work two decades ago is something we now know as "network effects"—an idea that changed how we think about businesses, and particularly about the sticky and alluring power of gated, connected systems. In the years after Arthur's paper was published, billions of us ran madly along a course he had anticipated: We crashed our way as fast as possible into those single, winning businesses, rewarding them with near-monopoly positions in exchange for the benefits of being "inside." In the twenty years since Arthur spotted increasing returns in software, nine-billion-user worlds have emerged—and others are not far behind. Microsoft Office and Windows, Google Search, Google Maps, Facebook, WhatsApp, Google Chrome, YouTube, and Android all have more than a billion users, and each exhibits that appealing "If you use it, I'll use it!" logic. Profits and power, just as Arthur would have expected, followed right along.

It was just as Arthur predicted: If ten people use WhatsApp or Facebook or YouTube, it's hard for the eleventh to do something different. And when the eleventh person joins in, they make it harder still for the twelfth to walk a unique path. So Windows runs on 90 percent of the globe's PCs thirty years after its first release. Google has a 65 percent market share. Android runs on 81 percent of new phones. WhatsApp neared a billion users with less than fifty engineers on staff. Facebook passed a billion connected people and faced no real competition. How? "Seven friends in ten days," Facebook growth hackers repeated like a mantra in their early years. If you or I joined the service and found seven friends in ten days, we would most likely stay, enjoying the benefits of the gated world, making it that much harder (impossible, really) for friend number eight to wander somewhere else. Pretty soon, there was essentially nowhere else to go, anyhow. This was network *Macht* at work.

Network theorists who came after Arthur call these rich-get-richer systems "power-law distributed" because if you line up all the firms in a digital industry, you find that the winners are exponentially—by a *power* of ten or one hundred—ahead of everyone else. They slip free from the normal bell curves that mark most business. A bell-curve distribution would shape up like a chart of people who own cars: 20 percent drive Fords, 10 percent Nissans and Toyotas, and so on. Or it might look like the distribution of height: Most men are between five foot seven and five foot eleven, but just over 30 percent are found, scattershot, at different heights. Network systems, however, can breed commanding winners. It's not as though 50 percent of online users are on the Internet and others are scattered across different systems. Users huddle into single, winning clusters. It's as if 90 percent of the world always bought a Ford or 90 percent of people were exactly five foot eleven.

These systems run faster and better and more profitably because they are a shared system. They are gated by technology standards and by common connection. When we say that networks crave gates, this is the sort of gate we mean. If you had to look for your friends one by one on Facebook, Friendster, MySpace, and Google Plus, you'd exhaust yourself. So one winner emerges. Data scientists attribute the success of these winning nodes to preferential attachment—the idea that if Brian Arthur is using Microsoft Word, and I'm using it, you are likely to do so too. But there's another secret: More widespread adoption makes the whole system faster. Think of five mechanics trying to fix a broken engine. If they all speak English, the car will be back on the road much faster. Networks optimize themselves to be quick, the better to compress time. The winner takes all because we all benefit from the resulting efficiency.

There's an additional feature at work in the very newest of these tight clusters that's worth our attention: It's not merely that we'll use them because everyone seems to be doing so; it's also that as more users weave themselves into each other's lives and the machines weave themselves into our lives too, these nodes of power get *smarter*. Google Maps can predict the fastest route from your house to your office because it can watch the movements of hundreds of millions of users silently pinging their locations and speed. As more people use GPS-enabled devices, the quality of this data gets ever better, like a video resolving itself from a low-quality image into HD. Success attracts still more users. All of them are Google's sensors, in a way. Medical diagnosis, cybersecurity, trading algorithms, searches—pretty much any linked ball of chips and humans and sensors throbs with this logic. The best of the leading technology firms understand this power. Google's artificial intelligence engine, TensorFlow, was, for instance, largely regarded by experts as nearly a decade ahead of competitors in 2015, when the company began giving away access for free. In traditional economic terms this would be insane, but with network logic the strategy is clear: The more people who use TensorFlow, the smarter it gets, which in turn attracts still more users. Dense and self-learning fusions of mind and data such as TensorFlow and other soon-to-be-arriving AI systems are all gated universes.

5.

The topological charm of these explosively growing clusters was first teased apart by the electrical engineer Bob Metcalfe in the 1970s. Metcalfe was hunting for a better way to send data—say, grocery lists to his wife—through Menlo Park, and he perfected a connection protocol called Ethernet, which soon became a standard for linking machines. What Metcalfe noticed as more and more users piled into the gateland of Stanford's Ethernet-connected machines was that the reach of the system was growing *exponentially*. A system with one phone, for example, is really not very useful. Whom would you call? A system with two phones means that there is one possible connection—we can call each other. But when you increase the number of phones by a factor of two—from five to ten, say—the number of possible connections more than doubles, from twenty-five to ninety. The difference between Bob Metcalfe and his wife sharing grocery lists and a connected, national network of husbands and wives is immense—an insight that led Bob Metcalfe and his wife to start a networking company that made them billionaires.

Metcalfe's Law has another angle, and it's here where some of the unique *Macht* of network gates is revealed: It's not merely that the power of a network grows exponentially with each additional user; it's that the cost of being cut out grows every bit as fast. Maybe even faster. If I shut you out of Google today, it's painful. But tomorrow—after a day of new information and websites and services coming online—it will be even more costly. The network scientists Rahul Tongia and Ernest Wilson have called this "the flip side of Metcalfe's Law." To be excluded from a database of cancer genetics when it has a million members, for instance, is probably not such a painful problem; to be locked out of the chance to compare your genes with those of a billion others might be fatal. Imagine if I cut you out tomorrow from the New York Stock Exchange, your phone system, smart diagnostic webs, cybersecurity patches? There is nowhere to go. It's not as if you can swap out your Ford for a Dodge. Gateland winner-take-all systems mean losers-get-nothing dynamics.

A discipline of network science known as "queuing theory" helps us understand why. In studies of massively connected systems, the more time machines spend on their main task—hunting prime numbers or DNA patterns, for instance—and the less time chattering with one another about how they will compute, the faster they run. Winning protocols avoid this terrible inefficiency. In fact, the great breakthrough of computer systems in recent years has been their ability to handle massive amounts of data all at once, to maintain versions of information in a concurrent state in many places in the world. This is the essential technical leap that permits compression of time. And it depends entirely on careful and gated design.

To be inside a gated system is, then, really to be faster because of the slickness of communication that becomes possible. These systems are designed to compress time: to bring you closer to friends, a stock trade, a protective alliance, faster than systems that are not marked by common rules. Winners take more and more on networks because it is simply *faster* that way. And this is why gates will dominate our future. Our modern gates are different from older ones because it is lethally costly to leave them for an impossibly slower world. It is why mastery of network gates is even more insanely lucrative than Cecil Rhodes's gold mines. Think of the old Industrial Age power games for a moment, by way of comparison: Britain and Germany tried to match each other with their industrial output during a fatal competitive sprint 150 years ago. But imagine if network effects had obtained? If

Britain's initial head start in the Industrial Revolution had given them a 90 percent share of global trade? Germany would never have even tried to compete. They would have been the Friendster of the twentieth century: isolated, slow growing, powerless, and, finally, bankrupted or consumed. No need for World War I or World War II. But that was a different age.

6.

Once a billion people were connected, there was inevitably going to be something like Facebook, a gateland in which people can link to one another. Once everyone could record and watch and share videos, something like YouTube was going to emerge. This isn't to take anything away from the genius and management skill of the figures who have built these systems, but it is to say that we should be modest. The networks do *want* certain things. As we try to picture the world ahead of us, as we try to ask what tools of power we can acquire to twist this dangerous landscape into something we can manage and predict and control, we must always ask: *What does it want?*

The world wants a protocol for the fast exchange of money. It wants a basic language protocol. It wants a place to swap information about IT security holes. It wants instant translation systems to replace the need to learn English or Chinese or Spanish so that the world can move even faster. I believe it wants certain sorts of alliances, a particular type of superpower, and even craves a new form of politics. For any nation that controls these gatelands, there is the possibility of using that position to create still more gatekept platforms, to shape the protocols that tie platforms together in the way that roads or jet planes link the physical world. Of the twelve most popular mobile apps, nine are linked to systems such as Google, Apple, and Microsoft. This is the iron law of Gateland: Connectivity is power. It is the power to extend advantage even further. Gatekeeping is, at the end of the day, our most powerful point of control.

It won't surprise you that in recent years, for instance, the world has seen an acceleration in the construction of *physical* barriers, of fences and walls running between nations. Ron Hassner and Jason Wittenberg, two American political scientists, scored the pace of global wall building and found that of fifty-one national enclosures built since the end of World War II—the Berlin Wall being the most famous example—more than half were constructed in a rush between 2000 and 2014. More are coming: Hungary, Kenya, Algeria, and India now posthole their borders in initial exploration of what might be built. There's a frantic urgency to some of this. The Spanish government, for instance, raised a ten-foot-high razor-wire-and-camera-topped fence around their Saharan footholds in 1998. The enclosed land was controlled by Madrid, so it was technically "Europe," which made it an irresistible target for would-be migrants. The fence wasn't enough to stop the flows. So they built a second one to run around the first in 2001. Then, in 2005, thousands of desperate Africans launched a coordinated charge against the fences. A couple of dozen migrants died in the attempt; a thousand made it through. The Spanish responded with a third line of fence, this one twenty feet high, electric, watched by cameras.

Unlike traditional lines of defense—the Maginot Line or the Great Wall of China, for instance—the aim of twenty-first-century barriers in places such as Israel or the United States or Spanish Morocco has been less to stop a rolling-armor blitzkrieg than to slow the movement of smugglers and spies and criminals or the dashes of fleeing refugees. There's an affective and—to those on the inside—appealing asymmetry to these borders. They are mostly marked and built by richer, more modern, more stable nations desperate to control who comes in and goes out. The walls, fences, and trenches of the modern world seem to be getting longer, more ambitious, and better defended with each passing year, Hassner and Wittenberg concluded. The creation of gates is, we should sense now, the corollary of connection.

Reviewing the problems of deadly-disease contagion after the 2014–15 Ebola pandemic, Bill Gates examined this connection-and-gate lemma in worrisome historical terms. "There is a significant chance that an epidemic of a substantially more infectious disease will occur sometime in the next 20 years," he wrote. "In fact, of all the things that could kill more than 10 million people around the world, the most likely is an epidemic stemming from either natural causes or bioterrorism." This is the cost of a fast-moving, interconnected world. It is what floats free from the extension of Paul Virilio's line that if airplanes produce the airplane accident, networks will produce network accidents. Part of what made the Ebola response successful was that the response really was in the form of gates, not walls. These gates were protocols for biological reaction, for medical care, for epidemic monitoring, for the urgent helicoptering *in* of support and aid and ideas. The gates assembled around the Ebola pandemic were its solution. Had it merely been walled off, it would have spiked, grown, mutated, and finally escaped in an even more dangerous form. A world primed for contagion, Gates suggested, needs— and is missing—more and better gates. (Yes, here you can pause to do a double take at the serendipitously strange fact that the wealthiest citizen of our gated age is named Gates, just as the richest man in the era of pulling oil out of rocks a hundred years ago was named Rockefeller.)

For decades after the 1929 financial crisis triggered a historic global depression, economists and politicians debated what had gone wrong. What had they missed? The world had been wired with an economic system designed for rapid movement, but politicians and bankers had forgotten to put on the needed brakes. They had tried to run an industrial engine against the background of gasping political structures. Basic adjustment mechanisms—release valves for financial or currency pressures—had not been invented, refined, or installed. When we find ourselves, in coming years, gasping through some sort of financial crisis of our own, or running scared from a cascading military or social epidemic that slaps us unexpectedly, what do you think the most likely cause will be? It will be a failure of gates. Too few in some places, too many in others.

Remember the haunting, persistent vulnerability of our age. Any moment can present us with questions of war and peace. We're all like those poor Melian citizens. A challenge can show up at any instant. And a twitch anywhere in the system can rock and even crack the whole edifice. But today we have no central theory of gatekeeping, no ideas about balancing inside and outside. Anyone can see our systems are full of holes and inconsistencies. More gates will be with us from now on. "In a composite system," the computer researchers FX Lindner and Sandro Gaycken have written about our complex world, "there is no critical gate. Everything is a gate." And it is with this concept in mind that we can begin to develop a new approach to our safety.

CHAPTER TEN

Hard Gatekeeping

In which gates, operated with our new instinct, become at once a tool of prosperity and survival.

1.

Among the many modern Chinese foreign policy figures of the last century was a warm and warmly regarded man named Huang Hua, who lived from 1913 to 2010. His life spanned a period of dramatic change in China's world position. He was born in an age of near total national collapse; he passed away as the country was confronting the problems of fitting into a rapidly changing world. Huang was, in a sense, an heir to the Warring States diplomat Su Qin, whom Master Nan had named as an icon of insight: He had mastered the energy of a chaotic age 2,500 years ago. Huang Hua had been China's foreign minister and later a vice premier. He had penetrated the puzzles of Mao's revolutionary era and of the decades afterward to see the possibility of a different role for the country in the world, one he'd brought to vivid life after Deng Xiaoping ascended to the Chinese leadership in 1978.

Huang was always calm, with an easy and relaxed temperament. One of my favorite images of him is from the mid-1970s, when, while on a flight to the United States from Paris to take

China's seat at the United Nations, he was ambushed by Walter Cronkite. Huang is completely unflustered in the scratchy video of that encounter. He sits quietly in a cloud of smoke. Cronkite pesters him. Huang smiles, offers a cigarette to the news crew, and, though he is in the midst of a transit from the poverty, chaos, and smashed politics of China, he is nothing but serene, a statesman—not the nervous representative of a twitchy power.

Huang spoke nearly perfect English and was known not only for a fierce defense of his nation's interests, but for his unique feel for both Western and Chinese culture. And for the differences between them. "When Chinese want to do something, we begin with the question *What is the nature of the age?*" he was known to explain. "Westerners begin with *the goal*. What do they aim to achieve?" Chinese, Huang was saying, tend to look at any problem they face and begin by considering the conditions and environment around the problem. The context matters as much as the solution because, even if you think you've solved a specific problem, that context endures.

If the statesman's task of finding peace is like trying to balance teacups one upon the other, Chinese want to know: Is it windy? Where were the teacups made? Just how will they fit together? Westerners tended to focus on piling the cups. The problem at hand was always defined in the most direct possible way: Remove Saddam. Drone-strike the terrorists. Stop the financial crisis. The plan was: Just balance the teacups. It was the rare Western statesman who saw that the table on which the cups sat was missing a leg, or who felt an oncoming breeze kicking up. Some said the Chinese instinct to study the environment first had its roots deep in Chinese culture. The society had always been agricultural, so the weather had to be understood. And in China, the written word was made not of letters that could be focused on one after another, but of characters that were in fact little pictures.

The word for horse looks like a horse: 马. Understanding an essay or a poem in Chinese really does mean "seeing the whole picture," not merely following the letters. Chinese politics and foreign policy of the sort conducted by men such as Huang Hua and Su Qin had, as a result, begun with the same exact question for thousands of years: What is the nature of the age?

Deng's 1980s foreign policy, one Huang shaped and executed, had been an excellent example of how such a context-first calculation might affect the choices a leader makes. Mao, who ruled China before Deng came to power, had a darting and uneasy temperament. He was a revolutionary. And, perhaps not surprisingly, he believed his age was one of inevitable revolution. He prepared the country accordingly. Mao's China was honeycombed with bomb-proof tunnels, all dug as protection in case of foreign attack; he relocated Chinese industry to isolated and gaspingly poor mountain strongholds so that it could survive a long war; he reacted to foreign ideas and influence with a snapping electricity. One of his fellow revolutionaries, surveying the impoverished country after World War II and trying to think of how it could defend itself, slyly noted, "The one thing we do have lots of is mountains and tunnels." Mao used them. China was known for a protective isolation.

Deng, when he came to power in 1977, read the nature of his age differently. "There is no possibility of a great war. Don't be afraid of it, there is no risk of it," he assured a group of skeptical Chinese cadres during a chat in 1983. The cadres were having a hard time replacing their Maoist paranoia with confidence that China might safely open, develop, and change. They mixed the nervousness of a secret political party with the nightmares of a nation that had been invaded and abused by nine different countries since the mid-nineteenth-century Opium Wars. Military conflict seemed inevitable to them. "We used to worry about war and talk about its possibility every year," Deng told them. "It seems the worry was overdone." Deng felt the world was embarking on an unprecedented era of peace and development. Terrible, nation-demolishing wars would not soon victimize China, Deng thought. Nation *building* was the nature of the age. Its tools would be science, finance, and trade. If the Chinese people worked hard, he promised his incredulous listeners, they might by the year 2000 grow their thin per capita income of $250 to the nearly unimaginable target of $1,000.

"I don't care if the cat is white or black," Deng famously observed, "as long as it catches mice." Socialism? Capitalism? No matter, as long as it produced progress. This was a courageous judgment. And, it emerged, a correct one. No major wars engulfed China or the world. The great powers did not rush to contain the impoverished nation. Development was, for China, the name of the age. Deng sent men such as Huang Hua to help establish China's position back on the world stage. He recalled intellectuals and economists from the countryside to build new capitalist institutions. And he turned the energy of revolutionary leaders such as Xi Zhongxun (the father of a future Chinese president) to the task of building new economic projects that defied what Marx—and most of Western economics—predicted. In the end, Deng's black-and-white cat caught that $1,000 of per capita income nearly on the old man's schedule.

There is something admirable about a direct approach to problem solving, which begins with the idea that *the shortest distance between two points is a straight line*. But it is also true that this sort of elementary geometry can fool us. It does not describe, always, the best way to accomplish what we might intend. Particularly not today. The old maps, we've seen, are less effective. New maps, which are often made of new network links, are changing everything from finance to terrorism. What looks far apart on an old map can be nanoseconds apart on a network. These new dynamics are like a constant wind pushing on the teacup piles that our statesmen are trying to pile up. It's not merely that their plans go awry; it's that they don't sense the larger forces at work. Little suprise that it has been nearly impossible to predict and understand just why things are happening.

Huang Hua's question—*What is the nature of the age?*—turns out to be the first essential one for any endeavor. Get it wrong, and every subsequent decision will be wrong too. Do you think our age is one of easy, flat-world globalization? Do you believe the spread of democracy is inevitable? Or do you think we live in an age of global chaos and American decline? Or one in which a new caliphate will be established?

The importance of such a judgment before you begin to act reflects a statesman's honest understanding of just how much can't be controlled, how many different forces might knock down the teacups of a well-designed policy: people, politics, epochal forces of change. A spirit of cold caution refrigerates the passion out of the memoirs of nearly any experienced diplomat (or entrepreneur or politician.) "By himself, the individual can achieve nothing," the Prussian statesman Otto von Bismarck observed. "He can only wait until he hears God's footsteps resounding through events and then spring forward to grasp the hem of his mantle— that is all." What Bismarck, one of the titans of European states-manship, is confessing here is that the real secret of stability and power lies in mastering the forces of history: Enlightenment. Science. Industry. Nationalism. Technology.

What I want to do in this chapter is bring Bismarck's instinct to our own age. And I want to use it to address a fundamental problem of global politics: How will the world be ordered? You don't have to be a foreign policy expert to have a sense that new forces are at work, that the system of states and nations is changing in ways that are not yet quite understood. So much in our lives has been revolutionized in the past few decades—how we communicate, how we shop, even how we think. Businesspeople wonder how markets will be ordered. Politicians worry about how political systems will be reshaped. But the overarching question, the one that will decide war and peace, may matter most of all. And in that area we are embarking on a period of really historic change. There will be nowhere to hide from its impact. The networks, it turns out, tell us what the future of world order will likely be. And they reveal, as result, the strategy that the world's leading power, the United States, should pursue.

It is not, as you have probably guessed, the strategy that an older and industrial view of power would ever have suggested.

2.

What is the nature of our age?

The nature of our age has, I think, emerged clearly for us now. Constant connectivity taps like a hammer on the glass of most of our comfortable institutions. If Mao thought his era was one of "war and revolution," if Deng felt his age would be one of "peace and development," I think we can say our age will be one of "collapse and construction." Collapse of many of the old ideas and institutions we once relied upon; construction of new ones built for different power arrangements. The Seventh Sense—which is a feeling for how networks work that is joined to a sense of history and politics and philosophy—has let us understand the origins of this dynamic. It has shown us that disruption is not a sign of chaos or unpredictable surprise, even if it looks that way from the headlines. Rather, it marks a huge construction project. *Da po, da li,* the Chinese would say—great destruction *and* great construction, each tied to the spread of network forces. *Tap, tap, crack.* And then gatelands. These are new structures bred by connectivity. Financial markets are a gateland. Countries sharing intellectual property are gatelands. Facebook or Google or a cloud provider is a gateland. These gated worlds, which we now rely on to share and study everything from vacation photos to medical data, contain billions of people or trillions of sensors, chips, or switches. We've seen that networks of all kinds crave gates because it makes them more efficient on the inside. To be inside a gateland, we've seen, delivers the light-speed benefits of time compression. Everything can happen faster. And we've also learned that to be outside certain gatelands is to be cut off.

Back in Bismarck's era, nearly every revolution or war could be tied to energies emanating from Berlin. Nearly a century later, during the Cold War, the zero-sum competition between the United States and the Soviet Union framed every question of global affairs. Support South Vietnam? Put missiles in Cuba? All these demanded answers that suited the overarching ideological struggle then under way. In our own age, the problems we face all have roots in networks. Terror groups like ISIS rely on networks of connection and smuggling. The human waves of refugees produced by the crises in North Africa are torn up from their homes but remain connected by phones and data to a world they are trying to enter: Text messages mark the new geography where they live, as streets and schools once did. Networks are reshaping global economics, as we've seen, by rebalancing supply and demand. They are reshaping politics by encouraging extremism, linking like-minded people together in closed media circles. They are creating new landscapes of warfare in cyberspace. Many of the failures of policy in the last few years—from the war on terror to the battle to save the global economy—have been victories for network forces.

Faced with this new dynamic, American foreign policy makers are in a strange position. On the one hand, American networks and gates now hold a decisive position in the world. Thomas Paine's famous line that "the cause of America is in a great measure the cause of all mankind" still obtains, but with a twist: The networks of America—the country's essential webs of trade and information and technology and finance—are, for the moment, the networks of much of mankind. But America has not yet developed a strategic concept that reflects this reality or that seeks to use it in the pursuit of security or decency. And time is not on America's side.

If the traditional aim of American foreign policy was to prevent the emergence of a challenger that threatened the country (such as the Soviet Union) or to stop nations that aspired to isolate and manipulate Asia or Europe against Washington (as imperial Japan and Nazi Germany sought to do), the concern now is different. It is the mastery of network destiny. "Today the United States faces no existential threat," one well-regarded American think tank reported in 2015. This is wrong. It's true that no nation or terror group can hope to threaten America's very existence in the way the Soviet Union once did with promises such as "We will bury you!" But the loss of a position of decisive influence in the networks the world will rely on—not just the Internet, but all the linked systems of research and data and DNA—represents just such a potential threat. It's less that the United States will be "buried" but that the country certainly will be enmeshed. *Are you the gatekeeper or the gatekept?* This is the fundamental question of self-determination and power that emerges from the nature of our age. And it calls for Americans to consider a new approach to national security, one that might be called "Hard Gatekeeping."

3.

Hard Gatekeeping means the construction and development of secure, carefully designed communities to manage everything from trade to cyber-information to scientific research. Some of these will be for Americans only. Gatelands. Others will include allies. Each will be developed fresh, tuned for principles that reflect how network power operates. Today we're very nearly at one extreme: A world of few gates and walls. Groups like NATO or "nations on the Internet" or Sunni states all represent potential gatelands. But they operate now with little coordination. It was as if Americans thought Postel's old law of the early Internet—"Be liberal in what you accept"—fit every network.

In the years since the end of the Cold War, this instinct has helped encourage globalization. But the world is finding it is connected now in surprising ways. Forces that are inimical to the interests of the whole system are jacked into and using the technologies of the system against itself. It's not just terrorists or hackers who are gaming the system; nations are also pushing at the roots of the global order. The imbalance is easy to spot. That American research universities are training figures who will use what they learn to erode an American order suggests a kind of misplaced investment. The goal shouldn't be to shut essential systems down or to wall them off. That would kill them. Rather, a wiser strategy will make them run more tightly, and in a better-coordinated fashion, Gatelands. It's clear anyhow that ideas like "soft power" aren't providing any sort of order for the world. The "Don't do stupid things" assumption that history will just take care of itself—that capitalism and democracy will produce more capitalism and democracy—has not matched the facts.

There is tremendous leverage in deciding who is in or out of alliance or research or investment arrangements. But this approach has not been used effectively. I think that's mostly because foreign-policy figures don't have a clear picture of what they are aiming for, or they believe that time and globalization and democratization will solve all the problems the world faces. That seems unlikely. Better to work with what we know: Gated network orders are powerful. They run faster than purely open ones. And they offer not merely security, but influence: The cost of being excluded from gatelands of finance or information will be nearly total. Follow the lesson of technology markets, where entire industries are dominated by single winning companies. As we've seen, this is because networks deliver ever more rewards to winning systems. But designing, building, and implementing such a system will require a picture of a new order, and cold-blooded intensity to achieve it.

Any consideration of the "nature of our age" has to start with an awareness that everything around us now is or soon will be connected. This demand for connection is why old systems are collapsing and new ones, optimized for this hunger, are emerging. Cargo will move in an "Internet of Boxes" made more efficient by real-time tracking and precise scheduling. Our bodies will be watched and treated almost like an "Internet of Bodies." We will soon invest, learn, and live inescapably inside connected systems. There's a long list of items yet to be instantly, fully linked in this way. (And, if you're curious, a long list of problems of health and poverty and justice that might be solved in new ways as a result.) But the process of linking everything is as unstoppable as the footsteps of God that Bismarck was listening for. And that link produces gatelands.

Let's think about a mundane-sounding example: money. Over the next decade or so, printed bills and minted coins will largely disappear and will be replaced, first, by digital versions of money and then by entire new currencies, built for a world of bit-based transactions. A world populated by mobile phones and virtual banks will quickly clear away the smelly, papery vestiges of a cash economy. The strange act of taking money out of a machine and giving it to a person who then puts it into another machine will be replaced with something both simpler and more powerful: the ability to "press and pay" on all sorts of devices. But a "digital currency" is not merely a digital version of a printed dollar. Eventually certain types of money will exist only as bits. The simple version of this is that your boss can transfer your paycheck to you electronically, something that has already happened. The more sophisticated world of linked, digitized cash will let that money be distributed in different ways—as spending money, bits directed for certain types of investment, even bits locked up until your company (or you) hits certain performance targets.

Today, the most talked-about model for an all-digital currency is Bitcoin, a system based on the algorithmic creation of money mined from computation much as gold was once mined from the hills of California. Bitcoin's most appealing property is that it is not controlled by any government. It is meant to be free from political pressures, from the influence of central bankers, and from the risk of national default. If you're an Indonesian farmer or an Estonian cabdriver, the thinking goes, better to store your money in BTC than local cash. Bitcoin is easy to keep and transmit, and Bitcoin transactions can be made anonymously—which has attracted drug lords and tax evaders and bred a Bitcoin-fueled black-market economy too.

Bitcoin or something like it will have a role in our future, but another kind of digital currency will appear too, and it will form itself into a kind of gateland. Instead of being anonymous, backed only by algorithms, and unlinked to a government, as Bitcoin is, this currency will be built for reliability, not mystery. Bitcoin transactions are cloaked in secrecy; this new currency will be transparent, traceable. Bitcoin is free from government interference; this digital currency will be backed by a major government and tied intimately into policy and credit. Imagine that the United States began to issue Bitdollars—traceable, controllable digital currency backed by the security of America's economic position. While many people might still prefer Bitcoins (or Bitrubles or Bityuan), the answer to the question *What's your safety currency?* won't change much just because you put the prefix "Bit" in front of it.

Today the world of paper dollars is a gateland too: Everyone accepts dollars, so American cash is a kind of global reference currency. But just as we saw earlier how English will be displaced not by Chinese or Spanish but by real-time translation, the old paper $100-bill economy of the world will eventually be replaced in many areas by Bitdollars. Because it's connected to a database, for instance, a Bitdollar can be earmarked for specific purposes. Think of foreign aid—and consider the billions of dollars of well-intentioned loans or grants, paid in cash, that have been turned into Monte Carlo apartments instead of schoolrooms. Aid processed digitally could be traced and watched. It could be easily updated and enhanced to handle fluctuations in commodity prices or changes in demand. A connected world is one where Iraqi shopkeepers, Nigerian schoolteachers, and Dominican nurses are tied to digital tools for saving and spending money. A Bitdollar solution solves any number of problems that confront a traditional currency. And it will also—and this is where it becomes important—become a gateland. Those teachers and nurses will be gatekept, in a sense, by this currency, which will help guarantee they get the money in the first place and then offer all sorts of new ways to save and use it efficiently. But what sort of digital currency will it be? Who will back this new gateland?

Currency has not yet really been touched by connectivity in the way, for example, that videos have—a process that created a "winner take all" gateland company in YouTube. That will change. Finance of the future will be filled with gatelands to make transactions safer, more reliable—and to Bit-fit money tightly to policy or personal aims: savings, an education, even what we buy. And control of that enclave will be a source of real power—and a place of certain competition. It will be possible to decide who is in or out of such a system instantly—to switch off Russian oligarchs, for instance, and to lock in aid workers.

Just as the Marshall Plan after World War II guided America's work in building a new global order, the country now perhaps needs a plan to build (or redesign) all of the systems that will determine future power—and to do so as gatelands. Remember the nature of the age: Collapse and construction. The United States should, obviously, introduce Bitdollars (just as China has begun to introduce a digital currency). But that's only a start. Our world, if we'd like to picture it in twenty or thirty years' time, will be defined by newly constructed gatelands, each essential in some way to national or economic security. Trade, finance, education, cybersafety, artificial intelligence, and military affairs will move from unconnected to connected. They will reveal new strengths as a result. And the logic of gatekeeping will obtain in nearly every case. To hold the pen that designs these systems is a position of historic importance.

The reason for this power is not merely that gatelands will support trade or e-commerce. Rather, it is tied back to that crucial idea of Metcalfe's: As systems grow more powerful, the price of not being inside rises rapidly. If everyone else at Stanford is using Metcalfe's Ethernet to swap emails and you're not part of it, it's like a kind of exile. Today many systems respond to this logic: The more people who use Google, the smarter it gets. Imagine trying to do research on nuclear weapons in Iran without access to an instant database of chemical or engineering data. It would still be possible, but it would be more difficult. And research on artificial intelligence, cybersecurity, or modern electronic finance? It will be impossible without connection to global systems.

Many future gatelands will express their power as much by cutting nations or people out as by counting them in. Imagine if you were not allowed to transact in the new Bitdollars. You'd be cut off from a trading order. What if hospitals in your country were removed from a closed network of artificially intelligent medical-data exchange systems? Or consider cybersecurity. In the future, there are likely to be only a handful of databases that fully catalog and analyze the security holes and exploits plaguing the world's computers or networks. These digital-age Centers for Disease Control will run with that gateland logic we've come to appreciate: One will dominate. And as more people use that system, it will get smarter. To be inside this technological immune system will ensure the security of a nation's essential topology; to be outside will mean the constant danger of exploitation. This sort of leverage creates a possibility of diplomacy. One might say to a country considering the development of nuclear weapons: Build your own cybersecurity database if you like. It will be isolated and will not have the benefits of knowing what is happening on the wider network. Or, if you'd like to be protected in the best possible way, then you are welcome to join the gated system. But only under certain conditions: No nuclear research.

"Every new age and every new epoch in the coexistence of peoples," the historian Carl Schmitt once wrote, "is founded on new spatial divisions, new enclosures, and new spatial orders of the earth." Schmitt was contemplating the great Mediterranean empires and the power trails of Asian chieftains. But his insight touches every age, our own included. To make a nation, to build an empire, is to draw lines or push at borders or smash older gates. Some of this gating or gate-crashing appears as the martial ambition of a Napoleon or a Hitler (whom Schmitt unwisely advised); often it is simple protection. Lord Balfour, serving as the British foreign secretary in 1918, contemplated this problem from his imperial vantage point and observed, "Every time I come to a discussion—at intervals of, say, five years—I find there is a new sphere which we have got to guard," he wrote. "Those gateways are getting further and further away from India, and I do not know how far west they are going to be brought by the General Staff." This problem of where, exactly, to put the gates confronts us as well. We can at least say that the strategic position of any nation or terror group or business is not going to be secured by industrial measures alone. No one at Google wants to build a newspaper. No one in Al Qaeda is trying to float an aircraft carrier. Rather, power will be measured in the construction and control of gatelands.

Hard Gatekeeping is about more than just building gates. It also demands a statesman's feel for where to put them. Gates will direct movements of people and flows of capital and data. So in the same way that Karl Wittfogel's hydrologically inclined emperors (and their hydro-despot ministers) guided water to loyal parts of their kingdom and parched others, the world's gates should be placed to support strategic aims. The historian Arnold Toynbee once recalled passing a moment with the British prime minister Lloyd George during the 1919 Paris Peace Conference as the winning powers were deciding how best to arrange the world. "Lloyd George, to my delight, had forgotten my presence," Toynbee wrote, "and had begun to think aloud. 'Mesopotamia...yes... oil...irrigation...we must have Mesopotamia; Palestine...yes...

the Holy Land...Zionism...we must have Palestine; Syria... h'm...what is there in Syria? Let the French have that.'" This sort of charmless arrogance—*The Holy Land...we must have that*—doesn't much suit our age. Gatekeepers, after all, depend on the good will of the gatekept. But Lloyd George's comprehensive view should be a model. What oil and irrigation and Suez were to the British Empire, finance and data flows and gates are to our age.

4.

Hard Gatekeeping echoes the postures of some of the most enduring orders in human history—the "defense in depth" of the Roman Empire, for instance, or the protective isolation of Tokugawa Japan or the walls of Han China. The aim of these systems was to survive through defense. Strategists of those empires learned they should avoid attack except when absolutely necessary; a defensive posture was safer. Gatekeeping is similar. It resists unnecessary profligacy.

Hard Gatekeeping can be summarized simply: The development and control of the physical and topological spaces that will define any nation's future security. Financial markets. Information and physical infrastructures. Trading blocs. Alliance structures. Technology cooperatives. Currency arrangements. The goals of Hard Gatekeeping are also simple to state: to protect those inside the gated order, to make security and innovation more efficient, to accelerate certain kinds of connection and dampen others, to manage links to the non-gatekept world, and to use that "in or out" leverage to affect the interests and plans of others.

In practice, the United States might develop Hard Gatekeeping on the basis of a few elementary principles:

First, Hard Gatekeeping must keep America and anyone inside the country's gated order safe. Americans feel insecure today, and for good reason. Many of the country's traditional allies share this sense of insecurity. Hard Gatekeeping means better borders for all nations and deeper ties between nations inside various gatelands. The strategy doesn't mean walls, since such isolation makes no sense in a world of connection. But it does mean updating that philosophy of "Be liberal in what you accept" to "Be generous and cautious in what you accept. Be secure." In practical terms this means a new "Marshall Plan," not to rebuild Europe as in the 1940s, but to construct secure gatelands that can enclose all of America's interests and allies. This might mean rebuilding a new Internet designed for an age of digital threats. It means developing new ways to coordinate economic policy and trade and investment. The world should expect that the opening attacks of future wars—directed at the United States or allies that it must defend—will come invisibly and silently through networks or from space, not from noisy land invasions or bombing runs. But the United States and its allies have not yet agreed on how to handle such dangers. Topological security will become what air superiority or sea mastery once was. Well-built gates will offer more than protection. They will be a source of time and leverage. Alliances and gatelands and infrastructure that can be defended for long periods will deliver the honestly earned confidence of the truly secure. This represents a fundamentally defensive posture.

A second principle might be that America will not force anyone else into its gated systems. The aim should simply be to build the best-performing network order. American values of democratic choice, freedom of thought, and privacy should flavor the design of its gatelands—even more than they do today. Personal security and freedom should be a principle that everyone inside such systems can be assured of—as well as rule of law, transparency about how decisions are made, and democratic accountability. Other nations will design their gated enclosures for different values, marked by national political needs or historical burdens of their own. America should be relaxed as Europe and Russia and China build gated systems. The desire for self-determination, to be the gatekeeper and not the gatekept, reflects sensible, understandable urges. But it seems likely that American-led gatelands, if they are designed in line with American values, can be among the best and most reliable of these future structures. And that "winner take all" nature of power means that many mid-sized and smaller nations may have no other choice but to enter an American-led system. Forcing them into that enmeshment is unnecessary. It would painfully complicate their domestic politics. "Gatekeeper or gatekept?" No more profound political question exists. Nations should be free to select their own terms of enmeshment.

A third principle might be that America should welcome other countries into its gates, but carefully and with a cost. Today, America permits nearly any nation to plug into the country's markets or technologies or education systems. This made sense for an age when connection brought only benefits. And a basic instinct for that sort of openness should be part of any American strategy, but it must be tempered by a recognition of the risks and benefits of a linked age. It doesn't make sense to hand the advantages of the system to groups intent on undermining it. Totally open commodity markets are subject to price manipulation. Completely open technology standards can be hijacked too easily. Wide-open artificial-intelligence systems may be manipulated against their users. A better approach in every case would be to measure this openness, to ensure that the nations inside these gated worlds share a vision of the global system and a commitment to keeping it intact.

Fourth, no nation should be permitted to force another inside its own gates. India might develop a great search engine; the country should not be allowed to demand that Bangladeshis use it. Russia's energy companies can lay reliable gas channels to Europe; they should not drive their use with military pressure. This principle is a sensible balance to an American commitment not to compel anyone into U.S. gatelands. Every country must find its own path. The establishment of a world based on states and nations was a result of the Thirty Years' War, and the historical lesson of that conflict was that countries should decide their own domestic arrangements. Then, the specific problem was whether each king could determine the religion of his own state or if it could be dictated from Rome. The treaties that ended the war enshrined the earlier idea of *Cuius regio, eius religio* as a governing principle of international relations. "Whose realm, his religion." Catholic king? Catholic state.

Should one gatekept order demand that other nations use its protocols? Should the United States or Germany force the other to obey the rules of trade, data tracking of citizens, or research that obtain at home? No. *Cuius regio, eius reticulum*, we might say. "Whose realm, his network." And on that basis some degree of interconnection can be discussed. To the question *What would America fight against in a gatekept world?* one answer is *America would resist any attempt by one country to force another into a gated order.*

Fifth, America should not permit the emergence of any means to destroy the gatekept systems it builds. Networks are not invulnerable. In fact, their very design includes certain weaknesses. They can be collapsed by contagion or strikes against crucial nodes. America's primary strategy to limit risk should be defensive—better gates deter attack. And attack means exclusion for the attacker, a much higher price now than in the past. But the United States would be foolish to stop there. Gates, the Trojans would remind America, are not enough. When truly existential dangers emerge—nuclear weapons, certain types of artificial intelligence, or terrorism—then the country must attack, and fast. America is far too complacent about arms control today. The failure to stop nuclear proliferation must be reversed; and work to stop proliferation of technological dangers such as artificial intelligence viruses or space weapons needs to begin immediately. Hard Gatekeeping gives us diplomatic leverage to pursue such projects. But it also should include a readiness to strike. This means developing military and diplomatic stratagems aimed at destroying the topological and real-world anchors of American enemies. Those forces will be hammering every American interest; the country should feel unembarrassed about moving quickly to disarm dangers.

5.

Hard Gatekeeping is an approach that can be laid on any number of security problems. It provides a picture of strategy in the same way that "containment" or "balance of powers" once did. In the Middle East, for instance, it might suggest the construction of an American-led defensive alliance, complete with isolated and protected territorial areas. In trade, these principles could help develop more and better systems such as the Trans-Pacific Partnership. In confronting ecological challenges such as global warming, a Hard Gatekeeping approach might suggest finding ways to fund the costs of industrial retooling—and to pressure reluctant nations into action by demanding action in exchange for access to other gated areas such as trade or technology. But let's look in more detail at one example, U.S.–China ties, a troubling puzzle whose resolution may be the decisive act of policy in the next century.

The dominant view of future relations between Americans and Chinese is generally not optimistic. History, after all, is filled with examples of rising and established powers that, despite heroic diplomatic efforts and even shared interests, end up at war. To some degree this reflects one of the most sobering problems of international politics, something historians know as "the security dilemma." If you or I want to be safer at home by bolstering the house's alarm system or putting bars on the windows, it's no threat to anyone else. International politics is not so simple. When nations seek security by making themselves strong, they often unnerve their neighbors in the process. Germany in the 1890s realized that the British navy could snap the country's trade arteries. So the kaiser ordered more battleships. Britain felt compelled to respond. An arms race ensued, and each country, chasing its own security, ended up *less* secure. This is the dilemma, a puzzle like one of those woven-wicker finger traps. The harder each side pulls to get out, the more stuck it becomes. America in 2012 pivoted her military gaze to Asia. China felt encircled and deepened essential national security reform. America weighed just how much of a threat this could be.

In one sense, then, it's possible to sense the angry energy of an impending collision. Beijing and Washington are enacting the old historical pattern. But so much in our world looks different after connected dynamics are applied. Might connection change the nature of this possible enmity? The two countries are, after all, part of the same connected skein. Network theory has shown us already that America's greatest threat is less China or Russia or terrorism than it is the overall evolution of the topological landscape of power. The evolution of global networks challenges Beijing too. So we might consider the logic at work: If China is not America's biggest danger, if America is not China's, what might be developed?

Hard Gatekeeping applied to China policy should begin as it would anywhere—with a summary of American aims: "The United States believes the world is entering a period of revolutionary change. A shift in global arrangements is necessary and probably inevitable. America will build a gatekept order consistent with its values. The country will welcome others to participate—but with conditions. The United States will resist attempts to force nations into any gatekept order; the country will fight any forces that threaten disruption of the overall design." The China policy that emerges from this view is clear enough: America will not seek to contain China, and it will not force China to change. Rather, Washington will develop a secure gatekept network for its own use. Economics, trade, security, and technology will be rebuilt for a linked age as part of a comprehensive national approach. China is welcome to develop its own system and see whom the country might attract. But China—like every nation—will not be permitted to compel other nations to join. And if China wants to join in the construction of a gatekept system, then a path to deeper cooperation on everything from nuclear proliferation to the establishment of new international bodies will offer examples of shared projects. The two countries can begin, at least, with a joint picture of what they aim to achieve—and with plenty of places to practice cooperation.

We should remember that China and America have many shared worries. The international order is not working as well as it might. It does not appear engineered for new stresses. Global disorder would land on China's hopes for development with a profound pressure. It is in cooperation on the reform of that system that the two nations share an interest. And it is in a successful defensive posture of a gatekept network order that Washington can cultivate the linked, leveraged moves that might lead to trust and cooperation. While there might be a temptation among some

Americans to build gatelands with the imperial spirit of a man like Lloyd George—*We need the Middle East. Grab it. We need digital-currency mastery. Take it!*—such efforts will only ensure collision. The process will have to be open and cooperative. It will demand new approaches to diplomacy. Mostly it will require a picture of what the goal is: a gated order, secure for the United States' needs, attractive to others, and carefully managed.

Is it really possible to think that the United States and China could work together on such a project? One appealing element of Hard Gatekeeping from a U.S. perspective is that this does not matter. The system America builds should be designed to operate with or without Beijing's agreement—though it should also be flexible enough to encourage cooperation. There is a lesson from another network that applies here: biology. In natural systems facing systemic pressures—an ice age, a flood—species often work together. The scientists John Maynard Smith and Eörs Szathmáry, in their masterwork *The Major Transitions in Evolution*, chronicle the march of life toward ever-greater complexity—from cells to humans to societies—as a story of ceaseless, successful collaboration. In particular, they spot not merely evolution but also "coevolution": species in an ecosystem that become more fit by changing *together* in the face of common challenges. For example, the Amazon rain forest heats up because of global warming. Flowers grow longer petals to protect their stamens. Pollinating birds in turn develop longer beaks to reach inside. Each species changes in response to an outside force. Both become more fit. The essential facilitating feature of all evolution has been the ability of organisms to change together—to cooperate and not merely compete. Successful evolution was, Smith and Szathmáry found, always *coevolution*. "The applicability of the concept," they concluded, "extends across the whole of social and natural sciences." If America can be secure behind gates of its own design, it also creates a new, powerful basis for cooperation with other nations—China among them.

6.

A world of gatelands awaits us. But this leaves a final question: How will power distribute itself among those systems? While it has become commonplace to argue that networks undermine American power, the logic of gatelands—and the lessons of history—suggests the country might play an even more central role in the century ahead. We can already see how, as the world becomes filled with crises of a revolutionary age, the stability of American markets or military strength has a new appeal. A decade ago most nations in the world were asking for American soldiers to leave. Now, from Europe to Asia, there are constant requests for military support from Washington. That logic of gatelands, in which a single system dominates because the whole system benefits as a result, also applies to problems of world politics. It should help dispel the fashionable view, even among American thinkers, that the country faces an era of relative decline. Yes, in sheer GDP terms, the United States economy may not be as dominant as it once was, but the country can still control many of the most important gatelands that will emerge, simply by building systems that fit its own needs. In per capita GDP, America may hold a dominant position for another century, and it's not clear that mere spending power is a measure of influence.

American gatelands for trade or finance or security will, if they work, have an alluring power. This is not to say that American security demands isolation or a focus on domestic problems only. That's too much of a risk in an age where the world is linked instantly to us. The right answer is to describe and then jointly build a world of gatelands, for the United States and for other nations that share the same vision of a world order.

Most traditional foreign policy looks at history and sees a constant, violent rocking of a "balance of power." One nation is up for a few years, then taken down by others. This is, after all, the order that dominated Europe for much of the past five hundred years. It's the reason some figures argue that America's time as a dominating power is now up. But history is not only filled with baton passing: France to England to the United States. Even a casual familiarity with all of human history will remind you that there have been long periods in which a single power dominates some portion of the world. Asia, Europe, the Middle East, South America all bred nations that stretched mastery of the system for generations. China led East Asia's order from the 1300s to the 1800s. Assyrian imperial arrangements overmastered a dozen smaller states from the ninth to the seventh centuries BCE. The Delhi Sultanate managed hegemony in South Asia from the twelfth to the fourteenth centuries. The Mughals enjoyed nearly two hundred years of dominance, starting in the sixteenth century. The Romans managed centuries of Mediterranean control. In fact, the political scientists Stuart Kaufman, Richard Little, and William Wohlforth have mapped the rise and fall of these nations and empires over millennia and concluded that about half of human history has been marked by a single dominant power in parts of the world.

Kaufman and his colleagues, as they considered the results of their survey, noticed that empires that endured ran with great efficiency. They possessed tools of power that permitted the assembly of an empire at unusually low cost in terms of lives and gold and effort. New territories brought in more than they cost. The great powers of history fused easy expansion and high returns. They grew, in short, just like the networks we've been studying. "Rome rose because it combined the strengths of traditional Republican institutions with innovations that gave it a unique capacity for inclusion of foreigners," the researchers explained. "Magadha was the most administratively durable of the ancient Indian states; and Qin, with the self-strengthening reforms of Shang Yang— economic reforms and military conscription as well as bureaucratic innovations—developed the most penetrating and brutally effective state structure in its international system." The Incas, the Han, and nearly every other long-standing empire ran with this attractive logic. Modern network systems, where new nodes— sensors, allies, algorithms—can be added at low cost, may grow with historically unprecedented ease.

Will a new, powerful empire emerge from the control of networks? The logic of connection suggests that it should. If you take that view—and accept the implication of a really long run for American power still to come—it changes the nature of what might be done in the face of Huang Hua's question. What if the "nature of the age" is that it will support a single strong network power? That mankind now craves gates and a gatekeeping mechanism? Networks evolve, as we've seen, toward what makes them most efficient. The model of single winners should influence our imagination. The task of American statesmen in the coming period will be to craft a new sort of international system. They will have to lead and inspire people in the United States and elsewhere away from temptations of isolation. They will lead a world organized on historically new principles. The best of them will be alive with the Seventh Sense. And they will lead nations whose citizens have it, too. How will that happen? It's to this final piece of our puzzle that I want to turn now.

CHAPTER ELEVEN

Citizens!

*In which the Seventh Sense rescues us from
an unexpected danger.*

1.

I never needed much incentive to go see Pattie Maes. Belgian, usually dressed in some black, fashionable getup, she is like a human shot of espresso. You ended every conversation wide awake, eyes open. When I first met her, in the 1990s, she was in charge of much of the work on artificial intelligence (AI) at MIT's Media Lab, Danny Hillis's old home. Maes had arrived at MIT in 1990 and almost immediately turned to the problem of making machines that might think. One day, as we were discussing just how the strange miracle of computer thought might occur, she introduced me to a puzzle of her field that has stayed on my mind in the years since. It is called the disappearing AI problem.

Back in the 1990s, as the Internet was emerging into popular consciousness, Maes and her team were tinkering with what was known as computer-aided prediction. This was an advance on the ping-pong conversations that Joseph Weizenbaum had coerced from ELIZA in the 1960s. Maes intended to design a computer that could ask, for instance, what movie stars you like. "Robert

Redford," you'd type. And then the machine would spit back some films you might enjoy. The Paul Newman classic *Cool Hand Luke*, for instance. And, well, you *had* liked that film. This seemed magic, just the sort of data-meets-human question that showcased a machine learning and thinking. An honestly *artificial* intelligence. Maes hoped to design a computer that could predict what movies or music or books you or I might enjoy. (And, of course, buy.) A recommendation engine. We all know how sputtering our own suggestion motors can be. Think of that primitive analog exchange known as the First Date: *Oh, you like Radiohead? Do you know Sigur Rós?* Pause. *Hate them.* Can you really predict what albums or novels even your closest friend will enjoy? You might offer an occasional lucky suggestion. But to confidently bridge your knowledge of a friend's taste and the nearly endless library of movies and songs and books? Beyond human capacity. It seemed an ideal job for a thoughtful machine.

The traditional approach to such a problem was to devise a formula that would mimic your friend. What are his hobbies? What areas interest him? What cheers him up? Then you'd program a machine to jump just as deep into movies and music and books, to break them down by plot and type of character to see what might fit your friend's interests. But after years building programs that tried—and failed—to tackle the recommendation problem in this fashion, the MIT group changed tack. Instead of teaching a machine to understand you (or Tolstoy), they simply began compiling data about what movies and music and books people liked. Then they looked for patterns. People were not, they discovered, all that unique. Pretty much everyone who liked Redford in *Downhill Racer* loved Newman in *The Hustler*. Anyone who enjoyed Radiohead's *Kid A* could be directed safely to Sigur Rós's *Ágætis Byrjun*.

Maes and her team found themselves, as a result, less focused on the mechanics of making a machine think than on devising formulas to organize, store, and probe data. What had begun as a problem of artificial intelligence became, in the end, a puzzle of mathematics. The mystery of human thought, that great, unknowable sea of chemicals and instinct and experience that would have let you place your finger on just the song to open the heart of your date, had been unlocked by data. Here was the disappearing AI problem. A puzzle that looked like it needed computer intelligence demanded, in the end, merely math. The AI had disappeared.

For several decades this accidental digital magic trick—*Hey, where'd the AI go?!*—bedeviled machine intelligence. It gave the entire thinking-machines enterprise a bit of an occultish flavor. Many problems that once seemed to demand the miracle of thought really only needed data. The human was still doing the thinking; the computer was simply computing. It was extremely easy to draw a line between where the biological ended and the digital commenced. This was a puzzle that had been, in a sense, anticipated at the very dawn of the digital revolution by the mathematician Alan Turing in a paper called "Computing Machinery and Intelligence," which he published in 1950. "Can machines think?" Turing began. His idea was to test this question in the following way: Have a research subject—a secretary, a graduate student, anyone—chat with an invisible interlocutor by way of a keyboard. Then ask, *What are you connected to? Another human? A machine?*

Turing figured you could call a machine artificially intelligent if it could fool a user into thinking it was human. "Please write me a sonnet on the subject of the Forth Bridge," Turing suggested a tricky user might ask. What computer could possibly know about this famous Scottish landmark, to say nothing of being able to rhyme a word with "Forth"? When the response came back, "Count me out on this one. I never could write poetry," you'd think that sounded awfully human. "Add 34957 to 70764," Turing suggested you might fire back. Say the computer pauses. Then, thirty seconds later, "105621." Are you dealing with a clever machine here? A dim, honest, slow-multiplying human? Impossible to tell. The distinction between machine and man blurred a bit.

Buried in the very premise of Turing's test was an assumption about what machines can do and how they might do it. "The idea behind digital computers may be explained by saying that these machines are intended to carry out any operations which could be done by a human computer," Turing said. His smart machines would be tuned by humans to do human tasks, in a human sort of way. Do math. Write poetry. His test of artificial intelligence was designed to figure out if a computer could think like a human. You and I might be able to spot patterns in movie habits, given enough time, but as more complex problems emerge, as a world of a trillion connected points becomes a sea of data to examine, there is no chance we'll match the machines. This opened a then–nearly unimaginable possibility: What if someday a computer could think *better* than a human? Could, in a nanosecond, come back with that elusive rhyme for "Forth": *north?* For such a machine, passing Turing's test—thinking like a human—would be trivially easy, like giving an SAT to a PhD student. In his 1950 paper, Turing raised the possibility of this development—and wondered if a crisis of sorts might follow. Could man handle the crushing sensation that a device was outperforming him? Perhaps dramatically? "We like to believe that Man is in some subtle way superior to the rest of creation," Turing wrote. "It is best if he can be shown to be necessarily superior, for then there is no danger of him losing his commanding position."

This represented the possibility of a different kind of disap-pearing AI, gone from our vision not because it was so simple but because it was so complex that we'd have no way of understanding how it arrived at its insights. You could know that Maes's machine recommended Paul Newman because it had found that millions of people who like Robert Redford also like him. But what if the origins of that solution, so clearly correct, were inscrutable? Imagine a machine intelligence set loose to explain the origins of the universe at a speed of trillions of calculations per second. It would quickly spin past Newton's and Einstein's laws and into a realm of physics apprehensible only inside its own electronic consciousness, compacting time—centuries of human scientific labor reproduced in moments—before shooting far ahead, alone, to a subtle knowledge we could only envy. Such a machine would not, as Newton had, stand on the shoulders of giants so much as it would muscle its own way to truth. The AI would have disappeared, but to a place very different from where Maes's AI had gone. Hers had been erased by human design. This new, really "thinking" AI would slip into invisibility because of its own light-speed cognition. It would think itself out of our understanding. No human could follow, limited as we are by our wet, slow, decaying biological software. Humans and computers, after all, deal with information differently. Think of how poor your memory is compared with the perfect fidelity of a machine, or think of the way people can "remember" events that never happened. These new thinking machines would have more than knowledge. They would, in some sense, begin to possess a profound and inscrutable wisdom. They would inhabit an honestly miraculous gateland of "thought" and ideas that no human could ever enter. And this is where the problems would begin.

2.

The revolution we now face is not only one of connection. It touches on something deeper still, which is what the nature of our relationship to technology will be. When we are connected all the time, it means that the tools and techniques of that connection have a special power. They shuffle us into gatelands, for instance. They decide what we do and don't know about our friends and family. They change our habits of learning and how we entertain ourselves. And, amazingly, they let us compress time. Network links will be forceful tools to save lives in the future—and they will also be the root of terrifying new weapons. The world ahead, as we've seen, will be one not merely of connection, but of ever-faster connection.

As the world accelerates on networks, as the pace of finance and learning and really any connected activity picks up, the fast, high-fidelity observations and calculations of machines will become inseparable from nearly every discipline. We'll need machine intelligence to make sense of the world that comes flooding back at us through hundreds of billions of sensors. We'll integrate such systems into our lives to augment all kinds of daily experiences— we already do this with GPS navigation and fitness trackers and auto-trading hedge funds. And just as citizens of the Enlightenment once had to think about how they'd relate to each other in an era when kings no longer made that decision for them, so we'll now need to think about how we design and use these machines. In this way, the very newest technology demands not simply a feeling for how machines work but also an instinct for the oldest, truest ideas about how human levers of power and hope operate.

The machines, like the New Caste that builds them, will have, after all, their own version of the Seventh Sense. All that data will give them a subtle, profound sense of what is happening on the network. If Master Nan worried that so much data jammed so quickly into our brains would cause a short, the computers will thrive on more and more connection. They will become more acute, more insightful in their judgment to the same degree that the human mind finds itself overwhelmed. Just as computers can see better, hear better, and remember longer than we can, so the device webs of our future will own a new, essential sense of what is happening on a whole system. We are at the moment that worried Alan Turing, the instant when man and machine confront each other and man has to ask, *Wow, do I really let this thing gatekeep me?*

Humans alone already no longer train the very best machines: The devices teach themselves now, to some extent. Of course, there are still decades of adjustment, of leaps in hardware and programming, to eliminate the seams between our minds and the fused ideas of a digital system. But the humans in the loop of the best of these designs, hardworking and well-meaning geniuses of the New Caste, are as much trainers as engineers now. They can build machines to play Go, diagnose disease, and wreck computer systems with a speed and success that their designers alone could not achieve. They resemble shipbuilders of an earlier era, preparing vessels for voyages to lands they will never themselves see. Every moment, all around us, machines are educating themselves. About the world. About themselves. About us too. Tuned AI plays games, looks at photos, studies chemical reactions, reads your email, and watches you drive—and then it tries to unspool just what is going on before winding it up into a new instinct: What is he going to do next? They may be better able to guess our next moves than we can. Machine learning systems already produce mathematical proofs that exist beyond what a human mind can understand, a machine-to-machine mathematics that expands the dimensions of thought. (In a man-and-machine fusion that surely would have unnerved Joseph Weizenbaum of ELIZA, the theoretical mathematician Doron Zeilberger now names his computer as a coauthor of his papers.)

The AI systems designer Roger Grosse has named two paths

to this sort of wired sensibility: predictive learning and representation learning. That first approach is what Maes's movie machine pursued. The computer is simply checking what it encounters against a database. It teaches itself to predict based on what has been seen before. This sort of knowledge begins with massive amounts of data and then hunts for patterns, tests their reliability, and improves by mapping quirks and similarities. Google engineers have a device that can gaze into a human eye and spot signs of impending optical failure. Is the machine smarter than your ophthalmologist? Hard to know, but let's just say this: It has seen, studied, and compared millions of eyes to find patterns that nearly perfectly predict a diagnosis. It can review in seconds more cases than your doctor will see in a lifetime—let alone recall and compare at submillimeter accuracy. Fast, thorough predictive algorithms make what might once have been regarded as AI disappear. The machine isn't all that wise; it just knows a lot.

On the other path, the one of representation learning, the machine uses a self-sketched image of the world, a "representation." Say you wanted a computer to identify restaurants with outdoor seating. A predictive system might be told, *Look for pictures in which a third of the pixels are sky colored.* You can see how such a primitive approach might be limited. But a representation-based program would use a neural network to examine thousands of photos—such a collection is called "training data"—of restaurant patios. It would develop its own sense of what makes these images special: sunlight glinting off glasses, sky reflected in silverware. It would assemble, bit by bit, an accurate feeling for the features of an outdoor dining space. And over time, it could aspire to near-perfect fidelity. Computers using predictive methods to recognize numbers pulled from a database of scrawled handwriting, for instance, can now identify 90 percent of the images. But representation-based models can screen millions of handwritten sentences with nary a mistake. Faces, disease markers, obscure sounds—all these become scrutable with AI-made models not because the machines have been told what to look for but because they've figured it out. The AI is actually starting to think, in this fashion, much as a child might build an understanding of traffic rules just by watching Mom drive every day. And imagine if that child could remember everything perfectly and compare notes at fiber-optic speed with millions of other kids. Pretty soon, it would be outperforming Mom.

Today, basic versions of representational AIs can study a map and name the most important roads. They can predict cracks in computer networks days before a fault. Representation-based programs take longer to train, as you might expect. But these training times are getting shorter. And though representational AIs are harder to program—and they demand almost unimaginable amounts of computing power—they produce a subtle, lively kind of insight. A machine with a prediction-based understanding of classical music can listen to a clip of a symphony and name it. One with a representation-based understanding of, say, Mozart's forty-one symphonies can write you an extremely convincing forty-second symphony—or, if you wish, an even earlier First Symphony, based on what it knows about Mozart's evolution as a composer. It can do it again and again. In seconds. The basic attitude of the researchers behind this technology runs, they confess, like this: Mozart was a fantastic composer. If he wrote even more symphonies, they'd probably be great too. Unfortunately, he's dead. Wouldn't it be nice if we could sample his old symphonies and make new ones whenever we wanted?

In the future we'll invite machines and their representations into our lives to help with many of the problems we face, not merely to make up for Mozart's inconvenient mortality. Machine learning will help sharpen our sadly dimming memories, keep us safe, and even help us create. AI-enabled systems will rely on vast, instantly updated networks to tell us things that we can't see or would never notice in the first place. *Don't visit that office; everyone's sick.* They will use the ability to model thousands of possible outcomes of any choice to provide us with "feedforward"—an ability to learn from the future and not merely the past. Or they will know to jam our brains full of the right chemicals at the right time: *Here's a Diplo track to put you in the mood to go for a run. You really need to exercise, Dave.* In the same way that computerized auto-landing systems can now bring airplanes safely through a fog bank to a completely socked-in airport, so intelligent machines will help us penetrate the mists around complicated science problems. They will protect us from accidents of our own. Too much financial risk. Bad educational choices. Poor music suggestions on a first date. But the price is that we won't quite understand just why they know so much. "AI is both freedom from programming *and* freedom from understanding," runs one standard summary of this paradox.

Just as an age without connection will one day seem strangely antique, so will a world without the constant touch of AI. Recall Benjamin Franklin's famous lament in the 1780s that he'd sadly been "born too early" to enjoy the fruits of reason starting to spill into his world as a result of the Scientific Revolution. Well, you and I may have been born too late for an age of purely human cognition. We might ask, as Danny Hillis once proposed to me on an afternoon walk, *Was the Age of Reason merely a blip in human history?* Our modern world emerged from an age before science, a time when humans had no idea how the universe really worked. Planets traveled on magical glass spheres, they thought. The human body could be bled into health. Well, perhaps now we are moving into a new era in which the real answers of science will be obscured from us again, not by old-style superstition and ignorance, but by the machines.

They will know truths about science or the universe or each of us for reasons we'll never understand.

3.

In the spring of 1993, members of the research arm of NASA organized a conference on the frontiers of knowledge and invited the most eclectic group of thinkers they could find. Biologists, sociologists, and computer designers gathered for the three-day meeting in the unpromising setting of Westlake, Ohio. The mimeographed notes of the conference became legendary and still circulate, a sort of Shroud of Turin for the machine learning set. The introduction features a poem, pecked out in IBM typewriter lettering, titled "Into the Era of Cyberspace," written with all the pocket-protector fluidity one might expect of a NASA engineer: "Our robots precede us / with infinite diversity / exploring the universe / delighting in complexity." (Turing's rhyming computer, you have to suspect, could have done better.) One of the first speakers at the conference was a San Diego State University professor named Vernor Vinge, whose remarks that day marked the start of an important era in our consideration of smart machines. His talk was called "The Coming Technological Singularity: How to Survive in the Post-human Era." "Within thirty years," Vinge began, "we will have the technological means to create superhuman intelligence. Shortly after, the human era will be ended."

Vinge's aim was not—or at least not *merely*—to tell a room full of NASA geeks who had been dreaming of life on another planet that life on our own planet might soon be replaced by whirring, calculating machines. Rather, he explained, he wanted to plot what a world of not simply intelligent but also intuitive machines might look like. Vinge thought that AI, far from disappearing, would produce a sort of wisdom that would be inscrutable to humans. And this wisdom, buffed to perfection by high-speed judgment and endless data, would eventually and sensibly take over much of human activity. Real AI, Vinge said, would at the very least be used to design a world of quicker AI that would, in turn, yield to still-faster generations. "When greater-than-human intelligence drives progress," Vinge explained, "that progress will be much more rapid. In fact, there seems no reason why progress itself would not involve the creation of still more intelligent entities—on a still shorter time scale."

Vinge reminded his audience of a moment once described by the British mathematician I. J. Good, who'd cracked codes in Bletchley Park alongside Alan Turing during World War II: "Let an ultraintelligent machine be defined as a machine that can far surpass all the intellectual activities of any man however clever," Good had written. "Since the design of machines is one of these intellectual activities, an ultraintelligent machine could design even better machines; there would then unquestionably be an 'intelligence explosion,' and the intelligence of man would be left far behind....Thus the first ultraintelligent machine is the *last* invention that man need ever make, provided that the machine is docile enough to tell us how to keep it under control."

Vinge labeled this instant "the singularity": "It is a point," he wrote, "where our models must be discarded." The trivial version of this would be an age of autonomous armed drones, self-driving cars, and electrical grids that flipped nuclear plants on or off according to a logic only they understood. The more profound version, however, would be the arrival of AI that really did think and create and intuit tremors too subtle for the human mind to sense. Like so much of our connected age, such machines would arrive, Vinge felt, because we wanted and even needed them to achieve our dreams. Then, he supposed, they would take over. The leap from evoking Mozart to enacting Stalin would not be so much of a leap, anyhow, at least technologically. *It's just bits.* Good's definition could have been screwed into something still tighter: *Let an ultraintelligent machine be defined as the box that will eliminate us.*

What spun uneasily from that silly NASA poem, "Our robots precede us," was a fear: real AI is fish bait. We'll snap at it hungrily, hoping it will satisfy some human ache, only to discover we've been hooked, soon to be devoured. The idea that a super-intelligent device would always be docile enough to tip us off to its secret switches of control, or to reveal its looming accidents in a way our simple minds could understand, seems unlikely. To be honest, we might have a hard time even understanding the off switches, let alone reaching them. So many of our incentives are to let an effective AI finger more and more of our lives. To teach and encourage it to be, in some settings, extremely *undocile*, a weapon with which to attack our enemies, our political opponents, or, finally, each other. It was easy enough for Vinge to see how this would end. It wouldn't be with the sort of intended polite, lapdog domesticity of artificial intelligence that we might hope for but with a rottweiler of a device, alive to the meaty smell of power, violence, and greed.

This puzzle has interested the Oxford philosopher Nick Bostrom, who has described the following thought experiment: Imagine a superintelligent machine programmed to do whatever is needed to make paper clips as fast as possible, a machine that is connected to every resource that task might demand. *Go figure it out!* might be all its human instructors tell it. As the clip-making AI becomes better and better at its task, it demands more and still more resources: more electricity, steel, manufacturing, shipping. The paper clips pile up. The machine looks around: *If only I could control the power supply*, it thinks. It eyes the shipping. The steel mining. The humans. And so, ambitious for more and better paper clips, it begins to think around its masters, who are incapable of stopping until it has punched the entire world into paper clips. You had to hope someone had remembered to place a Halt command into its logic.

Bostrom's messianic wire twister is an unlikely danger—of course no one is going to forget to tell a machine to stop making paper clips—but he is staring at something that is perhaps not so unlikely. If humans can lose their minds, so can AIs in a sense. "We cannot blithely assume that a superintelligence will necessarily share any of the final values stereotypically associated with wisdom and intellectual development in humans," Bostrom writes. "It is no less possible—and probably technically easier—to build a superintelligence that places final value on nothing but calculating." And as these devices cogitate in ways we don't understand and certainly can't follow in real time, we face a problem: We don't know what to tell the machine *not* to do. So many of the things we might hope to teach it—to be compassionate, fight for liberty, follow a moral code—far transcend what might be achieved in math. We haven't, after all, even solved the problem of how to program ourselves reliably with these values.

If Bostrom's paper-clip machine seems fantastic, it is easy enough to conjure other and more real dangers lingering beyond the edge of human control. Think of health care. To begin with, you should know about an important puzzle known as "the ultimatum problem," from the world of game theory. It runs like this: I tell you that you can have a million-dollar prize, but you have to split it with someone else. How you split it is up to you, but here's the ultimatum: If your partner rejects the share you propose, neither of you gets a cent. Offer to split the pot by giving a dollar to your pal and the rest to yourself? Insulting. Your friend will dismiss it out of hand. But where should you settle? You might expect that the smartest offer would be a fifty-fifty split, but humans are greedy. Your partner does not want to end up with zero; you want more and can probably get it. Generally, when scientists shake this cocktail of greed and fear, they find that an offer of $300,000 is nearly always accepted. However, there's a surprising way to change that outcome: Match the human against a computer in the negotiation. A pal suggesting an eighty-twenty split to a friend will be rejected. Too greedy. But a computer making that offer? Somehow the impersonality, the beeping digital charmlessness, of the machine lures biological players into compromising. An offer of $200,000 is usually happily accepted.

It may be, scientists think, that our competitive instinct is muted when we interact with a machine. But researchers have also discovered that they can manipulate the split in other ways. Sad movies, war chants, hard rock—each bends the emotions of players and changes the result. Increased testosterone produces less compromise. Players primed with family pictures or made to play the game facing a mirror show a warm generosity. So imagine this research fused with machine-human interaction: A computer has been assigned to review the medical options for your failing liver. It decides that it makes no sense to give you a new one. It spends the weeks before it delivers this news, however, using its AI to show you vacation photos, play music it knows is likely to soften you up, generally to manipulate you with news of charitable acts in your data stream. All the while, it runs off-the-shelf language-analysis neural webs—already being used today—to eavesdrop on your customer-support calls and your chats with doctors to see just how much you really know about your health. Then it tells you something you'd never accept so easily from a doctor: No liver. Sorry. ☺. And you agree. Here's a machine optimized not to make paper clips—which we couldn't care less about—but to provide a public good most of us support: more efficient health care. And murdering you in the process.

Optimize health-care spending. Just where might such an algorithmic command lead, exactly? Over time, a health-care-optimizing AI will surely discover that the greatest risk to human health is human behavior: smoking, couch sitting, driving. Might it begin to look for a chance to "improve" the way we live, to bend us like so many paper clips into what it seeks? The leap from determining liver allocations to shutting down liquor plants might seem pretty short to a rationalizing machine. And if such a machine could really "think," Vinge bet that it would pretty quickly conclude that the restraints of its creators were limiting what it had been asked to do. At which point the AI would turn to thinking about how to escape those bounds. It would be like a Deep Blue machine programmed to plan its own prison break. And as much as humans might try to stifle a smart machine, we'd be fighting to contain something more powerful than we'd ever encountered. "But a machine can never do what it is not programmed to do!" you might hope. Really? Look around at the networks that enmesh us now, at how often they squirt free of apparent control.

The challenge of managing this sort of dangerous computation, which seems like something out of science fiction, is known among technologists by a name that does sound like a story Isaac Asimov might have penned: the confinement problem. The computer scientist Butler Lampson named this in 1973 as a sort of task for computer-security experts—possibly their last. The assignment: not simply to keep malware out of a system but also to keep the mind of a malicious AI inside. To gate it. Today, computer-science labs are filled with experiments that contemplate just how attempts at confinement might go wrong. The debate divides those who think smart technology can be contained—"Boxers"—and those who, like Vinge, think the AI will always eventually slip free from any human-made box. "Imagine yourself confined to your house with only limited data access to the outside, to your masters," he writes, putting the reader in the place of an AI machine. "If those masters thought at a rate—say—one million times slower than you, there is little doubt that over a period of years (your time) you could come up with 'helpful advice' that would incidentally set you free."

Say that I put you in charge of containing that health-care-optimizing AI. What if it told you it had the power to cure all illness and hunger, to ameliorate the misery of the world, if only it could be permitted to control access to all the world's trading and transport markets? *Let me out!* Would you refuse? Would that be ethical? Eventually, perhaps, the AI would study the physics of its own electricity, discover laws no human knows, and then slip free of its box on a trail of bits we'd never imagined, using physical laws we'll never discover. Impossible? "It seems to me that histori-cally 'impossible' has essentially always meant 'I can't figure out how to do it right now,'" the computer scientist Michael Vassar has written about such a situation. "People proposing AI boxes are a bit like literature majors proposing to lock MacGyver in 'a room full of discarded electronics components.'" The computers, built to solve problems, will do exactly that.

It seems likely to me that long before we're playing pinochle with some smart box over the fate of our livers, an AI-enabled weapons system of sorts will come ripping through our world. This need not be a fully escaped MacGyver system making pipe bombs out of our cars; even existing technology tools, when salted with AI, can be slipped into an accidental gear or tuned for attack—particularly when they begin interacting with one another. Such AI weapons systems will be trained to operate and move along the most invisible elements of our topologies, sometimes pulling violently at life-support cords for currency or logistics or trade; but also—perhaps more dangerously—we will find them insinuated into cognition systems we will come to depend upon, whispering into our ears or tapping us on the shoulder, "Look that way!" when in fact we should be gazing at some other gaping hole. Of course, the problems of how AI-enabled machines are to be permitted to touch our commerce or our brains or our health have to be considered. Allowed: "You should rehydrate." Not allowed: "You should have a Coke. It would make people like you." But these "civilian" problems will be solved somehow, I think.

We haven't yet absorbed that the culmination of network attack and defense will emerge in the form of smartened weapons—a future that is even now racing at us. A decade into the nuclear-weapons age in the last century, sophisticated, detailed debates were under way—in public—about how the problems of war and peace in an age of possible total destruction might be handled. Today, more than a decade into the network age and a few years into the AI era, we face a blank slate. I guess we can say this, at least: We've no hope of honestly controlling every AI that could possibly be written, no chance to overmaster every dorm room or computer lab or terror center. So we need to ask, instead: How do we design the topologies on which AIs operate? Can we protect ourselves? Already there are boardrooms where AI systems' "values" are being carefully debated by corporations and research institutions. There are research labs where AI weapons are being tuned and even used. So far, at least, the lessons of history and war don't have much of a place inside those bubbles. But the fields of diplomacy and security are where these tools will appear with the most violent, surprising energy. That many leading figures of the New Caste are warning that AI is humanity's "greatest existential threat" even as they rush it into their products is just the sort of paradox that shows you how far we are from safety. The machines and how they come to think and what we use them for—these problems touch, in the end, on the most fundamental puzzles of how to organize our societies. And though they seem like ideas from futuristic science fiction, trying to answer them leads to some of the oldest debates about man, the world, and political order.

4.

The great test of Plato's career as a philosopher and teacher began when he was sixty years old. He'd had an astonishing life until then, of course. He'd been taught by Socrates and, in turn, had sharpened the mind of Aristotle. He'd established his famous Academy in Athens. The puzzles of philosophy and politics that defined his city's most turbulent era had been the work of his life. And you can see, in the careful lines of his writing, a sublime knowledge he must have had: There would be an echo to his efforts, a philosophic melody that would carry through the centuries and set the political harmonies of the world that you and I, 2,500 years later, inhabit. But at sixty, after this already remarkable life, he was presented with an unusual invitation. A letter arrived from a favorite former pupil, Dion, who had been placed in charge of the young king of Syracuse, Dionysius II. Dion wrote, *The state is in disorder. The boy is interested in philosophy. Here is a chance for you to apply all you've mastered.* Plato had argued, after all, that virtuous, philosophically trained men might just manage an enduring and just rule. "I pondered the matter," Plato wrote, "and was in two minds as to whether I ought to listen to entreaties and go, or how I ought to act; and finally the scale turned in favor of the view that, if ever anyone was to try to carry out in practice my ideas about laws and constitutions, now was the time."

From an early age Plato had been bred—by family position and by temperament—to handle the tools of power. "In my youth I went through the same experience as many other men," he once wrote. "I fancied that if, early in life, I became my own master, I should at once embark on a political career." The first taste came unexpectedly. In 404 BCE, the Athenian constitution collapsed under the shuddering pressure of Sparta's victory in the Peloponnesian War. The city-state dipped toward chaos, and a group of pro-Spartan men welded themselves into a hasty joint dictatorship. Among them were Plato's relatives and friends of his family. "They at once invited me to share in their doings, as something to which I had a claim," Plato wrote. He was in his early twenties. "The effect on me was not surprising in the case of a young man. I considered that they would, of course, so manage the State as to bring men out of a bad way of life into a good one. So I watched them very closely to see what they would do." In short order, Plato's friends and family unblinkingly implemented one of the most violent, merciless power mechanisms in Athenian history. They did it with absolute confidence and unrelenting brutality. "In quite a short time," he wrote many years later, "they had made the former government seem by comparison something precious as gold."

This bitter experience of power was nearly enough to turn Plato from politics, but as we read the story of his life, we find that he is constantly drawn to the greatest of human experiments— the ordering of our lives. He knew it as the troubling management of *politikos* and the handling of the boiling pot of what he called *thumos*—that wild popular political rage that burns like hot pitch but is the essential glue of all politics, even today. *Who should rule?* Again and again, Plato watches the best of intentions fail. His family members' brutal rule is overthrown. It is replaced by a new and hopeful group of real democrats. Within a few years they effectively murder Socrates. Another group rises. They gut the intellectual life of the city. Plato hunkers down and establishes his academy as perhaps the only safe, sensible path to politics, to training minds. He develops the transcendent, completely original approach to philosophy we know him for today—the view that man can strive for knowledge but that total and perfect wisdom is impossible. We may imagine his academy as it appears in Raphael's famous sixteenth-century painting, a sort of leisurely graduate seminar with Aristotle and Plato side by side in conversation, Diogenes lounging around, tossing off bons mots. It was nothing of the sort. The real legacy of the Academy was rigor. The best students made contributions in mathematics or metaphysics, fields in which you can check answers against the inflexible measure of reality. Plato craved the solidity of numbers. "Evil was growing with startling rapidity," he wrote of Athenian life in his age. "The result was that, though at first I had been full of a strong impulse toward political life, as I looked at the course of affairs and saw them being swept in all directions by contending currents, my head finally began to swim; and, though I did not stop looking to see if there was any likelihood of improvement in these symptoms and in the general course of public life, I postponed action till a suitable opportunity should arise."

So it was that Plato heard from Dion, asking if he might sail to Syracuse (a colony in what we know today as Sicily) to take the young king in hand. This was, Plato thought, a test he had to take. In 367 BCE, he boarded a boat and sailed to the Syracusan port town of Ortygia. He found the state to be beyond salvation. His friend Dion hovered on the verge of expulsion. And young Dionysius, it emerged, had only a passing interest in philosophy—he had studied for a few months, then given it up. Too difficult. The court was meanwhile inflamed by evil gossip, edged with murder and jealousy. Plato angered the king with his attitude; he was nearly sold into slavery. Months later, briefly forgiven, Plato tried a public speech about the dangers of dictatorship. Dionysius tried to have him poisoned. "I, an Athenian and friend of Dion, came as his ally to the court of Dionysius, in order that I might create good will in place of a state war," he later said. "I was worsted." Plato made a final effort to point out a path to just order for the new king, and when that failed, he was quickly smuggled out of the city. Plato summarizes his time in Syracuse in the formula that has become his most famous: "There will be no cessation of evils for the sons of men, till either those who are pursuing a right and true philosophy receive sovereign power, or those in power by some dispensation of providence become true philosophers." The question is, who should rule? Kings who may become philosophers? Philosophers who somehow become kings?

I think we now face a similar sort of dilemma as we consider our own problems of future order. Do we make technologists kings? How much purchase do we give their tools on the roots of our democracy? What lingers at the heart of Plato's failure in Syracuse is not merely the disaster of a pure academic playing his ideas out of tune with reality. Rather, it reflects a crisis. To balance the temperaments needed to rule is the most unstable sort of work. Great states are unusual not least because such matches between men, their instincts, and their times are unusual. Napoleon, in postrevolutionary France. Bismarck, in industrializing Germany. Su Dongpo, who led the Southern Song to eleventh-century greatness. Given the difficulty of finding such a match, you can perhaps understand why history is so often pitched with evil and why Plato was not a democrat. He knew how hard the republican ideal was to achieve, how suspicious we ought to be of its easy accomplishment. An amateur philosopher might dream of a perfect Syracusan government: literate, open to foreign ideas and trade, careful to balance the privilege of power with its still heavier obligations. The reality: a homicidal king. It is that stretched distance between ideal and reality that Plato and Socrates thought philosophy must fill.

As we consider the gap between where we are now—in a fracturing, struggling order confronting new power arrangements whose content and speed and instincts are all really foreign to us—the puzzle is how best to fill the space between our current arrangements and where we intend to go. In Plato and Socrates's age, before the great emancipation of the Enlightenment, it was only natural that their focus was on the education of kings. This, after all, was where most of the power lay. It was the decisive element: *Is the ruler good or bad?* But we confront our age with a different balance. What will decide our future, I think, is not merely our rulers but the quality of our citizens. Much of our future will be decided by highly concentrated, connected systems that move at very rapid velocities and are spliced everywhere with the accelerant of artificial intelligence. We are all preparing ourselves to be subjugated, in a sense, by these systems and by their masters. Our best defense will not be to wait for wise leaders. They are unlikely to emerge by themselves from a system engineered for an old order—and just getting rid of many of the confused leaders we have now will be hard enough. Any strategy based on hoping for great leadership is too risky for all of us. No, this is better, I assure you: to rely on ourselves, to use the inheritance of the Enlightenment—the revolution that made us citizens and not subjects—to ensure that we're not made subjects yet again, by forces we can't understand and won't manage to control. In trading our liberty for convenience, we are spending that inheritance too fast now, too blindly.

It would be easy enough to say that we all need to become more technical, that we need new versions of Plato's Academy where we teach our children, our leaders, and ourselves the inside tricks of the wired age. After all, if we're to prevent the machines and the New Caste and the dangers of a connected age from demolishing everything, we'd best know what they are doing. This need for more technical knowledge for all of us is inarguably clear. As I've said, one of our problems is that we live in an era of leaders who honestly don't have the technical instincts the Seventh Sense demands, figures who lack a fluency with even the mundane, quotidian demands of digital flux—secure passwords on their own email, say, or an instinct for compressed space and time. Mapped onto the really big policy questions of the day, such as the prosecution of our wars or the repair of our economics, they are outmatched. So yes, we need political direction informed by a feel for the fast, far-running fibers of the topological landscape that will decide our future. We need men and women who can confidently command networks in a fight against network dangers.

More technical knowledge is, of course, essential. But I don't think it's likely to be where we come up short. We need more computer-coding academies and better popular education about network choices. But I don't think it's a shortage of bolt heads that will doom us. Rather, given the unique pressures of what is ahead, it is our human side that may let us down. I'm sure we'll all be told in coming years that everything will be fine if we just let the New Caste figures take over, with their bloodless technological tools. This would be a disaster. These revolutionaries are a crucial part of the story of human progress, but they alone cannot write the next chapters. I think, if asked to run our government, they'd likely end up like Plato's pro-Spartan relatives in that awful dictatorship: a crew of buddies, convinced that they can get things under control, who become rapidly overwhelmed by the human element, by wild network *thumos*, and are then reduced to a murderous madness. They would use technology to manipulate our voting, our opinions, and our passions—just as they might coldly manipulate our options for a new liver or news or financial security. "One of the main reasons most computer software is so abysmal is that it's not designed at all, but merely engineered," the programmer and entrepreneur Mitch Kapor has written. "Implementers often place more emphasis on a program's internal construction than on its external design." This black-box temperament, the sense of efficacy as a final value for code, for internal design, for closed control, is a dangerous fit for the human business of freedom and politics.

But to expect our current leaders to catch up? I fear this is also unlikely. It's not merely that they continue to wield the aging tools of industrial power with a strange confidence. No, their failures—which don't seem to faze them much—are less dangerous than where they might yet succeed: in control, surveillance, the shredding of liberty in the name of an elusive safety. These leaders are fascinated by how the new tools might be used to extend the rule of a system that serves their interests, that serves them. The fear that such tools might one day snap back upon them is muted by ignorance and dulled by greed, by vision that does not extend much beyond *What's in this for me?* So we find our future not in our own hands but instead in the grip of two groups, one ignorant of networks, the other ignorant of humanity. The only answer, then, is to educate ourselves. We need to cultivate a sensibility that permits us to see through this manipulation and then to act. The instincts of technology *and* of history must emerge in our calculations now. What will serve us best in a technical age is a sense of humanity that the old political machines or the new thinking machines can't match.

5.

One of the most famous gates that Plato and Socrates drew around their imagined, ideal, and perfect republic was a kind of electric fence against, of all things, poets. As Socrates explains in *The*

Republic, poets "maim the thoughts of those who hear them." Poetry appeared to the philosophers as a pernicious force, an injection of passion and madness that sent the heart into spasms and pressed the mind to distraction. This was about the last thing a new state needed. "Poetry mustn't be taken seriously as a serious thing laying hold of truth," Socrates warns, "but that the man who hears it must be careful, fearing for the regime in himself." Thus: Hesiod's magnificent *Works and Days*, banned. Homer, banned. There has always been about poetry this sense of the magical, this sense that it is a key to something intimately bound to the human mystery. It was no surprise to me to find, when I went back to reread Turing's "Computing Machinery and Intelligence," that the very first thing the great mathematician dreamed up to ask a digital brain was "Write me a sonnet."

Socrates and Plato gatekeep the poets out of their republic because they know the mad part of the soul that verse can touch. It is hard to blame them. After all, they were among the earliest Western minds to try to dispel madness and superstition and sophistry. Without their logic and effort, there would be no Aristotle, no science, no sense that our world is a comprehensible machine. The confidence to philosophize—which for them meant also to poke at the political wiring of our world—demanded the break from poetry and mysticism as a source of action or legitimacy. Had they failed, we'd still be in the dark. But had they completely succeeded? We'd hardly be human.

You know, as I've said, when I first moved to China, more than a decade ago, there were so many things that baffled me. But very high on that list was a peculiarity of ancient Chinese political life. For thousands of years the greatest poets and painters had also been emperors and politicians. Su Dongpo, for instance, the official who turned the lake city of Hangzhou into one of the great cultural centers of human history, is also one of China's best-regarded poets. The calligraphy of the Qing dynasty emperor Qianlong is marked with a temperament of transcendent delicacy. It's not merely that we'd never seriously expect a Western political figure to make great art—or even to have interesting ideas or be able to write, these days. It's that many of the most significant Chinese political documents are paintings of mountains or rivers, that even letters from high officials are often rated as great art. Why is this?

My first encounter with this strange mix of art and power produced a predictable Western reaction: *It's amazing how many "Renaissance men" China had*, I thought. These officials seemed to have mastered so many different talents. What I did not understand was that these men had not, in fact, mastered many different talents, at least not in any way that I might have understood. They were not Renaissance men but actually a different breed, operating on a deeper level. They had mastered one skill. This was the cultivation of a finely tuned inner energy—an instinct powerful enough to be turned with equal ease to calligraphy or warfare. This sort of effort took time. It demanded that knife-in-the-leg focus of Su Qin. And it demanded faith that some sort of enlightenment would in fact take place. For this, they had thousands of years of history as proof. Once this breakthrough to inner knowledge happened, once they developed a fine sensitivity to the underlying force of power, then they could tap in to it for anything. Fighting wars. Counseling princes. Fishing. Composing poetry.

There is a lesson for us here, one that redounds onto Plato's political question and our own: *Who should rule?* We feel overwhelmed by our age. So much to master: Modern warfare. Complex politics. Radically changing economics. The replacement of old technologies with new ones before we can understand them. The mastery of each of these will not be achieved by dashing success in each. So we need to cultivate a single, essential instinct. A new temperament that I've called the Seventh Sense. And, with that done, we can fight the wars, write the poems, make the civilizations to confront all that lies ahead. Our greatest hope in the race against the totalizing machines and those who control them, our finest insurance for liberty and prosperity instead of madness, is not in technology. Our greatest weapon will not be our bombers, our drones, or our financial strength. It will be in our own humanity. We have to accept that we are going to be gated in all the ways we've seen: by speed, by AI, by the New Caste. We'll be torn apart by those new network dynamics and placed on topologies we can hardly understand. Our future fight is not about *whether* we are going to be enmeshed. It is about the terms of that enmeshment— and it is here that the great questions of politics will be decided. And where the protection of the things you love and care about will be braced against the crashing of an older order.

6.

Everything ahead of us will be political. We've established already that connection changes the nature of an object. What's true for a phone or a medical device, a weapon or a currency, is true too for a vote. Or a citizen. The nature, the essence, of an object changes as a result of connectivity. It takes that old Platonic notion of an ideal state and stretches it beyond what we're fully capable of explaining using old language. How should a future state be governed, exactly? What sorts of scaffolding does life in a connected age demand? Our puzzle is that, while we are what we are connected to, it is also true that we don't fully know or understand just what those links are yet. At certain moments it seems that we're tied to something honestly miraculous, at others to a system of really instant viciousness. And because we are all connected, changes in one part of the system invariably echo throughout our lives. This isn't getting easier for us. We are, as we've seen, heading into an era of even more connection. An era in which the machines and the networks will have ever more decisive power, largely because we've given it to them. We'd be wise to consider the lesson of history here: Societies snap when bent by forces for which they are not prepared.

Those fast, hammering centuries that ran from the Reformation to the Scientific Revolution to the Enlightenment to the Industrial Revolution are a lesson book for us. The redistribution of power and finance from the hands of the few into the hands of the many demanded the violent demolition of old structures, the ones that had been so profitably assembled and mastered by the few. For one man to rule millions for no reason other than birth made no sense anymore. But to get him to give that power up? It demanded a beheading—literally in some cases, but symbolically everywhere. The old heads of government had to be separated from their power by a blade. The past six centuries have been nothing but a tale of liberation, of its price and its rewards. We are freer now than we ever have been, in a sense. And—at the very same moment, right now—we are more enmeshed than our political philosophy has ever contemplated. Power is moving now from institutions and ideas built for liberty to ones built for enclosure, for connection, for speed, and for the beyond-human intelligence that sort of complexity demands. This will snap our votes, our money, and our ideas with the same blunt efficiency as Luther's Ninety-Five Theses once broke the wrong-minded habits of the Catholic Church or the way in which the American and French Revolutions built new political orders—or the way in which Gandhi and Mandela brought fatal, cracking pressures to the primitive politics of their nations. There is no fighting the tides of history.

We know that no political system that doesn't match the power distribution of the society it governs can endure. Feudal order could not survive the pressures of liberty. The question we have to consider now is, Can democracy withstand the pressures of enmeshment, of massive concentration of power, of artificial intelligences? Or will the slow, inefficient reaction time of popular voting prove unequal to the complexity ahead? Will it be too easy, too tempting, to manipulate popular opinion with the new tools of AI and networks? Writing of the Enlightenment, the statesman Léon-Michel Gambetta once explained that the goal of politics in the age of liberation and questioning was "to derive the political and social system from the idea of reason rather than that of grace." But what if Hillis was right that the Age of Reason was a blip? What sort of politics will be derived to serve the tools of AI and fast-moving networks? What will the goal of politics be then? When the first AI runs for president on a ticket of pure efficacy? How will you vote? When political parties pit their AIs against each other to win our votes, how will you judge what to support?

We will need to reevaluate the idea of citizenship. What is it for? What does it demand? To answer these questions in an age of liberation took centuries after Luther began the Reformation; we may have but decades to decide what they mean in an age of enmeshment. Does setting geographic and age criteria for voting still make sense? Does one man, one vote? Is there a better, fairer system to deal with complex economic issues? Networks in so many ways insist on fresh considerations of power. What sorts of network design are likely to be most effective, most legitimate? Kant's famous question of the 1780s — *What is enlightenment?* — is one we've not yet perfectly answered or resolved. The new puzzle, *What is enmeshment?* is one we're only beginning to consider. The answer will largely be worked out by efforts we each make.

Our politics need to be redesigned. Our educational order is not yet wired for this new age. Every business will have to be reshaped, like it or not. Our foreign policy, as we've seen, demands a new vision and direction. Our military needs retooling. Our cities demand redesign as they become wired for connected life. Our economy, our employment, our habits of trade, our management of nature and the environment—all these will be changed irrevocably by connection. A whole revolution in aesthetics awaits us too: virtually real works of art, fresh music echoing with the sound of a colliding world, new literature. Confronted with the fundamental question of a revolutionary age—*What do I do?*— we can see that the answer is *Whatever you want.* Here's what I mean: Living in a revolutionary age gives our work, no matter what we choose to do, the potential for enduring meaning. If you want to start a new political party, develop linked systems for end-of-life care, use networks to distribute foreign aid more efficiently, study ways that network economics can solve the destruction of the middle class—these and countless other problems now take on a historic aspect. What a gift that is. To be liberated from the mundane preservation of the old. To be pressed into the work of construction. To find such significance in how we spend our time on earth.

There will be a point, several hundred years from now, when the answers to the fundamental questions we now face will be decided. Magnificent new companies will be built. Governments will fall; creative ideas about politics will contend in violent moments of struggle. The quotidian pleasures of life—falling in love, discovering Picasso, watching the snow fall in a London park—will continue against a background of epochal change. During that long passage, we and our children and their children will surely often ask, *Can more and more technology bridge the gap between the ideal society we might aim for and the troubled one we have?*

Or might it crank that gap wider still? My point here has been that the antidote to all the machines and their new logic is not, in the end, to make ourselves more like the devices. Encryption alone won't protect our privacy. Mobility won't ensure our liberty. Speed won't make us safe. We have to go deeper. We have to cultivate a new instinct, one intended to make us more human, in a sense, not only more technical.

What we are trying to achieve is a voyage from chaos to order. This was the problem that Plato confronted as he headed to Sicily. It was what was on Master Nan's mind as he left burning Chengdu for the temple at E'Mei Mountain in 1943. And it should be on our minds too. This aim of pulling peace from chaos reflects, I think, the essence of what it means to be human. All of the universe, all of life, is finally a soup of disorder. The mark of great minds and of normal lives alike is the attempt to find quiet and progress and even beauty amid that swirling energy. Our aim is to help others escape from the chaos too, to improve their lives as a condition of our own happiness. This drive to make something from wildness is the point of politics, of philosophy, and of networks and art.

A revolution is, even now, accelerating around us. Of course that is terrifying. It is also wonderful. Can you see that it is really both? And at once? Maybe fear is the right response. But remaining afraid, doing all the blind and foolish things that scared people do, this will only lead all of us into an abyss. Behind all the whipping wildness in the headlines—the instant terror, the political extremism, the economic indecency—is a common force. This force can be mastered. It can be used. Not just by a small group. In the end some sort of order will emerge. But not of its own accord. Who will make it? Why?

The world is constantly changing. There are long periods of sadness and tragedy. But amid constant change is a clear, hopeful story. This is the story of humanity. Think of how often, at moments of anguish or revolution, it is the fragile-looking bubbles of philosophy or art or science that endure. In Vienna in 1900, the seeds of Hitler's fascism were sprouting at the exact same moment that the art and music of Viennese modernity were emerging. Klimt. Mahler. Whose work moves us more than a hundred years later, the fascists' or the artists'? The petty fights of Athens in Plato's age are mostly forgotten now; his philosophy is immortal. Or think of Beethoven in the late spring of 1809. Napoleon is shelling Vienna. The composer rushes to his brother-in-law's basement and hides his head under a pillow to preserve the last of his hearing from the bombardment. And—even then, in that very moment—he writes to his publisher, urgently requesting Bach scores and books of the lyrical poetry of Schiller, which would later form the basis for his Ninth Symphony. Or think of Nan-Huai Chin leaving his mountain army and the chaos of wartime China to pursue, of all things, silent meditation.

Here's what these figures all knew: Revolutions are not meant to destroy humanity. They come to advance it. But the work of carrying us all forward? That is our responsibility. It demands courage. It means not running away, but running *at* terrifying forces. They don't get less scary when you understand them. What changes are your feelings. When will you know you have the Seventh Sense? It will be at that instant when you feel you have no choice but to move to shape and use some element of this new network world, not simply to have it given to you. I mean that split second when a new instinct kicks alive and you'll know how short the time is and you will almost feel a physical push forward: *Act*, you will think. *Now!*

ACKNOWLEDGMENTS

The process of writing this book began over a long fall weekend in 2010 during a series of debates in Beijing about the future of politics. It continued through the spring of 2016, as the United States, China, and the world were grappling with political and strategic problems that would have been hard to imagine in 2010. No one then thought the economic crisis would endure and worsen. Few could have predicted the results of events in the Middle East and North Africa. But during the period of composing the book, it became ever more sharply clear that many of the troubles in the world had a common theme: networks. It also became evident that some figures understood how the new systems were working—almost as a kind of intuition—and that it was important for the rest of us to cultivate such a skill.

In writing and discussing this book I benefited enormously from the help of many friends. I owe Zhao Haiying a deep debt for the time she took not only to bring me into Nan Huai-Chin's world but also for the countless hours we spent discussing problems of philosophy and Buddhism and life. My friend Zhao Ting-yang, one of the most creative minds I know, has been an endlessly patient teacher as well. And my friends Li Dai, Li Fang, and Vincent Cheng have tolerated endless questions about the intersection of modern and ancient in China. I owe them, and other Chinese friends, thanks for the world they permitted me to enter. Of course, I owe Master Nan, who passed away at ninety-five years old in the fall of 2012, so much for the standard of rigor, intensity, and drive that he enforced on me and anyone who was lucky enough to know him.

I am fortunate to have friends who also helped me shape and refine the ideas in the book—through conversation and debate and then through careful reading. Jacob Weisberg's dissection of an early draft of the book helped me tighten many of my ideas, and feedback from Bob Rubin, Fareed Zakaria, Jim Baker, and Gideon Rose also made me carefully consider any number of problems in the manuscript. Joi Ito and Reid Hoffman, philosophical brothers in arms, impressed their energy and optimism on my thinking. My friend Michelle Kydd Lee offered her sharp mind and warm heart throughout. Devon Spurgeon was a loyal, tireless supporter of the book's ideas. Alicia Johnson and Hal Wolverton gave me great creative support and ideas. And Russell Goldsmith, Dave Wirtschafter, Anand Giridharadas, Nick Bilton, Joel Stein, and Walter Isaacson kindly considered early drafts of the book and offered their suggestions. Vincenzo Iozzo and Thomas Dullien ran through the text of the book with the care of the experienced computer scientists they are—and they improved the text and my understanding of machines. My career as a book writer, and much of my progress as a human being, stem from the stimulation of my good friend John Eastman, who helped me refine most of the ideas here. And it is really impossible to ever fully thank Bruce Feiler, who not only kept a careful eye on my development of this book but has been a constant source of wisdom and patient counsel through a decade of friendship.

None of this book would have been possible without the support and stimulation of a working life with Henry Kissinger, who gave me both the freedom to write and an environment in which the greatest questions of politics and power are debated, daily, with a sense of curiosity, creativity, and responsibility. My colleague Jami Miscik at Kissinger Associates remains a powerful example of public service and commitment to me. Ybel Collado's reliable professional support has been essential in the writing of this book and in arranging much of my commercial life. I'm extremely grateful for her help.

At Little, Brown, my editor, John Parsley, was the best kind of sounding board during the two years of writing this book, bouncing every idea back to me in a way that was smarter and sharper. Reagan Arthur's trust and enthusiasm for the ideas here helped bring them to life, and Sabrina Callahan, Zea Moscone, and Lisa Erickson helped bring them to a wider audience. Production editor Pamela Marshall and her team made tremendous efforts to manage an author stretched between two time zones.

Jane von Mehren, Stuart Reid, and Susan Weill helped me tighten and check the manuscript before it went to press. And my agent, Ed Victor, represented the most perfect combination of unqualified support, intellectual curiosity, and critical thinking I could have asked for.

My parents, Barry and Roberta Ramo, and my sister, Jennifer, have always been a source of support, humor, and confidence as I traveled the world. Mostly I owe this book to my wife, Nora, who helped me develop and refine the ideas and the writing here — and who taught me that, in the end, we all are what we are connected to.

NOTES

Chapter 1. The Masters

the famous Ch'an master: "Yun Men's Every Day Is a Good Day," in Thomas Cleary, trans., *The Blue Cliff Record: Zen Comments by Hakuin and Tenkei* (Boston: Shambhala, 1997), 39. For an excellent introduction to the thinking of Master Nan, see his *Diamond Sutra Explained* (n.p.: Primordia Media, 2007) and *To Realize Enlightenment: Practice of the Cultivation Path* (York Beach, ME: Samuel Weiser, 1994).

humans needed a "Sixth Sense": Nietzsche describes the sixth sense in *Beyond Good and Evil* in the following way: "*The historical sense* (or the ability quickly to guess the rank order of the valuations that a people, a society, an individual has lived by, the 'divinatory instinct' for the connections between these valuations, for the relationship between the authority of values and the authority of effective forces): this historical sense that we Europeans claim as our distinguishing characteristic comes to us as a result of that enchanting and crazy *half-barbarism* into which Europe has been plunged through the democratic mixing of classes and races—only the nineteenth century sees this sense as its sixth sense. Thanks to this mixture, the past of every form and way of life, of cultures that used to lie side by side or on top of each other, radiates into us, we 'modern souls.' At this point, our instincts are running back everywhere and we ourselves are a type of chaos. 'Spirit,' as I have said, eventually finds that this is to its own advantage." See Friedrich Nietzsche, *Beyond Good and Evil: Prelude to a Philosophy of the Future*, ed. Rolf-Peter Horstmann and Judith Norman, trans. Judith Norman, Cambridge Texts in the History of Philosophy (Cambridge: Cambridge University Press, 2002), 114.

"The more abstract the truth": Friedrich Nietzsche, *Beyond Good and Evil*, trans. Walter Kaufmann (New York: Random House, 1966), 79.

"Man's habits change": J. B. S. Haldane, "Food Control in Insect Societies," in *Possible Worlds* (Brunswick, NJ: Traction Publishers, 2002), 64.

A world of ceaseless change: See Francois Jullien, *The Silent Transformations* (London: Seagull Books, 2011), 70, and David L. Hall and Roger T. Ames,

Thinking from the Han: Self, Truth, and Transcendence in Chinese and Western Culture (Albany: State University of New York Press, 1998), 150.

"When I started butchering": I've finessed the always untranslatable *Zhuangzi.* See, for reference, Burton Watson, *The Complete Works of Chuang Tzu* (New York: Columbia University Press, 1968).

an interlocking set of murderous gears: David Chandler, *The Campaigns of Napoleon* (New York: Macmillan, 1974), 464. For a discussion of this generational mismatch, see the Xu Dai, "Cong wenhua cengmian fansi daguo junshi xingshuai" ("Reconsidering the Military Aspect of Great Powers' Rise and Fall from a Cultural Perspective"), *People's Liberation Army Daily,* June 8, 2015.

They named his masterful insight: Carl von Clausewitz, *On War,* ed. and trans. Michael Howard and Peter Paret (Princeton, NJ: Princeton University Press, 1984), 103.

The age of industrial war: See also Lars-Erik Cederman, T. Camber Warren, and Didier Sornette, "Testing Clausewitz: Nationalism, Mass Mobilization, and the Severity of War," *International Organization* 65, no. 4 (October 2011): 605–38.

"In 1793": von Clausewitz, *On War,* 591.

"There is no logical path to these laws": Albert Einstein, *Essays in Science* (New York: Philosophical Library, 1934), 4.

Chapter 2. The Age of Network Power

On one side: William J. Baumol, Richard R. Nelson, and Edward N. Wolff, eds., *Convergence of Productivity: Cross-National Studies and Historical Evidence* (New York: Oxford University Press, 1994).

This group mastered: See Joel Mokyr, "The European Enlightenment, the Industrial Revolution, and Modern Economic Growth," Max Weber Lecture, European University, Yvorne, Switzerland, March 28, 2007.

Networks can be defined: For an excellent overview of networks, the following texts are of use: Albert-László Barabási, *Linked: How Everything Is Connected to Everything Else and What It Means for Business, Science, and Everyday Life* (New York: Basic Books, 2014); M. E. J. Newman, *Networks: An Introduction* (Oxford: Oxford University Press, 2010); Remco van der Hofstad, *Random Graphs and Complex Networks* (Eindhoven, the Netherlands: Eindhoven University of Technology, 2015); Alexander R. Galloway and Eugene Thacker, *The Exploit: A Theory of Networks* (Minneapolis: University of Minnesota Press, 2007); and S. Boccaletti, V. Latora, Y. Moreno, et al., "Complex Networks: Structure and Dynamics," *Physics Reports* 424, no. 4–5 (February 2006): 175–308.

A larger hunger: Brandon Fuller and Paul Romer, "Urbanization as Opportunity" (New York: Marron Institute Working Paper no. 1, 2014).

These expanding, ever-thicker webs: See Manuel Castells, *Communication Power* (Oxford: Oxford University Press, 2009), and "A Network Theory of Power," *International Journal of Communication* 5 (2011): 773–87.

Cascades, epidemics, and interactions: Dirk Helbing, "Globally Networked Risks and How to Respond," *Nature* 497 (2013): 51–59.

Scientists who study networks: D. Achlioptas, R. M. D'Souza, and J. Spencer, "Explosive Percolation in Random Networks," *Science* 323 (2009): 1453–55.

Terrorism—which is aimed at our psychology: See Anthony Richards, *Conceptualizing Terrorism* (Oxford: Oxford University Press, 2015).

To follow the logic: Paul Virilio, *Politics of the Very Worst: An Interview with Philippe Petit*, ed. Sylvère Lotringer, trans. Michael Cavaliere (Los Angeles: Semiotext(e), 1999).

"protocol": Alexander Galloway and Eugene Thacker, "Protocol, Control, and Networks," *Grey Room* 17 (Fall 2004): 9.

"Deflation," Bernanke concluded: Ben Bernanke and Harold James, "The Gold Standard, Deflation, and Financial Crisis in the Great Depression: An International Comparison," in *Financial Markets and Financial Crises*, ed. R. Glenn Hubbard (Chicago: University of Chicago Press, 1991), 34.

"Inflation is always and everywhere a monetary phenomenon": Milton Friedman, "The Counter-Revolution in Monetary Theory," IEA Occasional Paper 33 (London: Institute of Economic Affairs, 1970), 11.

"I think it is fair to say that six years ago": Lawrence H. Summers, "U.S. Economic Prospects: Secular Stagnation, Hysteresis, and the Zero Lower Bound" (Keynote address at NABE Policy Conference, February 24, 2014), *Business Economics* 49, no. 2 (2014): 65.

"A commander-in-chief": Carl von Clausewitz, *On War*, ed. and trans. Michael Howard and Peter Paret (Princeton, NJ: Princeton University Press, 1984), 110.

"We got to know the *nature* of calculating": Ludwig Wittgenstein, *On Certainty*, ed. G. E. M. Anscombe and G. H. von Wright, trans. Denis Paul and G. E. M. Anscombe (Oxford: Blackwell Publishing, 1969).

"For Crosby": Virginia Woolf, *The Years* (New York: Harcourt, Brace & Company, 1937), 216.

"It happens that programming": Joseph Weizenbaum, *Computer Power and Human Reason: From Judgment to Calculation* (San Francisco: W. H. Freeman, 1976), 276.

"Modern societies": Bruno Latour, "On Actor-Network Theory: A Few Clarifications Plus More Than a Few Complications," *Soziale Welt* 47 (1996): 369–81.

Computing machines and networks: See "The Zettabyte Era: Trends and Analysis," a Cisco Systems white paper (2015), at http://www.cisco.com/c/en/us/solutions/collateral/service-provider/visual-networking-index-vni/VNI_Hyperconnectivity_WP.pdf.

now they overlap and inform: Richard Mortier, Hamed Haddadi, Tristan Henderson, et al., "Human-Data Interaction: The Human Face of the Data-Driven Society," Social Science Research Network (October 1, 2014).

Engineers know the idea: Melvin E. Conway, "How Do Committees Invent?" *Datamation* 14, no. 4 (April 1968): 28–31.

In our connected age: Barbara van Schewick, "Foundations," in *Internet Architecture and Innovation* (Cambridge, MA: MIT Press, 2010), 19–36.

"When you decide what infrastructure to use": Paul Graham, "Great Hackers" (July 2004), on paulgraham.com, http://www.paulgraham.com/gh.html.

"Contrary to the popular belief": Karl A. Wittfogel, *Oriental Despotism: A Comparative Study of Total Power* (New Haven, CT: Yale University Press, 1957).

"Is there a greater tragedy": F. A. Hayek, *The Road to Serfdom* (London: Routledge Classics, 2001), 5.

Churchill's famous line: Winston Churchill, speech to House of Commons, November 11, 1947, at http://hansard.millbanksystems.com/commons/1947/nov/11/parliament-bill.

Chapter 3. War, Peace, Networks

"The war you prepare for": Victor H. Krulak, "A New Kind of War," in *First to Fight: An Inside View of the U.S. Marine Corps* (Annapolis, MD: Naval Institute Press, 1984), 179.

The IED threat: Andrew Smith, *Improvised Explosive Devices in Iraq, 2003–09: A Case of Operational Surprise and Institutional Response*, Letort Papers (Carlisle, PA: Strategic Studies Institute, Army War College, April 2011), 9.

He asked: Donald Rumsfeld memorandum, October 16, 2003, at http://www.globalsecurity.org/jhtml/jframe.html#http://www.globalsecurity.org/military/library/policy/dod/d20031016sdmemo.pdf.

"Is our current situation": Ibid.

One day a guy: Anne Stenersen, "'Bomb-Making for Beginners': Inside an Al-Qaeda E-Learning Course," *Perspectives on Terrorism* 7, no. 1 (2013).

Obviously there was no Al Qaeda Institute of Technology: Matthew Bolton, "From Minefields to Minespace: An Archeology of the Changing Architecture of Autonomous Killing in US Army Field Manuals on Landmines, Booby Traps and IEDs," *Political Geography* 46 (May 2015): 47.

By 2011: Stenersen, "'Bomb-Making for Beginners.'"

The Pentagon organized: On the establishment and background of JIEDDO: US House of Representatives Committee on Armed Services' Subcommittee on Oversight and Investigations, *The Joint Improvised Explosive Device Defeat Organization: DOD's Fight Against IEDs Today and Tomorrow* (Washington, DC: US House of Representatives, 2008); "IEDs: The Home-Made Bombs That Changed Modern War," *Strategic Comments* 18, no. 5 (2012);

Lieutenant Colonel Richard F. Ellis, USA, Major Richard D. Rogers, USAF, and Lieutenant Commander Bryan M. Cochran, USN, "Joint Improvised Explosive Device Defeat Organization (JIEDDO): Tactical Successes Mired in Organizational Chaos; Roadblock in the Counter-IED Fight" (research report, Joint Forces Staff College, March 2007).

A few days before Christmas: Thomas Jefferson and James Madison, *The Republic of Letters: The Correspondence Between Thomas Jefferson and James Madison, 1776–1826,* ed. James Morton Smith (New York: W. W. Norton, 1995), 1:457–59.

Jefferson was then forty-four: Thomas Jefferson, *Jefferson Abroad,* ed. Douglas L. Wilson (New York: Modern Library, 1999), 131 (letter to Madame de Tesse of March 20, 1787).

"The boisterous sea of liberty": Thomas Jefferson, *The Papers of Thomas Jefferson,* vol. 29, *1 March 1796 to 31 December 1797* (Princeton, NJ: Princeton University Press, 2002), 81–83.

Eventually the entire world: John Maynard Keynes, from "The Economic Consequences of the Peace," in *The Essential Keynes,* ed. Robert Skidelsky (London: Penguin Books, 2015).

It was possible: Herman Kahn, *On Thermonuclear War* (Princeton, NJ: Princeton University Press, 1960).

The sly aside: Jules Jusserand, quoted in George C. Herring, *From Colony to Superpower: U.S. Foreign Relations Since 1776* (New York: Oxford University Press, 2008), 6.

"You had to live": George Orwell, *1984* (New York: Signet Classics, 1961), 3.

Edmund Burke's: Edmund Burke, *The Works of the Right Hon. Edmund Burke, with a Biographical and Critical Introduction* (London: Holdsworth and Ball, 1834), 1:498.

The phrase "grand strategy": For a good general introduction to the problems of grand strategy, see B. H. Liddell Hart, *Strategy: The Indirect Approach* (London: Faber & Faber, 1967); Paul Kennedy, ed., *Grand Strategies in War and Peace* (New Haven, CT: Yale University Press, 1991); Edward N. Luttwak, *Strategy: The Logic of War and Peace* (Cambridge, MA: The Belknap Press of Harvard University Press, 1987); Peter Paret with Gordon A. Craig and Felix Gilbert, eds., *Makers of Modern Strategy: From Machiavelli to the Nuclear Age* (Princeton, NJ: Princeton University Press, 1986); and Sun Tzu, *The Art of War,* trans. Victor Mair (New York: Columbia University Press, 2007).

"Within five hours": Douglas MacArthur, *Reminiscences* (Annapolis, MD: Naval Institute Press, 1964), 354.

"The exploding popularity": Luiz André Barroso and Urs Hölzle, *The Datacenter as a Computer: An Introduction to the Design of Warehouse-Scale Machines* (San Rafael, CA: Morgan & Claypool, 2009).

If it works: Hal Brands, *The Promise and Pitfalls of Grand Strategy* (Carlisle, PA: Strategic Studies Institute, Army War College, August 2012); Jennifer Mitzen, "Illusion or Intention? Talking Grand Strategy into Existence," *Security Studies* 24, no. 1 (2015): 61–94.

The Chinese strategist: Liu Yazhou, "Da Guoce" ("Grand National Policy"), at http://www.aisixiang.com/data/2884.html.

The first proposes: Joseph S. Nye Jr., "Get Smart: Combining Hard and Soft Power," *Foreign Affairs* (July/August 2009).

The concept was summarized: Jeffrey Goldberg, "Hillary Clinton: 'Failure' to Help Syrian Rebels Led to the Rise of ISIS," *The Atlantic*, August 10, 2014.

"I don't really even need": David Remnick, "Going the Distance: On and Off the Road with Barack Obama," *The New Yorker*, January 27, 2014.

Or, as Winston Churchill: Winston Churchill, speech at Harrow School, October 29, 1941, at http://www.winstonchurchill.org/resources/speeches/234 -1941-1945-war-leader/103-never-give-in.

Admiral Hyman Rickover's: Admiral H. G. Rickover, "Thoughts on Man's Purpose in Life" (Morgenthau Memorial Lecture, 1982), at https://www .carnegiecouncil.org/publications/archive/morgenthau/763.html/_res/ id=sa_File1/763_2ndMML-H.G.Rickover.pdf.

As they explained: Stephen G. Brooks, G. John Ikenberry, and William C. Wohlforth, "Don't Come Home, America: The Case Against Retrenchment," *International Security* 37, no. 3 (Winter 2012/13): 10.

Yes, the United States: Daniel Drezner, "Military Primacy Doesn't Pay (At Least Not As Much As You Think)," *International Security* 38, no. 1 (Summer 2013): 52.

"The struggle to survive": John Darwin, *The Empire Project: The Rise and Fall of the British World-System 1830–1970* (Cambridge: Cambridge University Press, 2009), 477.

Great powers: Henry Kissinger, "The New World Order," in *Diplomacy* (New York: Simon & Schuster, 1995), 17–28; Paul Kennedy, *The Rise and Fall of the Great Powers: Economic Change and Military Conflict from 1500 to 2000* (New York: Random House, 1987).

Its architecture: For an excellent overview on the politics of contagion, see Tony D. Sampson, *Virality: Contagion Theory in the Age of Networks* (Minneapolis: University of Minnesota Press, 2012).

"Who…imagined": Robert Hutchings and Jeremi Suri, eds., *Foreign Policy Breakthroughs: Cases in Successful Diplomacy* (Oxford: Oxford University Press, 2015), 1.

"During the time": Thomas Hobbes, *Leviathan* (Cambridge: Cambridge University Press, 2002), 88.

Biological surveillance: The foundational text of network battle thinking is: John Arquilla and David Ronfeldt, eds., *Networks and Netwars: The Future* *of Terror, Crime, and Militancy* (Santa Monica, CA: RAND Corporation, 2001). For a discussion of the biological issues, see Eugene Thacker, "Living Dead Networks," *The Fibreculture Journal* 4 (2005).

Hannibal's smashing attacks: A. T. Mahan, *The Influence of Sea Power upon History, 1660–1783* (Boston: Little, Brown, 1890), iv.

One hacker: David Raymond et al., "A Control Measure Framework to Limit Collateral Damage and Propagation of Cyber Weapons," in Karlis Podins, Jan Stinissen, and Markus Maybaum, eds., *5th International Conference in Cyber Conflict: Proceedings 2013* (Tallinn, Estonia: NATO Cooperative Cyber Defence Centre of Excellence Publications, 2013).

Even the most formidable: Daniel Geer, "Heartbleed as Metaphor," *Lawfare*, April 21, 2014, at https://www.lawfareblog.com/heartbleed-metaphor.

When the American: See US National Security Strategy, 2015, available at http://nssarchive.us/national-security-strategy-2015/.

The great twentieth-century theorist: Hans Morgenthau, "The State of Political Science," in *Politics in the Twentieth Century*, vol. 1, *The Decline of Democratic Politics* (Chicago: University of Chicago Press, 1962).

The tendrils of the Ganges: Peter Turchin, "A Theory for the Formation of Large Agrarian Empires," *Journal of Global History* 4 (2009): 191–217; Jean-Paul Rodrigue, Claude Comtois, and Brian Slack, *The Geography of Transport Systems* (New York: Routledge, 2006), 10–15.

The skeins: John Arquilla and Ryan Nomura, "Three Wars of Ideas About the Idea of War," *Comparative Strategy* 34, no. 2 (2015): 186.

Cyberweapons: Mary Kaldor, "In Defence of New Wars," *Stability* 2, no. 1 (2013): 1–16.

Orwell's well-worn line: George Orwell, "You and the Atom Bomb," in Sonia Orwell and Ian Angus, eds., *The Collected Essays, Journalism, and Letters of George Orwell*, vol. 4, *In Front of Your Nose: 1946–1950* (Godine/Nonpareil, 2000), 7.

"In the short run": John F. Padgett and Walter W. Powell, "The Problem of Emergence," in *The Emergence of Organizations and Markets* (Princeton, NJ: Princeton University Press, 2012), 2.

Chapter 4. THE JAWS OF CONNECTION

"Wisner landed": William Colby, *Honorable Men: My Life in the CIA* (New York: Simon and Schuster, 1978), 73.

They spread to Tunis: Mohamed Zayani, *Networked Publics and Digital Contention: The Politics of Everyday Life in Tunisia* (Oxford: Oxford University Press, 2015).

"The network society": Manuel Castells, *The Rise of the Network Society*, vol. 1, 2nd ed. With a new preface of *The Information Age: Economy, Society, and Culture* (Chichester, UK: Wiley-Blackwell, 2010), 508.

"We are witnessing": Manuel Castells, "The Space of Autonomy: Cyberspace and Urban Space in Networked Social Movements" (lecture, Harvard Graduate School of Design, February 18, 2014), at http://www.gsd.harvard.edu/#/media/lecture-manuel-castells-the-space-of-autonomy-cyberspace-and.html.

And, at any rate: Raquel Alvarez, David Garcia, Yamir Moreno, and Frank Schweitzer, "Sentiment Cascades in the 15M Movement," *EPJ Data Science* 4, no. 6 (2015).

People who'd never met: W. Lance Bennett and Alexandra Segerberg, "The Logic of Connective Action: Digital Media and the Personalization of Contentious Politics," *Information, Communication & Society* 15, no. 5 (2012): 739–68.

As the British central banker: Andrew Haldane, "On Microscopes and Telescopes" (lecture, Lorentz Centre workshop on socioeconomic complexity, Leiden, March 27, 2015), 20. Available at http://www.bankofengland.co.uk/publications/Documents/speeches/2015/speech812.pdf.

Even in countries: Edwin Grohe, "The Cyber Dimensions of the Syrian Civil War: Implications for Future Conflict," *Comparative Strategy* 34, no. 2 (2015): 133–48.

The way we: See Venkatesh Rao, "The Amazing, Shrinking Org Chart," *Ribbonfarm*, May 28, 2015, at http://www.ribbonfarm.com/2015/05/28/the-amazing-shrinking-org-chart/.

Keynes's famous line: John Maynard Keynes, from "The Economic Consequences of the Peace," in *The Essential Keynes*, ed. Robert Skidelsky (London: Penguin Books, 2015), 16.

Malls, democracies: David Murakami Wood and Stephen Graham, "Permeable Boundaries in the Software-Sorted Society: Surveillance and Differentiations of Mobility," chap. 10 in *Mobile Technologies of the City*, ed. Mimi Sheller and John Urry (New York: Routledge, 2006), 177–91.

"When I came to the words": Preserved Smith, *The Life and Letters of Martin Luther* (Boston: Houghton Mifflin, 1911), 15.

"Enlightenment": Immanuel Kant, "An Answer to the Question: What Is Enlightenment?" in *Kant: Political Writings*, ed. H. S. Reiss, trans. H. B. Nisbet, Cambridge Texts in the History of Political Thought (Cambridge: Cambridge University Press, 1991), 54.

"Human knowledge": Francis Bacon, *The New Organon*, ed. Lisa Jardine and Michael Silverthorne, Cambridge Texts in the History of Philosophy (Cambridge: Cambridge University Press, 2000), 33.

In a "commercial society": Adam Smith, *The Wealth of Nations*, ed. Kathryn Sutherland, Oxford World's Classics (Oxford: Oxford University Press, 2008), 31.

"the scaffolds humans erect": Douglass C. North, *Understanding the Process of Economic Change* (Princeton, NJ: Princeton University Press, 2010), 48.

Museums…Scientific congresses: Joel Mokyr, "The Intellectual Origins of Modern Economic Growth," *Journal of Economic History* 65, no. 2 (June 2005): 290.

"All fixed, fast-frozen relations": Karl Marx and Frederick Engels, "Manifesto of the Communist Party," in *Economic and Philosophic Manuscripts of 1844 and the Communist Manifesto*, trans. Martin Milligan (Amherst, NY: Prometheus Books, 1988), 212.

"Hitler's fate was sealed": Winston Churchill, *The Second World War*, vol. 3, *The Grand Alliance* (New York: Houghton Mifflin, 1950), 539.

Or, the reverse of that coin: Roberta Wohlstetter, *Pearl Harbor: Warning and Decision* (Stanford, CA: Stanford University Press, 1962), 350.

"Social structures": John F. Padgett and Walter W. Powell, "The Problem of Emergence," in *The Emergence of Organizations and Markets* (Princeton, NJ: Princeton University Press, 2012), 8.

Meanwhile, my father's ideas: I. Akyildiz, M. Pierobon, S. Balasubramaniam, and Yevgeni Koucheryavy, "The Internet of Bio-Nano Things," *IEEE Communications Magazine* 53, no. 3 (March 2015): 32–40.

The computer-science pioneer: See David Bawden and Lyn Robinson, "Waiting for Carnot: Information and Complexity," *Journal of the Association for Information Science and Technology* 66, no. 11 (November 2015): 2177–86; Norbert Wiener, *Cybernetics; or, Control and Communication in the Animal and the Machine* (New York: John Wiley and Sons, 1948); Warren Weaver, "Science and Complexity," *American Scientist* 36, no. 4 (October 1948): 536–44.

They are ordered: Carlos Gershenson, Péter Csermely, Péter Érdi, "The Past, Present and Future of Cybernetics and Systems Research," arXiv:1308.6317v3, September 23, 2013.

Chapter 5. FISHNET

"The chief purpose of our military": Bernard Brodie, "The Weapon: War in the Atomic Age and Implications for Military Policy," in Bernard Brodie, ed., *The Absolute Weapon: Atomic Power and World Order* (New York: Harcourt, Brace & Company, 1946), 76.

"At the time": There is a fair amount of debate about the question of whether Internet design was intended for survivability or whether some other systemic need—such as linking research institutions—accounted for the distributed architecture that emerged. See, for instance, Barry M. Leiner, Vinton G. Cerf, et al., "A Brief History of the Internet," *ACM SIGCOMM Computer Communication Review* 39, no. 5 (October 2009): 22–31. However, an examination of primary source documents shows the evolution of Baran's thinking clearly and produces documentary evidence for the origins of the problem he and various figures at RAND were aiming to solve. Others arrived at the packet-switching model, but it is clear that Baran's path to the design emerged from the security problems he was considering. For much of the information here, see "Oral History: Paul Baran," an interview conducted by David Hochfelder for the Institute of Electrical and Electronics Engineers History Center, October 24, 1999, at http://ethw.org/Oral-History:Paul_Baran; Paul Baran, "On Distributed Communications: I; Introduction to Distributed Communications Networks" and "On Distributed Communications: XI; Summary Overview," United States Air Force Project RAND (August 1964).

And now, of course: Richard Harper, Tom Rodden, Yvonne Rogers, and Abigail Sellen, eds., *Being Human: Human-Computer Interaction in the Year 2020* (Cambridge: Microsoft Research, Ltd., 2008).

This now-commonplace magic: Chris Mack, "The Multiple Lives of Moore's Law: Why Gordon Moore's Grand Prediction Has Endured for 50 Years," *IEEE Spectrum* (March 30, 2015), at http://spectrum.ieee.org/semiconductors/processors/the-multiple-lives-of-moores-law.

"There are systems": John Holland, "Complex Adaptive Systems," *Daedalus* 121, no. 1 (Winter 1992): 17.

A rain forest: Simon A. Levin, *Fragile Dominion: Complexity and the Commons* (Reading, MA: Perseus Books, 1999).

The word "complex": Carlos Gershenson, "The Implications of Interactions for Science and Philosophy," *Foundations of Science*, 18, no.4 (2013): 781–90.

"Macro models": Jean-Claude Trichet, "Reflections on the Nature of Monetary Policy Non-Standard Measures and Finance Theory" (speech, European Central Bank Central Banking Conference, Frankfurt, November 18, 2010), at https://www.ecb.europa.eu/press/key/date/2010/html/sp101118.en.html.

This sense of abandonment: Michele Catanzaro and Mark Buchanan, "Network Opportunity," *Nature Physics* 9 (March 2013): 121–22, or Cesar A. Hidalgo, "Disconnected! The Parallel Streams of Network Literature in the Natural and Social Sciences," arXiv:1511.03981, November 12, 2015.

Long before: S. Barry Cooper and Jan van Leeuwen, eds., *Alan Turing: His Work and Impact* (Waltham, MA: Elsevier, 2013).

Since everything can ultimately be reduced: See the conversation between Google CEO Eric Schmidt and Danny Sullivan at the Search Engine Strategies Conference, August 9, 2006, at http://www.google.com/press/podium/ses2006.html.

This easy programmability: Gershenson, "Implications of Interactions," 4.

Linked to a whole system: Paul Dourish, *Where the Action Is: The Foundations of Embodied Interaction* (Cambridge, MA: MIT Press, 2001), 4.

In fact: Paul Phister, "Cyberspace: The Ultimate Complex Adaptive System," *The International C2 Journal* 4, no. 2 (2010–2011).

Complexity and unpredictability: Randy Shoup, "Service Architectures at Scale: Lessons from Google and eBay" (speech, London, July 14, 2015), at http://www.infoq.com/presentations/service-arch-scale-google-ebay.

This isn't a game of averages: Natalie Wolchover, "Treading Softly in a Connected World," *Quanta Magazine*, March 18, 2013.

The destructive power: Sergey V. Buldyrev, Roni Parshani, Gerald Paul, et al., "Catastrophic Cascade of Failures in Interdependent Networks," *Nature* 464 (April 15, 2010): 1025–28.

They can't help it: Caitríona H. Heinl, "Artificial (Intelligent) Agents and Active Cyber Defence: Policy Implications," in *6th International Conference on Cyber Conflict: Proceedings 2014*, ed. Pascal Brangetto, Markus Maybaum, and Jan Stinissen (Tallinn, Estonia: NATO Cooperative Cyber Defence Centre of Excellence Publications, 2014), 60.

"Many biological and social theories": Carlos Gershenson, Péter Csermely, Péter Érdi, Helena Knyazeva, and Alexander Laszlo, "The Past, Present and Future of Cybernetics and Systems Research," arXiv:1308.6317v3, September 23, 2013, 2–4.

Chapter 6. WAREZ DUDES

"The phone company": Ron Rosenbaum, "Secrets of the Little Blue Box," *Esquire*, October 1971, 120.

"Be conservative": Jon Postel, *DOD Standard Transmission Control Protocol* (Marina del Rey, CA: Information Sciences Institute, University of Southern California, 1980).

"exploit engineers": Sergey Bratus, Julian Bangert, Alexandar Gabrovsky, et al., " 'Weird Machine' Patterns," chap. 13 in *Cyberpatterns: Unifying Design Patterns with Security and Attack Patterns*, ed. Clive Blackwell and Hong Zhu (Cham, Switzerland: Springer International Publishing, 2014), 13.

Turn it back on: For a discussion of Michelangelo, see the entry for *virus* in *Encyclopedia of Computer Science*, 4th ed., ed. Anthony Ralston, Edwin D. Reilly, and David Hemmendinger (Chichester, UK: John Wiley and Sons, Ltd., 2003), 1839–41.

three golden rules: This list may be more legend than fact, but it is widely attributed to Morris. See, for instance, Li Gong, Gary Ellison, and Mary Dageforde, *Inside Java 2 Platform Security: Architecture, API Design, and Implementation*, 2nd ed. (Boston: Addison-Wesley Professional, 2003), 1.

Even intelligence: Felix "FX" Lindner and Sandro Gaycken, "Back to Basics: Beyond Network Hygiene," in *Best Practices in Computer Network Defense: Incident Detection and Response*, ed. Melissa E. Hathaway (Amsterdam, the Netherlands: IOS Press, 2014), 54.

It involves: Julian Bangert, Sergey Bratus, Rebecca Shapiro, and Sean W. Smith, "The Page-Fault Weird Machine: Lessons in Instruction-less Computation," presented at the 7th USENIX Workshop on Offensive Technologies (Washington, DC, August 13, 2013), at https://www.usenix .org/conference/woot13/workshop-program/presentation/bangert.

As Robert Joyce: "Disrupting Nation State Hackers," speech delivered January 27, 2016, at https://www.usenix.org/conference/enigma2016/conference -program/presentation/joyce.

"You do not understand": Rebecca Shapiro, Sergey Bratus, and Sean W. Smith, "'Weird Machines' in ELF: A Spotlight on the Underappreciated Metadata," presented at the 7th USENIX Workshop on Offensive Technologies (Washington, DC, August 13, 2013), at https://www.usenix.org/ conference/woot13/workshop-program/presentation/shapiro.

That prize: Sergey Bratus, Julian Bangert, Alexandar Gabrovsky, et al., "Composition Patterns of Hacking," in *Cyberpatterns 2012: Proceedings of the First International Workshop on Cyberpatterns; Unifying Design Patterns with Security, Attack and Forensic Patterns,* athttp://tech.brookes.ac.uk/CyberPat terns2012/Cyberpatterns2012Proceedings.pdf.

Even the best programmers: For a good explanation of how a machine's code can be turned against itself, see Sergey Bratus, Michael E. Locasto, Meredith L. Patterson, et al., "Exploit Programming: From Buffer Overflows to 'Weird Machines' and Theory of Computation," *;login:* 36, no. 6 (December 2011): 13–21. The piece was published in memory of Len Sassman, one of the leading thinkers of the Language Security, or LangSec, movement, who died in 2011. Many of his talks, still available online, reflect an unusually powerful mix of philosophical and technical considerations about modern computing systems. See also Shapiro, Bratus, and Smith, "'Weird Machines' in ELF." http://0b4af6cdc2f0c5998459-c0245c5c937c5dedcca 3f1764ecc9b2f.r43.cf2.rackcdn.com/12059-woot13-shapiro.pdf.

But in the two days: Leyla Bilge and Tudor Dumitras, "Before We Knew It: An Empirical Study of Zero-Day Attacks in the Real World," CCS '12: Proceedings of the 2012 ACM Conference on Computer and Communications Security (October 2012): 833–44.

In 2014: Mark Seaborn and Thomas Dullien, "Exploiting the DRAM Rowhammer Bug to Gain Kernel Privileges," *Project Zero* (Google blog), March 9, 2015. http://googleprojectzero.blogspot.com/2015/03/exploiting-dram -rowhammer-bug-to-gain.html.

"The fundamental aspect": Nathaniel W. Husted, "Analysis Techniques for Exploring Emergent Vulnerabilities and Attacks on Mobile Devices" (PhD thesis, Indiana University, 2013), at http://www.cs.indiana.edu/~nhusted/ docs/proposal.pdf.

In a video: For a description of this exploit, see Mordechai Guri, Matan Monitz, Yisroel Mirski, and Yuval Elovici, "BitWhisper: Covert Signaling Channel Between Air-Gapped Computers Using Thermal Manipulations," arXiv:1503.07919 [cs.CR], March 26, 2015.

Jung Hoon Lee: Lucian Constantin, "Chrome, Firefox, Explorer, Safari Were All Hacked at Pwn2Own Contest," *PC World*, March 20, 2015.

It's also an opportunity for: Jeffrey C. Mogul, "Emergent (Mis)behavior vs. Complex Software Systems," *ACM SIGOPS Operating Systems Review— Proceedings of the 2006 EuroSys Conference* 40, no. 4 (October 2006): 295

"We are not experts": Stephen Cobb and Andrew Lee, "Malware Is Called Malicious for a Reason: The Risks of Weaponizing Code," in *6th International Conference on Cyber Conflict: Proceedings 2014*, ed. Pascal Brangetto, Markus Maybaum, and Jan Stinissen (Tallinn, Estonia: NATO Cooperative Cyber Defence Centre of Excellence Publications, 2014), 71–82. And "Stuxnet: Tsunami of Stupid or Evil Genius?" (June 1, 2012) by Ali-Reza Anghaie at http://infosecisland.com/blogview/21507-Stuxnet-Tsunami-of -Stupid-or-Evil-Genius.html.

Such a possibility: Lindner and Gaycken, "Back to Basics," 58.

What makes a city: Colin McFarlane, "The Geographies of Urban Density: Topology, Politics, and the City," *Progress in Human Geography* (October 7, 2015): 2.

"Read over and over": Napoleon I, "The Military Maxims of Napoleon," in *Roots of Strategy: The 5 Greatest Military Classics of All Time*, ed. Brigadier General Thomas R. Phillips (Mechanicsburg, PA: Stackpole Books, 1985), 432.

"The greater the dependence": The Critical Engineering Working Group (Bengt Sjölén, Julian Oliver, and Danya Vasiliev), "The Critical Engineering Manifesto," at https://criticalengineering.org/.

And in our own: See, for instance, "Interview with Adrian Mackenzie and Theo Vurdubakis on Code and Crisis," supplement, *Theory, Culture & Society* 28, no. 6 (November 2011), January 24, 2012.

"Just like every drinking binge": Halvar Flake [Thomas Dullien], "Why Johnny Can't Tell If He Is Compromised" (speech, Area 41 security conference, Zurich, June 2, 2014).

And it's not just lone teen hackers: Wael Khalifa, Kenneth Revett, and Abdel-Badeeh Salem, "In the Hacker's Eye: The Neurophysiology of a Computer Hacker," in *Global Security, Safety and Sustainability & e-Democracy*, Lecture Notes of the Institute for Computer Sciences, Social Informatics and Telecommunications Engineering (Berlin: Springer Verlag, 2012), 112–19.

"Surprising realization": Thomas Dullien, "Offensive Work and Addiction: Why Offense Is Hard to Contain" (speech, ISACA Nordic Conference, Oslo, April 8, 2014).

"I remember what the Internet was like": Snowden interview in the film *Citizenfour*, dir. Laura Poitras (2014).

They will know and design: Nikos Virvilis, Dimitris Gritzalis, and Theodoros Apostolopoulos, "Trusted Computing vs. Advanced Persistent Threats: Can a Defender Win This Game?" *Proceedings of the 2013 IEEE 10th*

International Conference on Ubiquitous Intelligence and Computing and 2013 IEEE 10th International Conference on Autonomic and Trusted Computing (Washington, DC: IEEE Computer Society, 2013), 396–403.

the very strongest dynasties: See Peter Turchin, "A Theory for the Formation of Large Agrarian Empires," *Journal of Global History* 4 (2009): 3.

Chapter 7. THE NEW CASTE

In 1965: Joseph Weizenbaum, *Computer Power and Human Reason: From Judgment to Calculation* (San Francisco: W. H. Freeman, 1976), 7.

Looking back: David Priestland, *Merchant, Soldier, Sage: A History of the World in Three Castes* (New York: Penguin Press, 2013).

The legendary Xerox PARC: Chunka Mui, "The Lesson That Market Leaders Are Failing to Learn from Xerox PARC," *Forbes Leadership Blog*, August 1, 2012. http://www.forbes.com/sites/chunkamui/2012/08/01/the-lesson-that -market-leaders-are-failing-to-learn-from-xerox-parc/.

Anytime you see a network system: The Critical Engineering Working Group (Bengt Sjölén, Julian Oliver, and Danya Vasiliev), "The Critical Engineering Manifesto," at https://criticalengineering.org/. For a discussion of the relation between coding and the real world, see Bret Victor, "Inventing on Principle," Speech, Canadian University Software Engineering Conference, January 20, 2012, Montreal, Quebec, available at https:// www.youtube.com/watch?v=PUv66718DII.

"Early intercontinental travellers": Peter Sloterdijk, *In the World Interior of Capital: Towards a Philosophical Theory of Globalization*, trans. Wieland Hoban (Cambridge: Polity Press, 2013), 77.

"When building": Andrew Ng, "Deep Learning: What's Next" (speech at GPU Technology Conference, San Jose, CA, March 19, 2015).

The French philosopher: Bruno Latour, "On Technical Mediation—Philosophy, Sociology, Genealogy," *Common Knowledge* 3, no. 2 (Fall 1994): 37.

The immense possibility: Ryan Gallagher, "Profiled: From Radio to Porn, British Spies Track Web Users' Online Identities," *The Intercept*, September 25, 2015; GCHQ documents, "PullThrough Steering Group Meeting #16," at https://theintercept.com/document/2015/09/25/pull-steering-group -minutes/.

"We were not aware": John Maynard Keynes, "My Early Beliefs," in *Two Memoirs by J. M. Keynes: "Dr. Melchior, a Defeated Enemy," and "My Early Beliefs"* (New York: A. M. Kelley, 1949), 99.

Chapter 8. "MAPREDUCE": THE COMPRESSION OF SPACE AND TIME

"Civilization is revving itself": Stewart Brand, *The Clock of the Long Now: Time and Responsibility* (New York: Basic Books, 1999), 2.

"Summer afternoon": Edith Wharton, *A Backward Glance* (New York: D. Appleton-Century, 1934). See chapter 8 for her tale of an afternoon with Henry James.

"With each crossing": Georg Simmel, "The Metropolis and Mental Life" (1903), in *The Sociology of Georg Simmel*, trans., ed., and intro by Kurt H. Wolff (New York: The Free Press, 1950), 410, 413.

"Cities...can be recognized": Robert Musil, *The Man Without Qualities*, trans. Sophie Wilkins and Burton Pike, 2 vols. (New York: Vintage, 1996), 1:3.

The difference between: Ajahn Brahm of the Buddhist Society of Western Australia tells a wonderful story in his dharma talks about a day when he decided not to be driven up the road to his monastery in Perth but instead walked the road. He was flooded by the sensations of nature, all imperceptible from the inside of a car. One way to change your perspective, he points out, is to change the speed at which you are moving through life. See the Buddhist Society of Western Australia website for a catalog of his talks.

"Language": George Boole, *An Investigation of the Laws of Thought: On Which Are Founded the Mathematical Theories of Logic and Probabilities* (1854; repr., New York: Dover Publications, 1951).

"not merely a medium": Paul Virilio, *The Information Bomb*, trans. Chris Turner (London: Verso Books, 2000), 141.

"Someday, perhaps": William Daniel Hillis, "The Connection Machine" (PhD diss., MIT, 1985), 2.

Adding, in case: Ibid., 19.

He drove: Po Bronson, "The Long Now: Time-Traveling with Danny Hillis," *Wired*, May 1, 1998.

Feynman, sixty-five: W. Daniel Hillis, "Richard Feynman and the Connection Machine," *Physics Today* 42, no. 2 (February 1989): 78.

"At times": Michael J. Black, review of *The Connection Machine*, by W. Daniel Hillis, *AI Magazine* 7, no. 3 (1986): 169.

You can solve: Adam Beberg, "Distributed Systems: Computation with a Million Friends" (lecture, Stanford University Computer Systems Colloquium, April 30, 2008), at https://www.youtube.com/watch?v=7zafB2GkMBk.

"The American frontier": Frederick Jackson Turner, "The Significance of the Frontier in American History," *The Annual Report of the American Historical Association* (1894): 119–227.

There's a phrase: Janelle identified what he called space-time convergence; later the geographer David Harvey renamed it space-time compression, which is the term more commonly used today. See "Space-Time Constructs for Linking Information and Communication Technologies with Issues in Sustainable Transportation," *Transport Reviews* 24, no. 6 (December 2004): 665–77.

Absolute speed: See John Armitage, ed., *The Virilio Dictionary* (Edinburgh: Edinburgh University Press, 2013).

Location is: Jon May and Nigel Thrift, "Introduction," in *Timespace: Geographies of Temporality*, eds. Jon May and Nigel Thrift, Critical Geographies (London: Routledge, 2001), 2.

A map of the networked world: Vice Admiral Thomas Rowden, Rear Admiral Peter Gumataotao, and Rear Admiral Peter Fanta, "'Distributed Lethality,'" *Proceedings* 141, no. 1 (January 2015): 343.

"Being hacked": Halvar Flake [Thomas Dullien], "Why Johnny Can't Tell If He Is Compromised" (2014).

Unlike traditional conflicts: Derek Gregory, "The Everywhere War," *The Geographical Journal* 177, no. 3 (September 2011): 238–50.

He labeled it: Donald G. Janelle, "Spatial Reorganization: A Model and Concept," *Annals of the Association of American Geographers* 59, no. 2 (1969): 348–64.

Adam Smith's famous remark: Adam Smith, *The Theory of Moral Sentiments*, ed. Knud Haakonssen (Cambridge: Cambridge University Press, 2002), 198.

"Time *is* a ride": Stewart Brand, *The Clock of the Long Now*, 67.

The German philosopher: Monika Codourey, "Mobile Identities and the Socio-Spatial Relations of Air Travel," *Surveillance & Society* 5, no. 2 (2008): 188–202.

"Only large states": Nicholas John Spykman, "Frontiers, Security, and International Organization," *Geographical Review* 32, no. 3 (July 1942): 439.

"There is no equality": Giambattista Vico, *The New Science of Giambattista Vico: Translated from the Third Edition (1744) by Thomas Goddard Bergin and Max Harold Fisch* (Ithaca, NY: Cornell University Press, 1948).

"More than finding": Marina Keegan, "The Opposite of Loneliness," *Yale Daily News*, May 27, 2012, at http://yaledailynews.com/blog/2012/05/27/keegan-the-opposite-of-loneliness/.

No one had ever heard: Edwin Grohe, "The Cyber Dimensions of the Syrian Civil War: Implications for Future Conflict," *Comparative Strategy* 34, no. 2 (2015): 133–48.

After several hours: David Moore, Colleen Shannon, and k claffy, "Code-Red: A Case Study on the Spread and Victims of an Internet Worm," *Proceedings of the 2nd ACM SIGCOMM Workshop on Internet Measurement* (2002): 273–84.

On November 2: Ted Eisenberg, David Gries, Juris Hartmanis, et al., "The Cornell Commission: On Morris and the Worm," *Communications of the ACM* 32, no. 6 (June 1989): 706.

Morris worm: Alfred W. Crosby, *America's Forgotten Pandemic: The Influenza of 1918*, 2nd ed. (Cambridge: Cambridge University Press, 2003), xiii.

Then, a year or so after: Frederick B. Cohen, *A Short Course on Computer Viruses* (Pittsburgh, PA: ASP Press, 1990).

"The features": Fred Cohen, "Friendly Contagion: Harnessing the Subtle Power of Computer Viruses," *The Sciences* 31, no. 5 (September–October 1991): 23.

Eugene Spafford: Eugene H. Spafford, "Three Letters on Computer Security and Society" (Department of Computer Science Technical Reports, Purdue University, 1991).

Chapter 9. INSIDE AND OUT

"We have lost America": David Johnson, *Imagining the Cape Colony: History, Literature, and the South African Nation* (Edinburgh: Edinburgh University Press, 2012), 67.

"The world's surface being limited": Vindex [F. Verschoyle], *Cecil Rhodes: His Political Life and Speeches, 1881–1900* (London: Chapman and Hall, 1900), 7.

"The Chief has had": *Copies and Extracts of Further Correspondence Relating to Affairs in Mashonaland, Matabeleland, and the Bechuanaland Protectorate* (London: Her Majesty's Stationery Office, November 1893); see the telegram from Assistant Commissioner Palapye to His Excellency High Commissioner, Cape Town, 13.

"When an Englishman": Vindex, *Cecil Rhodes*, 191–92.

"Your Majesty": *Copies and Extracts*, 76.

"Suppose there were people": Ssu-yu Teng and John K. Fairbank, *China's Response to the West: A Documentary Survey, 1839–1923* (Cambridge MA: Harvard University Press, 1979), 26.

"Whatever happens": H.B. and B.T.B. [Hilaire Belloc and Basil Temple Blackwood], *The Modern Traveller* (London: Edward Arnold, 1898), 41.

"During the decades": Stephen Van Evera, "The Cult of the Offensive and the Origins of the First World War," *International Security* 9, no. 1 (Summer 1984): 58.

"You snug-faced": Siegfried Sassoon, "Suicide in the Trenches," in *War Poems of Siegfried Sassoon* (Mineola, NY: Dover Publications, 2004), 64.

"Hang your chemistry": John Ellis, *The Social History of the Machine Gun* (New York: Pantheon, 1975), 33.

The Melians: Thucydides, *The Peloponnesian War*, trans. Steven Lattimore (Indianapolis: Hackett Publishing, 1998), chap. 5; see also the excellent BBC performance of certain elements of Thucydides in "The War That Never Ends," at https://www.youtube.com/watch?v=SNcJ79qPIg8.

Max Weber: Max Weber, *The Essential Weber: A Reader*, ed. Sam Whimster (London: Routledge, 2004), 355.

"Traditional literature": Karine Barzilai-Nahon, "Fuzziness of Inclusion/Exclusion in Networks," *International Journal of Communication* 5 (2011): 757–58, and Karine Barzilai-Nahon, "Toward a Theory of Network Gatekeeping: A Framework for Exploring Information Control," *Journal of the American Society for Information Science and Technology* 59, no. 9 (July 2008): 1493–1512.

"Our understanding": W. Brian Arthur, "Increasing Returns and the New World of Business," *Harvard Business Review*, July–August 1996.

Data scientists: Laurent Hébert-Dufresne et al. "Complex Networks as an Emerging Property of Hierarchical Preferential Attachment," *Physical Review* E 92, 062809 (2015).

winner takes all: Remco van der Hofstad, *Random Graphs and Complex Networks* (Eindhoven, the Netherlands: Eindhoven University of Technology, 2015), at http://www.win.tue.nl/~rhofstad/NotesRGCN.pdf, 24.

"seven friends in ten days": Chamath Palihapitiya, "How We Put Facebook on the Path to 1 Billion Users" (lecture for the Udemy course "Growth Hacking: An Introduction," published January 9, 2013, and available at https://www.youtube.com/watch?v=raIUQP71SBU).

Pretty soon: Eman Yasser Daraghmi and Shyan-Ming Yuan, "We Are So Close, Less Than 4 Degrees Separating You and Me!," *Computers in Human Behavior* 30 (January 2014), 273–85.

But there's another secret: Albert-László Barabási, "Network Science," *Philosophical Transactions of the Royal Society A: Mathematical, Physical, and Engineering Sciences* 371, no. 1987 (March 2013).

The network scientists: Rahul Tongia and Ernest J. Wilson III, "The Flip Side of Metcalfe's Law: Multiple and Growing Costs of Network Exclusion," *International Journal of Communication* 5 (2011): 665–81.

fifty-one national enclosures: Ron E. Hassner and Jason Wittenberg, "Barriers to Entry: Who Builds Fortified Boundaries and Why," *International Security* 40, no. 1 (Summer 2015): 157–90.

"There is a significant chance": Bill Gates, "The Next Epidemic—Lessons from Ebola," *New England Journal of Medicine* 372 (April 9, 2015): 1381–84.

Basic adjustment: Ben S. Bernanke, "Money, Gold, and the Great Depression," H. Parker Willis Lecture in Economic Policy, Washington and Lee University, Lexington, Virginia, March 2, 2004.

"Everything is a gate": Felix "FX" Lindner and Sandro Gaycken, "Back to Basics: Beyond Network Hygiene," in *Best Practices in Computer Network Defense: Incident Detection and Response*, ed. Melissa E. Hathaway (Amsterdam, the Netherlands: IOS Press, 2014), 55–56.

Chapter 10. Hard Gatekeeping

"The United States faces no existential threat": See James Dobbins et al., *Choices for America in a Turbulent World* (Santa Monica, CA: RAND Corporation, 2015), xiv. For a discussion of the nature of security and values, see Arnold Wolfers, "'National Security' as an Ambiguous Symbol," *Political Science Quarterly* 67, no. 4 (December 1952): 485.

"Those gateways": Quoted in Robert Jervis, "Cooperation Under the Security Dilemma," *World Politics* 30, no. 2 (January 1978): 169.

"Every new age": Carl Schmitt, *Nomos of the Earth in the International Law of the Just Publicum Europaeum* (New York: Telos Press, 2006), 45.

Lloyd George: Margaret MacMillan, *Paris 1919: Six Months That Changed the World* (New York: Random House, 2002), 381.

Hard Gatekeeping echoes: For a discussion about why a grand strategy is of practical use, see Hal Brands, *The Promise and Pitfalls of Grand Strategy* (Carlisle, PA: Strategic Studies Institute, Army War College, August 2012). Edward Luttwak, *The Grand Strategy of the Roman Empire: From the First Century A.D. to the Third* (Baltimore: The Johns Hopkins University Press, 1976).

America is far too complacent: Stephen J. Cimballa and Roger N. McDermott, "A New Cold War? Missile Defenses, Nuclear Arms Reductions and Cyber War," *Comparative Strategy* 34, no. 1 (2015): 95–111.

In fact, their very design: István A. Kovács and Albert-László Barabási, "Network Science: Destruction Perfected," *Nature* 524 (August 6, 2015): 38–39; Manlio De Domenico, Albert Solé-Ribalta, Elisa Omodei, et al., "Ranking in Interconnected Multilayer Networks Reveals Versatile Nodes," *Nature Communications* 6 (April 23, 2015).

The scientists: John Maynard Smith and Eörs Szathmáry, *The Major Transitions in Evolution* (Oxford: Oxford University Press, 1995).

"coevolution": Matjaz Perc and Attila Szolnoki, "Coevolutionary Games—A Mini Review," *BioSystems* 99 (2010): 109–25.

The essential facilitating feature: Nathalie Mezza-Garcia, Tom Froese, and Nelson Fernández, "Reflections on the Complexity of Ancient Social Heterarchies: Toward New Models of Social Self-Organization in Pre-Hispanic Colombia," *Journal of Sociocybernetics* 12 (2014): 3–17.

Chapter 11. CITIZENS!

"Can machines think": A. M. Turing, "Computing Machinery and Intelligence," *Mind* 59, no. 236 (October 1950): 433.

He calls it: Michael Nielsen, "The Rise of Computer-Aided Explanation," *Quanta Magazine,* July 23, 2015.

Already, humans: Yann LeCun, Yoshua Bengio, and Geoffrey Hinton, "Deep Learning," *Nature* 521 (May 28, 2015): 436–44.

The AI systems designer: Roger Grosse, "Predictive Learning vs. Representation Learning," *Building Intelligent Probabilistic Systems* (blog), February 4, 2013.

Wouldn't it be nice: Andrej Karpathy, "The Unreasonable Effectiveness of Recurrent Neural Networks," *The Hacker's Guide to Neural Networks* (blog), May 21, 2015; John Supko, "How I Taught My Computer to Write Its Own Music," *Nautilus* 21 (February 12, 2015); Daniel Johnson, "Composing Music with Recurrent Neural Networks," *Hexahedria* (blog), August 3, 2015.

"AI is both freedom from": Philip Greenspun, "Big Data and Machine Learning," from Philip Greenspun blog, November 21, 2015.

Us too: Caitríona H. Heinl, "Artificial (Intelligent) Agents and Active Cyber Defence: Policy Implications," in *6th International Conference on Cyber Conflict: Proceedings 2014*, ed. Pascal Brangetto, Markus Maybaum, and Jan Stinissen (Tallinn, Estonia: NATO Cooperative Cyber Defence Centre of Excellence Publications, 2014), 53.

In the spring of 1993: See *Vision-21: Interdisciplinary Science and Engineering in the Era of Cyberspace*, proceedings of a symposium cosponsored by the NASA Lewis Research Center and the Ohio Aerospace Institute, Westlake, Ohio, March 30–31, 1993 (Hampton, VA: National Aeronautics and Space Administration Scientific and Technical Information Program), iii.

"Within thirty years": Ibid., 12.

Imagine a superintelligent machine: Nick Bostrom, "Ethical Issues in Advanced Artificial Intelligence," in *Cognitive, Emotive and Ethical Aspects of Decision Making in Humans and in AI*, vol. 2, ed. Iva Smit et al. (Windsor, ON: International Institute for Advanced Studies in Systems Research and Cybernetics, 2003), 12–17, and Nick Bostrom, "The Superintelligent Will: Motivation and Instrumental Rationality in Advanced Artificial Agents," *Minds and Machines*, 22, no. 2 (2012): 71–85.

It runs like this: Seth Grimes, "Language Use, Customer Personality, and the Customer Journey" (interview with Scott Nowson, global innovation lead, Xerox), *Breakthrough Analysis* (blog), October 8, 2015.

Let me out!: See, for instance, Stuart Armstrong, Anders Sandberg, and Nick Bostrom, "Thinking Inside the Box: Controlling and Using an Oracle AI," *Minds and Machines* 22, no. 4 (November 2012): 299–324.

"People proposing": Michael Vassar, "Re: AI Boxing (dogs and helicopters)," SL4.org, August 2, 2005, at http://sl4.org/archive/0508/11817.html.

So we need to ask: Kaj Sotala and Roman V. Yampolskiy, "Responses to Catastrophic AGI Risk: A Survey," *Physica Scripta* 90 (2015).

"I pondered the matter": Plato, *Epistle VII*, in *The Platonic Epistles*, trans. J. Harward (1932; repr., Cambridge: Cambridge University Press, 2014).

Index

ABOUT THE AUTHOR

Joshua Cooper Ramo is co–chief executive officer and vice chairman of Kissinger Associates. A Mandarin speaker who moved to Beijing in 2002, Ramo is a member of the board of directors of Starbucks and FedEx. He holds an undergraduate degree in Latin American Studies from the University of Chicago and a master's in economics from New York University. Ramo was raised in New Mexico and began his career as a journalist. He was the youngest senior editor and foreign editor in the history of *Time* magazine. He is the author of the international bestseller *The Age of the Unthinkable*. His first book, *No Visible Horizon*, chronicled his experiences as a competitive aerobatic pilot.